Dollar, Dove, and Eagle

# Dollar, Dove and Eagle

## One Hundred Years
## of Palestinian Migration
## to Honduras

Nancie L. González

**WITHDRAWN**

*Ann Arbor*

THE UNIVERSITY OF MICHIGAN PRESS

Library of Congress Cataloging-in-Publication Data

González, Nancie L. Solien, 1929–
    Dollar, dove, and eagle : one hundred years of Palestinian
migration to Honduras / Nancie L. González.
        p.     cm.
    Includes bibliographical references and index.
    ISBN 0-472-09494-7 (alk. paper). — ISBN 0-472-06494-0 (pbk. : alk. paper)
    1. Honduras — Emigration and immigration — History.   2. Immigrants —
Honduras — History.   3. Palestine — Emigration and immigration —
History.   4. Palestinian Arabs — Honduras — History.   I. Title.
JV7419.G64   1992
325′.25694′097283 — dc20                                            92-28017
                                                                          CIP

To the memory of my friend and colleague, Edward A. Azar
  Lebanon 1938 — Washington, D.C. 1991
Founder and former director of the Center for International
Development and Conflict Management
University of Maryland, College Park

# Preface and Acknowledgments

This book required fieldwork in two quite different parts of the world — Central America and the Middle East. Both areas were the scene of ongoing civil conflict. The day I arrived in Honduras for my most extended stay a prominent politician was shot and killed only a few blocks from where I came to live. The American embassy in Tegucigalpa was attacked and badly damaged by firebombs during a general protest, which also included a similar attack on an Arab store in San Pedro Sula.

Nothing in Honduras, however, matched the daily tensions of living on the West Bank. Friends and colleagues frequently ask me if I was afraid for my own safety. Truthfully, I was not incapacitated by the specter of physical injury or death, even though I admit that occasionally, I did expose myself to such. Still, only once, when I was whisked inside a shop and heard bullets (rubber sounds the same as metal) whizzing past behind the metal doors which were hurriedly closed after us, did I feel that I might have had a close call.

Because some anthropologists have become concerned lately about the propriety, if not the ethics, of exposing ourselves to dangers of various sorts (Howell 1990), I think it important to address this issue at the outset. It is my view that anthropologists have always accepted, implicitly more than explicitly, the possibility that their fieldwork might be fraught with danger. Disease, intestinal parasites, inadequate diet, slippery cliffs, rushing waters, snakes, lions and tigers, overcrowded and poorly maintained transport facilities, reprisals for misbehavior resulting from misunderstandings of societal expectations — these are only a few of the more common pitfalls we have faced, and more than a few anthropologists have lost their lives in the field. How many have suffered permanent physical or mental health damage as a result of their work is less well known, perhaps because such cases are seldom admitted and even less often made public.

Having said all this, it is still my sense that we have chosen a profession with certain occupational hazards, but that with proper knowledge and forethought, we must make the best of whatever field situation we encounter. We learn to swim, we watch what we eat and drink, we take along preventive and curative medicines, we tread carefully and emulate our hosts' behavior in regard to all things unfamiliar and which they themselves fear. We recognize that even in our own society we cannot hope for invulnerability.

In both Honduras and in the West Bank I lived, insofar as was feasible, much as the people I was studying lived. I avoided going out during times of the day or night that were considered dangerous; I also avoided those zones thought to be most risky. Since I was not studying the violence or the intifada per se, I did not find it necessary to attend political rallies or protests, except in the West Bank, when I did sometimes join the women and children in such after determining that these rarely led to bloodshed. In short, I was a coward, but I lived like most of my informants, who also took only calculated risks. Indeed, learning to calculate them is part and parcel of learning any culture.

In chapter 1 I will outline other reasons why I believe that fieldwork in areas undergoing violent conflict presents new and perhaps insurmountable challenges. Here let me only say that, without the special help and guidance of my many Palestinian friends and collaborators in both field sites, I could not have done the work. At the same time I must also recognize and emphasize the importance of support given me by expatriate American (and sometimes European) friends, to whom I sometimes had to turn for psychological comfort, knowing that our non-Oriental background gave us a commonality of reaction which was sometimes different from that of our Middle Eastern associates.

Given Edward Said's 1978 critical perspective on scholarly discussions of foreign cultures in his influential book *Orientalism,* it is important to explain and clarify my position on this issue. As Lila Abu-Lughod has pointed out, "The totalizing opposition between East and West [postulated as the basis of orientalism by Said] does not have particular currency in anthropology, where other dichotomies such as primitive/modern, black/white, savage/civilized, and now self/other are more salient" (1989:269). Yet repeatedly in the discussion that follows I have used language suggesting a division between East and West as an explanatory factor in my analyses. Despite my basic agreement with Said's general argument, I find it important to note that, in everyday life, people are often pushed into taking sides, especially when violent conflict erupts between what are seen as two peoples or cultures. In the ongoing dispute between Israel and the Palestinian people increasingly being displaced by the expansion of that state, most Westerners have backed Israel, even when they have felt uncomfortable about some of its actions and policies. It is often suggested that, regardless of their religious or ethnic background, Westerners perceive Israelis as being more like themselves, that is to say, as being less "Oriental" than are the Arabs of different nationalities and religions who border their country.

Having spent some time in the area, it is my impression that this is a too facile conclusion and that Israel itself is a Middle Eastern, or Oriental, country, exhibiting many cultural patterns quite similar to those of its neighbors. Although I reject and do not intend to suggest any "cookie cutter" view outlining rigid ethnopolitical boundaries, there are many (but not all) areas of both everyday life and public policy wherein Israel and its Arab neighbors resemble and understand each other. In fact, the cookie cutter image is too often the cause of misunderstandings among nations whose leaders assume total congruity on the basis of a few perceived similarities. Too much, perhaps, has been made of the supposed Westernizing impact of life in the diaspora, especially upon European Jews, with the consequent assumption that the state of Israel would be modeled after those of Europe and America. On the other hand, too little attention has been given to the very real cultural differences that have arisen among Jews in the diaspora and which lead many of them to decline living in Israel at the same time that they celebrate its existence.

My message here is the opposite of Said's. Orientalism, as a "style of thought based upon an ontological and epistemological distinction made between 'the Orient' and (most of the time) 'the Occident' " (Said 1979:2–3), makes the mistake of overlooking similarities while at the same time emphasizing differences so as to create a false (and rigid) dichotomy. I suggest that the United States and other Western countries tend to emphasize Israel's similarities to themselves, thus excluding them from the Orientalist camp. This, too, I aver, is a falsification of reality. As I shall detail in the chapters that follow, the situation is, in fact, so complex as to bring about dismay and extreme mental strife among those who try to comprehend it.

There were, thus, many times when I needed to check my impressions concerning similarities and differences with others whose cultural upbringing had occurred outside of the area under consideration. These included not only persons of Arab descent raised in Honduras but also Americans and Europeans who had married or otherwise had an opportunity for intimate observation of Palestinians and Jews.

My special thanks for moral support, material and psychological assistance, and general hospitality in San Pedro Sula go first to Father Juan N. Chahín and the faithful of his Orthodox church, the only one of its kind in Central America; to the second-generation Pedro Canahuati family and their many relatives, especially Judy, whose Jewish background eventually made it difficult to maintain a public friendship in Honduras; to Victoria Arja de Larach of Beit Jala and her Honduran-born in-laws; to Soad and Nasri Ictech, she of Bethlehem origin; and to the several brothers of the Faraj family, their wives, and their sister, Feride, originally of Beit Sahur.

Many others in San Pedro Sula also eventually became my friends, but the initial stages of gaining rapport were extremely difficult, and it was the above-mentioned individuals and their families who first broke the ice and made me feel welcome. A long-distance telephone intercession on the part of Edward A. Hazboun, then president of the Bethlehem Association in the United States, was crucial in helping me establish my credentials with the Honduran Palestinians, many of whom were suspicious to the point of acute hostility, fearing that, if not a Jew myself, I was at least an undercover agent of the Israeli embassy in Washington. The fact that I was associated with the University of Maryland located in the Washington area exacerbated their suspicions.

Other Hondurans who were especially helpful in various ways included Julia de Kipps, Edgar Dumas, and Marvin and Vida Roth — the latter couple expatriate Americans with more than thirty years in Central America. Marvin's impressions as a secular Jew were especially valuable in assessing changing attitudes toward Jews in Honduras. Their hospitality, friendship, and insights on the relations between Palestinian and other Hondurans were invaluable for my morale and my understanding.

In Jordan special thanks are due President Hamdan of Yarmouk University in Irbid and Professor Dr. Moawiya Ibrahim, director of the Institute of Archaeology and Anthropology—both Palestinian Jordanians—as well as the rest of the faculty and administration of the institute. Frank Faneslow, my colleague in the anthropology section and a neighbor in the Yarmouk University faculty apartments, helped ease problems of housekeeping in a new land and struggles to teach introductory social anthropology to graduate students with a less than perfect understanding of English. The students themselves were an inspiration as well as a pool of friendliness and moral support.

On my trips to Amman I stayed at the hostel of the American Center for Oriental Research (ACOR), then directed by Bert (and Sally) DeVries, where I always found a warm welcome and interesting colleagues. Dr. Rick Roberts, an anthropologist and at that time cultural attaché of the United States Information Service (USIA), was especially helpful and cordial, and United States Ambassador Roscoe (Rocky) Suddarth took a special interest in my study, introducing me to several important local contacts and sharing with me his considerable knowledge of Middle Eastern affairs.

On the West Bank the Christian Brothers of Bethlehem University, as well as various lay faculty members, opened their doors to me to the extent permitted by the Israeli occupation forces. Executive Vice-Chancellor Brother Anton de Roeper and Academic Vice-President Brother Cyril Lytecky gave me a good bit of their time to describe the growth and development of the university, the impact of the Israeli sanctions, and their thoughts on its future, as did Sister Miriam, vice president for finance, and Sister Frances, the registrar. Several other members of the faculty extended their collegial support and in some cases their personal friendship as well. The latter included Adnan and Salweh Musallam, Qustandi and Sousa Shomali, Selim Soghbi, and Brother Jean Manuel.

Victoria Canahuati, director of the Bethlehem Museum and relative of the Canahuatis I knew in Honduras, deserves special recognition for the friendship and assistance she offered. The family of now Honduran Victoria de Larach was also especially warm and open, as were members of the Hasbun and Shehadeh families.

In Jerusalem Ali Kleibo and his wife, Elena, offered me the comforts of their beautiful home in the Old City of East Jerusalem as well as a Muslim perspective on the intifada. My research assistant at Maryland, (now Dr.) Massoud Eghbarieh, and his family were also important in this regard, especially because they were Israeli citizens as well.

Last, but perhaps most important, I will always be grateful to Ayoub Musallam of Bethlehem and his wife, Virginia, who took me into their home as a daughter, introduced me to local living patterns, tried hard to fatten me up, and were an important source of information on earlier patterns of emigration and on the Jordanian period (1950–67), during which he had been member of Parliament and minister of development for the West Bank.

Fieldwork in Honduras was made possible by a sabbatical leave from the University of Maryland plus travel funds for several preceding trips from the College of Behavioral and Social Sciences, the Center for International Development and Conflict Management (CIDCM), the Graduate School, the Department of Anthropology, and the Office of International Affairs. Dr. Edward Azar, a Lebanese-American and former director of CIDCM, made one trip to Honduras with me to help assess the potential for research, and I owe my interest in the subject of conflict to ongoing discussions with him starting as early as 1980. It saddens me greatly that he passed away just before this book went to press. I am grateful to all of the deans and directors of these units for their continuing faith in my work and prompt response to requests for financial assistance.

The Council for the International Exchange of Scholars (CIES) provided a Fulbright award for the work in the West Bank, and I particularly laud their responsible personnel for their imagination and venturesomeness in suggesting Jordan instead of Israel when it became apparent, because of the intifada, that I could not be assigned to a university in the West Bank. They allowed me to make the decision about whether one or two semesters would best serve my needs, and I appreciate their flexibility in this and other matters.

Louise Sweet's intimate knowledge of and continuing interest in Middle Eastern affairs were invaluable, for she led me to the best of the vast literature and helped correct some of my misinterpretations in the early stages of the research. Her strong support, along with that of Ozzie Werner, Doug White, and Tom Weaver, helped me secure the necessary funding. I was energized and informed by lengthy discussions with Cheryl Rubenberg concerning her sojourn in a Palestinian camp in Lebanon as well as by her published analyses of the Palestine Liberation Organization (PLO) and Israeli involvement in

Latin America. Mark Granovetter, Bill Stuart, Stuart Plattner, Lee Preston, and Suhail Bushrui were kind enough to read all or portions of the manuscript. All of these academic colleagues have my gratitude and respect; they should not be held responsible for remaining errors, omissions, or naïvetés, several of which were detected by the anonymous reviewers, to whom I am also grateful.

Getting the final draft together would not have been accomplished half so well without the editorial assistance of Ian González; bibliographical and secretarial services from Tracy Levine, Dana Holland, and Nabil Azar; and a last minute bailout provided by Edmund Sayed, who saved me from a computer disaster involving inadvertently "locked" and encrypted files. Megan Frame did the maps, and Tom Offit helped coordinate the final manuscript preparation. My heartfelt thanks go to all of them.

# Contents

# Chapter 1

# Introduction: Research Problems and Methodology

Your Dollar, Dove and Eagle make
A Trinity that even you
Rate higher than you rate yourselves;
It pays, it flatters, and it's new.
And though your very flesh and blood
Be what your Eagle eats and drinks,
You'll praise him for the best of birds,
Not knowing what the Eagle thinks.
— E. A. Robinson

And alone and without his nest shall the eagle fly across the sun.
— Khalil Gibran

Fieldwork in Guatemala and Honduras over the past thirty-five years with rural and urban Garifuna, Cakchiqueles, and Ladinos has given me a familiarity with the general social milieu in that part of the world. Like most other scholars and laypersons, I saw the Central American social landscape primarily in terms of the tripartite post-conquest ethnicities of American Indian, African, and European, acknowledging, of course, the enormous diversity within each category as well as the hybrid peoples and cultures that the encounter produced.

Some time ago, however, I began to wonder about the origin of certain local surnames in the Garifuna towns where I worked in Honduras, since they did not seem to fit the linguistic patterns of cultures I knew. I was told that *Sikaffy,* for example, was "Turkish," and, since the few such people with whom I came into contact were merchants, I assumed they were isolated cases, much like the occasional Chinese or Jewish merchants I had previously encountered in Guatemala and Belize. It was not until the early 1980s that I realized there was, in fact, a sizable Middle Eastern population on the north coast of Honduras; that it was not Turkish and resented being so called; and that most of these people identified themselves as Palestinians or descendants of Palestinians.[1]

During fieldwork in the Dominican Republic in 1966–68 I had also encountered Middle Eastern merchants — there, mostly Lebanese, or so I was informed. Carol Holzberg's pioneering doctoral research in Jamaica (Holzberg 1987) dealt with Sephardic Jews in that country, but she had also mentioned other Middle Easterners, including a significant number of Palestinians — all, she told me later, from Bethlehem. Holzberg's search of the literature in the late 1970s turned up few sources on any of these groups in the Caribbean, although Lowenthal had commented that in the Caribbean Arabs are "more widely dispersed than any other minority" (1972:208). A preliminary search of the literature for the Americas south of the United States disclosed only a few articles (Ammar 1970; Bray 1962; Chuaqui 1952; Crowley 1974) and three doctoral dissertations, all focusing on Lebanese rather than on Palestinians (Knowlton 1955; Maloof 1958; Páez Oropeza 1984). Crowley had spent time in San Pedro Sula, and, in addition to reading his published articles, I was able to obtain other manuscripts with invaluable information based on his observations there.

In 1984 I began collecting systematic data on what I then perceived as a distinctive but well-integrated and highly acculturated Central American ethnic group. Between January of that year and January of 1988 I made five research trips to Central America, during which I combined this new interest with other work I was doing on Garifuna settlement patterns (Cheek and González 1986) and the persistence of ethnic identity among that group of black American Indians (González 1988).

One of these trips included a survey designed to estimate the number and importance of Middle Easterners in the six Central American countries of Guatemala, Honduras, El Salvador, Costa Rica, Nicaragua, and Belize. Reasoning that merchants and other middle-class persons in cities and towns where the service was avail-

---

1. Through the years their names for themselves have changed with the times. At the turn of the century and until the 1950s they used *Palestinian* (*Palestino*), although they often further modified that by adding the village or town from which they came. At the time of the fieldwork *Arab* (*Arabe*) was becoming more common, since Palestinian conjured up the notion of terrorist, largely due to United States and Israeli propaganda. With the onset of the Persian Gulf War, even *Arab* may become less often used.

able would be likely to have telephones, at least for business purposes, I collected telephone books from all six countries, later entering into an electronic data base all the identifiable Arabic surnames and their addresses. (See chap. 6 for details on this methodology.) I also sought out and interviewed local Palestinians, Lebanese, and Jews to determine something of the nature of their past and present ways of life, the extent to which they considered themselves members of a distinct ethnic group or otherwise expressed ethnicity, and how they viewed events in their Middle Eastern homelands—indeed, whether they thought of their own or their ancestors' birthplaces as homelands at all.

Although all of the six countries had a good sprinkling of Arab surnames identified by Arabic-speaking informants in the United States and/or by Hondurans of Palestinian descent,[2] in the end I chose Honduras for more detailed study. In part this was due to the effects of the protracted conflicts in El Salvador and Nicaragua, which had provoked the (temporary?) emigration of large numbers of their citizens, including, I was told, a good portion of their people of Palestinian origin. I even went to Miami to interview some of these "conflict migrants." Costa Rica had a large colony of Jews, both Ashkenazim and Sephardim, but few identifying themselves as Arabs, while Belize had insignificant numbers of Arabs, mostly Lebanese. The Guatemalan Palestinian community, although relatively large and containing many prominent individuals, seemed not to have retained so much of its cultural identity as was the case in Honduras. Lately, however, there have been signs of what may be a reemerging separate Palestinian identity there.[3]

January through June of 1988 was spent in residence in San Pedro Sula, Honduras—a city of about 350,000 population in 1987—in which people of Palestinian origin have come to dominate the commercial and industrial, if not the social, elite. This book is largely

---

2. Most were Palestinian, but there were also numerous Lebanese, especially in Guatemala, and an occasional Egyptian or Syrian. Some were Sephardic Jews, with surnames only anciently derived from Arabic, if at all—such as Zemurray (Zimeri), for example.

3. Over the past decade Salvadorans have gone in large numbers to neighboring Guatemala. Among them, although I have no quantitative data to support this, are persons of Palestinian ancestry. It is interesting that, as of 1990, the Middle Eastern presence in Guatemala seems to be more visible than in 1987. In addition to an "Arab-Guatemalan Club," for example, there is now a store selling Middle Eastern delicacies, many of which, according

about them and their forebears — how they came to settle in Honduras and how they have fared since. In addition, this work has larger intellectual aims, one of which is to understand the nature of what I am calling "conflict migration" and its impact on culture change in both sending and receiving societies. Diaspora, as a special type of migratory stream, is a related concept and one that will be further discussed in chapter 2, along with other types of migration and their characteristics. Second, this book is intended to further our understanding of the way in which ethnic minority entrepreneurs take advantage of their detachment from the host population in furthering their own economic welfare. Granovetter (1990) uses the terms *coupling* and *decoupling* to describe the in-group solidarity versus the out-group distancing that often occurs in such instances.[4] I will here argue, with evidence from Honduras, that the activities of such entrepreneurs also enhance development in both their original and host communities.

Deciding that in order to understand better what I was seeing in Honduras, and since initial research had suggested that most of the Honduran, as well as the majority of Central American Palestinians had come from the region once known as Ephrata ("fruitful"), which comprised the town of Bethlehem and the closely associated villages of Beit Jala and Beit Sahur, I applied for and was awarded a Fulbright to teach and conduct research at Bethlehem University. The Council for International Exchange of Scholars (CIES) notified me of my nomination by phone on 8 December 1988. My appointment, if locally approved, was to have begun the following September, after my sabbatical stint of eight months in Honduras.

On 9 December the Arab rebellion, or intifada, burst into flames

---

to their labels, are manufactured in El Salvador. Guatemala is also interesting in that it has many families of Sephardic Jewish origin that have intermarried extensively with Palestinians. Many respondents were not able to tell me to which of the two categories certain people belonged. I take this to mean that these people are now basically Guatemalan Latins — Roman Catholics — with only a family tradition of Middle Eastern origin. Many of the Jews came from Germany or via Bessarabia when it was part of the Russian Empire; for the most part, they identify themselves as German-Guatemalans rather than as Sephardic Jews, although they are aware of that aspect of their heritage as well. There are also, of course, many Ashkenazim as well. Most of the latter are more recent immigrants.

4. Mark Granovetter's forthcoming book *Society and Economy*, seen in manuscript, describes and analyzes these in his chapter 4 on entrepreneurship, development, and the emergence of firms.

in the West Bank and in Gaza, and, with considerable pessimism about the possibility of completing the whole of my planned research project, I nevertheless left for Honduras. In April I was notified by CIES that there was little hope of my going to Bethlehem. I stopped taking Arabic lessons and prepared to stay in Central America for the remainder of my sabbatical year. Around the middle of June, to my great surprise, CIES asked whether I would like to go to Jordan instead. Knowledgeable people claimed I could get from Irbid to Bethlehem in an hour and a half. Despite misgivings about my lack of preparation for this new assignment, I decided to give it a try, since everyone involved seemed to understand and sympathize with my research aims in the West Bank.

Yarmouk University and the Institute of Archaeology and Anthropology were my hosts for the fall semester of 1988. I taught only one course for them — a seminar for beginning graduate students — which met once a week, thus leaving me relatively free for the research. Getting to Bethlehem, however, proved more difficult than had been suggested. Each trip required a special permit that could only be obtained in Amman, the capital, some two hours away by car — a three- or four-hour trip if one had to do it by bus. Therefore, I bought a rattletrap car, a more daring and complicated transaction in Jordan than elsewhere. Once having acquired the vehicle, red tape continued to plague my movements. Approval of each travel application — a two-page document with photo, good for only one trip — required two to three working days, thus necessitating two trips to Amman for the purpose, and, because of timing and logistics, the second one could not be combined with my actual trip to the West Bank. Thus, my trips were reduced to about one every three weeks, each lasting from seven to ten days. Crossing the bridge (called "King Hussein" in Jordan and "Allenby" in the West Bank)[5] was always something of an ordeal, although non-Arab foreigners were spared its worst terrors, leaving us to cope only with apparent rudeness, inconvenience, and seemingly pointless delays, searches, and confiscations of things such as a small, unopened jar of instant coffee. ("You can buy coffee in Israel," I was told.) An elastic clothesline with attached metal clothespins caused a sensation and a fifteen-minute delay while

---

5. General Allenby was the leader of the British forces occupying Jerusalem on 11 December 1917 after its surrender by the Ottomans.

it was taken around to all the other customs inspectors for their opinions as to whether it was safe to allow it in.[6]

Once I arrived in Bethlehem and its neighboring communities of Beit Jala and Beit Sahur, it was like old home week. I was received with interest and kindness by everyone. Most families had relatives in America, many in Honduras, and they were eager to invite me to their homes and to share with me their views on life in the diaspora and its meaning for those in the home community. English was commonly spoken, a legacy of the British Mandate; several people I met spoke Spanish, either because they had resided in Latin America or had made frequent visits to relatives there. Still, after the novelty of my presence wore off, it was difficult to keep their minds on the subject of diaspora, for they were living in intifada.

Peoples engaged in violent social conflict do not enjoy normal living arrangements, although in this case the inconvenience and suffering were far from equal for both sides. Too often I arrived in Jerusalem only to find telephone lines to Bethlehem disconnected or transportation difficult or impossible due to curfews or the closing of the highway by Israeli authorities. The Palestinians themselves called frequent strikes, during which they refused to appear at their places of employment, including their own businesses, which were normally closed (in protest) after noon each day. The people of the Bethlehem area were eager to talk about the intifada; I collected horror stories by the dozen. There was no one whose life had not been affected in numerous ways, ranging from deaths, imprisonment, or beatings of loved ones to petty humiliations and economic deprivations.

Outside of Jerusalem, where bus transportation was quite adequate for my purposes, it was something of a problem to get around without a car. While I stayed in Bethlehem, phone connections to Jerusalem and the other towns were often shut off, so it was difficult to make and keep appointments. Although communal Arab-driven taxis between Jerusalem and Bethlehem were reasonably cheap and

---

6. In fairness, I should note that Jordanian customs officials also sometimes make it difficult for people arriving from Israel across the Allenby / King Hussein bridge. Although I never was stopped for any reason, I observed others having to remove labels written in Hebrew from things such as towels and small jars of spices. I had been previously warned not to bring anything with Jewish symbols such as the menorah or the Star of David. A long-standing boycott of companies doing business with Israel, such as Helena Rubinstein, for example, prohibited their products from being imported into Jordan.

quick, they did not always run, and the Israeli bus service on that route was erratic. I managed quite well within each smaller town on foot, but moving between them was difficult without a car. Private cars are not permitted to enter from Jordan, so mine was left in the care of a farmer across the road from the bridge. Rental cars, available only in Jerusalem, carried Israeli license plates and would have been vulnerable to attack anywhere on the West Bank. Keeping one overnight in Bethlehem would have been especially foolhardy. My friends were very kind about chauffeuring me here and there, but there were many times when it was clear that they preferred being off the streets altogether. Trying to get to Beit Sahur from Bethlehem — only a few kilometers — was a major undertaking. Once I asked three different taxis to take me there, wait for half an hour, and return. All refused to make the trip, for Beit Sahur has a reputation for active and vociferous protest, with the result that Israeli soldiers were camped there for several months during my research, housed next door to one of my host families, in the closed junior high school.

For all these reasons I decided to cut my research stay to five months, for I began to experience diminishing returns on the emigration issue and found my focus gradually changing toward the intifada itself. The conditions under which I was working were mentally and physically exhausting, and, worst of all, I came to share many Arabs' passionate distrust and distaste for Israel. Even though I felt I had objective reasons for my generally pro-Arab stance, I nevertheless realized that I was no longer functioning as I felt an anthropologist should.[7] I returned to the United States at the end of January 1989, where I waited some months before pulling together the materials I had collected for this book. It has taken a while to recover from the experience, and in many important respects I never will.

At the Library of Congress I continued the literature search be-

---

7. I am aware that not all my colleagues would agree with this position. I am also under no delusion that we can ever be entirely objective about anything. But the degree of emotion I was experiencing led me sometimes to make wildly subjective interpretations of what I saw, accompanied by sometimes irrational reactions to incidents that were innocuous, if not trivial. I was behaving more and more like a local Arab! This problem — indeed perhaps a conundrum — of how far we can or should go in identifying with our hosts is one that has preoccupied anthropologists extensively. To obtain rapport and to understand their views we must identify with "our people" to some extent. Where to draw the line in order to arrive at useful description and meaningful conclusions is far from settled.

gun at the American Center for Oriental Research in Amman and at the Albright Institute in Jerusalem. I found nineteenth-century pilgrims' and travelers' accounts particularly valuable for information on conditions in the Holy Land just before and during the period of most intense emigration. The more I read, the more I realized the importance of historical factors in leading to the present impasse in the Middle East and its effects on Palestinians in the diaspora. In Jerusalem, where I spent a total of about ten working days, I interviewed several Jewish and Arab "notables"[8] and perused the Israeli National Archives and Library. I learned a great deal about Arab-Jewish relations merely by walking the streets, visiting public places, and exploring the city by bus. Since I was usually mistaken for a visiting Jew, I was repeatedly warned by well-meaning Israelis that I was risking my life by going into the old city and that I should not set foot in East Jerusalem (where my hotel was located).

I might well have simply concentrated my efforts on studying the Palestinian emigration to Jordan, except that my original research design was intended to complement my work in Honduras, and I was not really prepared, on such short notice, to take advantage of the altered field situation. There was a large camp of Palestinian Muslims near Irbid, for example, but I was not able to converse with them in Arabic, their only language. The Christian Palestinian community, many from the Bethlehem area, was concentrated in Amman, a city of about a million people in 1988, to which they have been drawn since the 1920s, when it was officially part of Palestine under the British.[9] The logistics of tracking them down there would have been formidable, even if I had been able to spend more time in Amman. Some believe that perhaps 75 to 80 percent of that city's inhabitants are

---

8. This is the term commonly used in English to refer to Middle Eastern men of informal or formal political influence and stature. They serve as intermediaries between government and the people, especially in urban settings (Hourani 1968:48; Muslih 1988:5). Although there is a class implication, it is not necessarily associated with extraordinary wealth. Its use in English goes back to at least the eighteenth century and perhaps before.

9. In 1950 King Abdullah absorbed the West Bank, an action that was recognized by the United Kingdom and by Pakistan but not by the rest of the world (Wilson 1987). Since the war of June 1967 — in which Israel defeated Egypt, Syria, Iraq, and Jordan — Israel has occupied the West Bank and Gaza and has annexed both East Jerusalem and the former Syrian territory of the Golan Heights. Most of the Sinai was returned to Egypt following the Camp David accords in 1977–78.

West Bankers (Day 1986:59), although Jordanian government estimates for public information are far lower. For many reasons the tensions between Jordanians and Palestinians are great, and an anthropological study of that situation is overdue but would require
time, preparation, and a thorough knowledge of Levantine Arabic.

On the positive side, my Middle Eastern residence helped me
refine my ideas about the diaspora and its Central American component. I came to realize how different the Palestinian/Israeli conflict
looks to individuals on each side of the world, as well as on each side
of the controversy, and that it would be a mistake to assume that all
emigrant Palestinians share the same hopes and fears. My primary
reference group and subject in this book are the Christian Palestinians of Bethlehem, Beit Jala, and Beit Sahur (a collectivity I frequently will refer to as Ephrata) and their coreligionists of Arab descent in Honduras. Yet I must place them in their larger context, both
historic and ethnic, and try to explain also the inexorable drive that
for one hundred years or more has sent them out of their home land
to virtually all parts of the world but which, at the same time, brings
them back in spirit, if not in person. One family of Beit Sahur has a
genealogical tree painted on their family room wall showing names
of relatives living in all five continents. Other families have made
similar records, albeit in less artistic form.

As a record of the Palestinian diaspora, this book does not pre-
tend to document the largest segment, comprised of Muslims who
also live all over the world but are more heavily represented in the
nearby Arab countries. Although he did not distinguish between
Muslims and others, one observer estimated that there were nearly
three million Palestinians outside Israel, the West Bank, and Gaza in
1986 (Salam y Massarueh 1986:27). Those in United Nations Relief
and Rehabilitation Administration (UNRRA) refugee camps in Jordan and Lebanon are, nearly without exception, Muslim (Rubenberg 1989). Many others live in the Arab gulf states, where, depending upon their education and skills, they may work as professionals
or as menial, often seasonal, laborers. There are also large Muslim
communities in the United States and Canada and in several European countries, including England, France, Germany, and Sweden.

Within the Middle East, emigrant Christian Palestinians are
concentrated in Jordan, Lebanon, and Egypt, where they are mostly
engaged in trade, banking, and the professions. By far their largest

numbers, however, have gone to Christian countries—especially those of the New World. In part this is due to their having begun the diaspora to the Americas so long ago. Having relatives already settled in another country provides the major impetus for choosing a particular destination.

Furthermore, this book is not comprehensive in relation to the emigration of Christian Palestinians to the New World, or even to South and Central America. Honduras must be seen as a case study, albeit of one of the more important Latin American diaspora communities. There are more Palestinians to be found in cities such as Santiago, Chile, and Monterrey, Mexico, but their numbers and local dispersion defy their study by traditional ethnographic techniques.[10] As anthropologists who have worked in urban areas know, the size of both the city and our particular reference group within it are important limitations. I estimate that persons of Palestinian descent make up about one-fourth of the population of the 350,000 who live in San Pedro Sula, but they are neither residentially segregated nor phenotypically distinguishable from other Hondurans. Thus, they tend to fade into the general fabric of Honduran life when that is viewed casually by outsiders.

Nevertheless, there are many social groups in San Pedro Sula made up exclusively of Palestinians, and their presence and distinct identity are recognized by virtually every Honduran, to whom they are known collectively (along with Lebanese and sometimes Jews) as "*Turcos.*" Many of the data presented here came from documentary sources as well as statistical compilations made by others, but a good bit resulted from personal interviews and the time-honored method of participant observation. Much of the latter occurred in connection with the diverse activities of the Orthodox church and its various sodalities.

Finally, rather than being merely a descriptive study of an emi-

---

10. Smith states, without giving a source, that by the 1970s there were eighty thousand Palestinians in Chile, thirty thousand of whom were from Bethlehem. She goes on: "In addition to the immigrants who had come after 1948 the community included several thousand who were descended from the original settlers who had left Palestine before the First World War to escape conscription by the Ottomans" (1984:128). The implication here, it seems to me, is that most of the eighty thousand were recent arrivals. It is difficult to imagine how Smith arrived at these figures; I suspect they were estimates given to her by an interested party, for to my knowledge there have been neither census data nor ethnographic surveys done on this population in Chile.

grant community, I have strived to contribute to our understanding
of the phenomena social scientists and others lump under the heading
of "ethnicity." Throughout my research I asked myself the same questions I often heard in both Honduras and Jordan from local officials
as well as academics: What is a Palestinian? A *Turco?* An Arab? How
does religion interface with customs and values deriving from use of
a common language, residence in a particular community, and loyalty to the shifting boundaries of different nation-states with rulers of
different ethnic origins? Is it possible in the Middle East to separate
state and religion, which the Christians within the PLO urge but
which is largely seen by their Muslim brethren (and, increasingly, by
their Israeli adversaries) as a European, western, solution?

It is my view that the Christian Palestinians are best considered
as a distinct ethnic category, of which the Bethlehemite portion is especially significant because of its lengthy history of migration to the
Americas—a process that long ago became incorporated into its way
of life. This does not mean that, as Christians, they feel no common
loyalties with Muslims deriving from the same general region, but
this is a complicated political stance with a long history. In fact, I
would argue that many, if not all, modern political movements in plural or pluralistic societies have found it useful to incorporate ethnicity
into their platforms or charters, even though it may be necessary to
bend the ethnic realities into a new "tradition."

Middle Eastern specialists have long emphasized that identity
there is based upon family, community, and religious or communal
affiliation, although those three cannot be separated, except analyti-
cally. In the diaspora the criteria remain crucial for the definition of
ethnicity, especially because Arabic (language usually constitutes a
critical component of ethnicity) has largely disappeared among the
second generation. Thus, because of differing life experiences in their
new homes, emigrants define their political allegiances in novel ways,
conforming neither to the desires and expectations of their hosts nor
to those of their kith and kin in areas they have left behind.

This book will not be popular with many of my Palestinian
friends who would like to have scholarly support for their struggle to
achieve an independent Palestinian state. Neither will it offer balm or
hope to those Palestinians who prefer the idea of a pluralistic Israel
in which both Jews and Arabs share power, wealth, and prestige. Although I sympathize with both those dreams and believe the present

situation of both Israeli Arabs and of those in the West Bank and Gaza is an abomination and a blot on the record of both Israel and its main supporters, this book was not conceived as a means of either reinforc- ing or refuting arguments made by any particular political party or position. The lack of cohesion among Arab, even Palestinian, inter- ests has not been helpful to the solution of their problems. Neverthe- less, I hope this book will improve the image of Palestinians in the eyes of their neighbors everywhere and contribute to a better understand- ing of how it is possible to maintain ethnic loyalties, while at the same time declining to fight actively to return to what would be, for many, a foreign land, with foreign neighbors. Even if an independent Pales- tine were to be achieved, it seems clear that it would not be completely secular (despite PLO rhetoric) and that Christians would perforce re- main second-class citizens. (See chap. 8.) Neither does it seem likely that a nation-state conceived by its founders and leaders as being of Jews, by Jews, and for Jews will be easily converted to pluralism (Domínguez 1989).

Even though it may be argued that they are second-class citi- zens, or even that they constitute an underclass at present, it is manifestly apparent that most of the Palestinian migrants to the New World — at least in Honduras — have done very well for themselves. Although not all are wealthy, a good number may be so considered, and few, if any, are in dire straits of poverty. Most have achieved a comfortable middle-class existence. There has been considerable prejudice against them, but, despite that fact, they have benefited the country in many ways. I will present evidence to demonstrate the enormous impact the Palestinian immigrant community has had and continues to have on the development of the north coast of Honduras. Only recently have some Palestinian Hondurans begun to seek active political roles, which is not unrelated to the observation that, increas- ingly, they see themselves and are accepted by others as Hondurans, rather than as temporary, exploiting sojourners. The continuing im- migration from the West Bank, however, today directly a result of the conflict there, stimulates and reinforces this group's presentation of self as "native" Hondurans and may eventually lead to a new decoup- ling of the more acculturated group — or part of it — from the larger Arab population in ways many of the latter will not appreciate.

In closing this brief introductory essay I should try to explain why I have chosen *Dollar, Dove, and Eagle* as the title for this book. It came from a poem by the American poet E. A. Robinson that struck me as particularly apt. In any conflict migration the pursuits of peace and of economic well-being cannot easily be separated. Much of the argument today about how to define a refugee centers on the fact that there may be multiple motivations for emigration. Poverty may make people more vulnerable to involvement in resistance or revolutionary movements, which in turn may increase the difficulty of staying alive — both because of efforts by rebels to win local support and because of governmental reprisals when support is given. But, in turn, protracted conflict adversely affects the entire economy: Loss of production and, consequently, of markets; scarcity of food and other necessities; rising prices; and inflation all tend to accompany internal strife. Death, whether by bullet or by starvation, is to be avoided, and sometimes flight is the only apparent solution. Terror, both random and targeted, as has been used at times by many belligerents — including, in this case, both the PLO and Israel — may be only the final straw in provoking an unplanned emigration.

In time, however, refugeeism itself becomes institutionalized as a strategy of conflict migration (see Burns 1989; McCommon 1989; and various essays in Carmack 1988). It is debatable whether such migration from a base of poverty is actually an effective means of improving the well-being of the emigrants. As these and many other studies have shown, oftentimes the new situation turns out to be less favorable than expected. Some of the disappointed will try to return, but many others, having burned their bridges, stay on — hoping that things will be better for their children. Such hopes perpetuate the strategy.

Poverty alone, of course, cannot account for all emigration. In any civil war or escalating conflict the more affluent, who are thought of as being more powerful, in some ways are also more vulnerable. If active politically, they are more identifiable by their opponents than are the poor and are thus subject to death threats, kidnapping, or deportation. Some of their property may be damaged or destroyed. On the other hand, they are also better able to raise capital and mobilize kin, media, and business networks in other countries and thus promulgate their personal and collective cause and improve their economic situation, at the same time that they escape local violence. These are the so-called fat cats, despised by many of their compatriots who envy what seems to be a more favorable position than their own.

Those left behind today in the West Bank cannot understand why the emigrants do not spend more of their time and money trying to remedy the Palestinian situation in the Middle East. The suggestion that many of their absent brethren have given up any thought of ultimate return is often vehemently denied as being impossible or, at least, incomprehensible.

Most of the Palestinians whose story appears on these pages left their homeland for multiple reasons, seeking both the dollar and the dove. Their new position is not one of unmitigated luxury and exalted social status, but neither do they necessarily desire to return, as we shall see. The eagle, as a symbol of strength, independence, and power, is also appropriate here in several ways. It is almost impossible to escape the all-pervading economic, cultural, and political influence of the United States in Honduras, and it has been so for more than one hundred years (See Posas and del Cid 1981). The prominence of our country in Israeli affairs has risen sharply since the Six Day War of 1967, although before that, as I read the evidence, the United States was reluctantly acquiescent, then moderately obstructionist, then indifferent.[11] The position of the United States today, up until the period of the Gulf War, has been strongly pro Israel. Clarke has made the following observation: "Except perhaps for El Salvador and Honduras, no other nation is so thoroughly dependent on the United States [as Israel]" (1989:232).

Palestinians resident in or citizens of Honduras for the most part approve and enjoy the policies of the United States in Central America but decry them in the Middle East, where they overwhelmingly stand behind the Palestine Liberation Organization as the only legitimate representative of the Palestinian people, both at home and in diaspora (see chap. 8). In truth, "they know not what the Eagle thinks," or, at least, they cannot make sense of it. They did not appreciate the Sandinista strength in Nicaragua, yet they were also chagrined by the fact that Israel was implicated in providing arms to Somoza and to the Contras (Bahbah 1986; Jamail and Gutiérrez 1986; Rubenberg 1986a and 1986b). Uncomfortable with Israel as an

---

11. The literature on this theme is vast. Much of it is highly political and emotional. But see the following for several different views: American Christian Palestine Committee 1948; Anglo-American Committee of Inquiry 1946; Blitzer 1985; Caldarola 1975; Chomsky 1983; Feintuch 1987; Findley 1985; Green 1988; Hadawi 1967; Jansen 1970; Neff 1988a, 1988b.

ally in Central America and an enemy in the Middle East, they seek peace on both fronts and economic and political security at both national and personal levels. They want the best of both worlds — to be accepted as first-class citizens of Honduras and also of an independent Palestinian state, even though most, if given the choice, would probably not choose to live in such a state. This book will try to show their views of these two dilemmas as well as the structural causes of their inability to come to terms with either.

*Chapter 2*

# Migrations and Diasporas

The great fear of the people is that once Zionist wealth is passed into the land, all territorial and mineral concessions will fall into the hands of the Jews whose intensely clannish instincts prohibit them from dealing with any but those of their own religion, to the detriment of Moslems and Christians. These latter, the natives of the soil, foresee their eventual banishment from the land.

—Chief Administrator Major-General H. D. Watson to the Foreign Office, August 1919

## Migration

This book is about the continuing self-relocation of people to places far away from their homelands. Specifically, it describes the experiences of Arabic-speaking Christians—who have called themselves Palestinians since at least the turn of the twentieth century and possibly for much longer—in Central America. It asks questions and tries to supply some answers about the nature of human migration and resettlement through time and how these relate to cultural persistence and change. It will be particularly concerned with documenting and analyzing the impact of conflict in the Middle East on the emigration of Palestinians to the New World.

The social scientific literature is replete on the subject of migration, long a favorite of historians, sociologists, geographers, and anthropologists. Most of the earliest studies, whether focusing on internal (usually rural-to-urban) or international movements, dwelt on the impact of migration on the receiving society and on the migrants' new lives there, probably because the social scientific observers were themselves part of that host society and were on hand to witness the adaptive process. Such studies have continued in all of the disciplines mentioned, many of those dealing with the United States stressing the differences between the massive European influx of the nineteenth century and the "New Immigration," since 1950, largely from Latin America, the Caribbean, and Asia. The latter movement, in contrast to earlier immigrant streams, is marked by a significant number of

17

"irregular" or undocumented entries, conflict refugees, and women. It has a large component of persons from non-European, non-Western cultures and is, therefore, extremely visible (Bryce-LaPorte 1980:xi).

Indeed, it would appear that one of the primary characteristics of the changing global sociopolitical reorganization is that peoples everywhere are on the move. Many traditional societies are no longer isolated, as development efforts carve roads through mountains and jungles, allowing more people, goods, and information from the outside world to enter the communities and lure away many of their inhabitants, often because their ancestral mode of production and sources of income have become disturbed by the development process. Increased health, formal schooling, and population growth — all products of development — also stimulate the outward flow. Finally, demands for both skilled and unskilled labor in the more industrialized countries, combined with rising expectations and demands on the part of native-born workers, have led to increased formal and informal recruitment of foreign workers. Typically, the latter are heavily represented in menial agricultural jobs, in domestic work, in the hotel and restaurant industry, and in the garment industry. Some United States cities have been so heavily settled by migrants from one part of the world that the ambience of the whole has been affected. The Caribbeanization of New York City is a case in point (Sutton and Chaney 1987). Similarly, Salvadorans in Washington, D.C., and Arabs in Detroit have left an indelible mark on those cities (Abraham and Abraham 1983; Aswad 1974). Anthropologists no longer need travel outside the borders of the United States, or even outside its major cities, to find exotic, even "traditional," communities for their perusal.

Economic development, natural disaster, and conflict situations have stimulated studies of "involuntary resettlements" (Cernea 1989; Colson 1971; Hansen and Oliver-Smith 1982; Scudder 1973) and of refugeeism (Burns 1989; Gersony 1989; McCommon 1989; Skinner and Hendricks 1979), although none of these is really a new phenomenon. Many of these movements have been necessitated and orchestrated by national or international entities trying to change the face of the globe for what they believe to be the betterment of one particular region. Nubians, for example, much of whose homeland today lies beneath the waters of Lake Nasser in Egypt, have become a dispersed minority, living in many different countries of the Middle East (Geiser 1973:184). The Bikini islanders, evacuated from their island to allow testing of the atom bomb following World War II, are another early example (Kiste 1974). Today the number of such incidents has increased to the extent that involuntary resettlement has become a topical specialization in the field.[1]

As anthropologists increasingly observed emigration from the so-called traditional — even isolated — communities they were studying, it became necessary to scrutinize its effects on the society left behind, especially in economic and demographic terms (Georges 1990; Shankman 1976) but also in relation to worldview (Seeger 1981; Hinshaw 1975), ritual (Kerns 1983), gender relationships (Brettell 1986), and family organization (González 1961; Murray 1981; Watson 1975), to cite only a few of the many extant works. The positive effects of emigration seem largely limited to improvements in the standard of living made possible by cash remittances to those left behind, plus some advantage for those who return in old age to live on dollar pensions that give a good exchange in a depressed economy. Anthropologists often conclude that the disadvantages in relation to culture loss and psychological trauma for both migrants and stay-at-homes outweigh the benefits for the home community (Ghosh 1989; González 1988:198–200; Rubinstein 1983:299; Zenner 1971:44–45).[2]

Most anthropologists began to study migration as they watched the villagers move to nearby cities and then followed them to their international destinations. Once they began to view these "peasants in cities" (Bock 1970; Foster and Kemper 1974) there developed a new anthropological interest in global industrial society and the ways in which the power and influence of the more developed nations affected life and social patterns elsewhere. Migration was clearly one primary effect, and, as people flocked to cities, first within their own country and later to those in foreign countries, the concept of a culture of poverty developed (Lewis 1959). Increasingly, too, as populations have become more diverse, anthropologists have concerned themselves

---

1. A Program on Involuntary Migration and Resettlement is currently being started at the University of Florida. It will promote research, offer expert consultation on planning and implementing policies and programs, and educate graduate students in the fields of refugee studies, disaster research and management, and population dislocation as a consequence of development projects (*Anthropology Newsletter* 1991).

2. For an immigrant's somewhat different, more optimistic view, see Shammas 1991.

with ethnicity and how it is defined and redefined to suit the ever-changing sociopolitical scene. In addition to documenting migrations from Third World countries, anthropologists have also studied migratory streams from one European or Middle Eastern country to another under various circumstances. Among these are studies of temporary, or "guest," workers (Center for Migration Studies 1986; Mandel 1989), Jews from many countries "repatriated" to Israel (Domínguez 1989; Goldberg 1977; Weingrod 1965), and the Palestinian refugees of Jordan (Allison 1977; Bailey 1966), Lebanon (Rubenberg 1989), and the Gulf States (Baster 1954; Aruri and Farsoun 1980).

## Motivations

The motivations underlying any particular act of migration, and, by extension, any discernible migratory stream, have always been a difficult research topic. Not only are individuals' motives usually multiple and only subconsciously realized, but they are necessarily voiced in terms that cannot easily be verified, much less quantified. The old idea that people move to the city because they want to experience the excitement and "lights" may well be true, but it represents a type of reductionism that is sociologically awkward and difficult to address. In the same category we must include moving to avoid a military draft, to find a better job, to escape a death squad, to be able to practice rituals freely and publicly — numerous reasons may be advanced. These discussions or responses are interesting facets of the story but are only partial explanations in and of themselves and not really subject to further scientific analysis, since, ultimately, individuals' proximate reasons for their decisions to migrate are legion, imprecise, and often inscrutable, even to themselves. This does not mean that statements regarding motivations should be excluded from consideration but that they should be viewed in context, as individual expressions of dissatisfactions and unrealized dreams. As such, they add to the total description of the movement, but I believe they hardly ever explain it.

On the other hand, statistical analyses of migratory streams sometimes induce social scientists to assign motives, even without interviewing the migrants, as when it is shown that migration rates correlate well with wages paid to unskilled labor in the receiving society or with unemployment at home (Todaro 1969) or that emigration from Central America rises during periods of violence against peasants (Feinberg and Carlisle 1989). Certainly, such studies are useful, especially when considering global phenomena, and, for anthropologists, as heuristic devices suggesting fruitful avenues or areas for ethnographic research.

## Migration Strategies

In order to gain a fuller understanding of the movement of peoples at both global and micro levels, it may be more useful to deal with migration strategies, which are subject to institutionalization, and to the character of the resulting settlement patterns. In the following I rely on the insights and suggestions of Hamilton (1985) as well as on my own early (1961) and recent work on migration.

Migration strategies underlie migration processes, and in Hamilton's model temporary and permanent migration form basic categories and have different consequences for settlement in the host country and also in the homeland. I agree with his major point, but, as I pointed out in 1959, at any given moment in time it is impossible to determine whether a given migrant will return home, remain, or move on to still another host community or country. Ethnographic evidence suggests that much of what starts out as temporary migration becomes permanent, and the opposite—return migration of those who came to stay—may also occur (Brettell 1979; Hernández Alvarez 1967; Kubat 1983; Rhoades 1979; various essays in Stinner et al. 1982).

Step migration, in which people move through a series of communities before finally settling down in one, has also been well documented. The tendency for this to happen leads to what has been termed "chain migration." In this process one views step migration from the perspective of the larger society, rather than of the individual migrants, in which case it may be seen as a type of settlement pattern in which a colony of migrants from a particular location develops in a nearby town then feeds other migrant communities in a more distant city or even a different country.

This strategy was quite different from that used by some other migrants who settled in Central America and the Caribbean, such as black and white Americans who left the South after its defeat in 1865. The latter sent reconnaissance parties to different places to examine the living conditions and economic potential of each. Most of these had agrarian as well as commercial intents, but few understood the problems of living and farming in the tropics. Still, they chose their locations carefully, adapted themselves to local conditions, and managed to survive.

The "colony" was an important migration strategy for centuries among Europeans seeking new lives in the Americas and elsewhere. Colonies were made up of entire families who joined with similar units in attempting to establish a new community similar to what they had left behind, often literally carving it out of a wilderness. Sometimes the colonists had previously been neighbors; more often they came from diverse communities, sometimes diverse nations. It is significant that many of these planned colonies failed due to their leaders' having received poor information or to outright fraud on the part of either local entrepreneurs or their representatives in Europe or the United States. Most often, the colonists were given inadequate information and resources with which to confront and conquer or conform to their new environment.[3]

Whether and how people from the same original community (town, country, ethnic group) congregate and interrelate in a new location are significant considerations. As suggested above, some try to recreate overnight a way of life identical to what they left behind. Others, no less organized but with different agendas and means, may live in workers' quarters or camps provided by employers or relief agencies such as the United Nations (UN). Others move in with their relatives, sometimes with no apparent residential ethnic clustering beyond that of the extended family, as is the case for Koreans in the Washington, D.C., area.[4] The latter do have considerable ethnic cohesiveness, but they live near the scattered small businesses they own and operate throughout the area. These and other cases, such as that

---

3. A few examples of such unfortunate colonies were those of the Norse in Newfoundland (Fitzhugh 1985:27–29); Isabela (1493–94), established by Columbus on the island of Hispaniola (Herring 1964:123–24); late eighteenth-century Spaniards on the Honduran Mosquito Shore (Sorsby 1972); early nineteenth century English at Abbotsville in Guatemala (Griffith 1965:222); Belgians at Santo Tomas (1840), also in Guatemala (Blondeel Van Cuelebrouk 1846); and New Englanders in North Dakota between 1886 and 1890 (Gardner and Olson 1986:11–20).

4. Dr. Ruth Krulfeld is presently studying Koreans in the D.C. area, and conveyed this information to me. She informs me that to date there are no publications on the subject.

of the Arabs who live in and around Detroit, Michigan (Abraham and Abraham 1983; Aswad 1974), as well as the Garifuna experience presented below, suggest that the geographical unit of analysis for effective anthropological analysis of migration strategies must be larger than the neighborhood—that it may be necessary to view the entire city along with its hinterland, or even the host country as a whole, since official immigration policies, even when largely ineffectual for the purposes intended, will inevitably influence the migratory stream in some way. They determine, for example, whether immigrants must evade detection by hiding themselves through dispersion among the general populace or whether they are encouraged to reside together and separate from the local citizens (Griffith 1972).

Thus, in addition to considering strategies and processes, I would add settlement type as an important categorizing device, if not an independent variable. In other words, where people settle may be important in determining whether they ultimately stay or return to their homeland. It has the further advantage of being directly observable, rather than merely postulated. By *settlement* I mean first the country chosen. Laws controlling who may enter and under what conditions citizenship or its rights may be acquired are important variables in the economics of choice. Opportunities for capital and labor investment may not be the same for all comers. Early nineteenth-century Honduras, for example, seems to have been less threatened by the possibility of immigration of "Asians" than were Guatemala and El Salvador, both of which hoped to "improve" the racial mix in their populations by encouraging people of European descent over others. This is undoubtedly reflected in the figures shown in chapter 5 for both Chinese and Palestinian entrepreneurs in Honduras.

*Settlement* also refers to the region of the country to which migrants are drawn. Neither Guatemala nor El Salvador experienced the turn-of-the-century banana boom over such a large extent of their territory as did Honduras. Most of the earliest Palestinians settled in the smaller towns and hamlets of the Honduran north coast, especially in those that served as sea or river ports, where cash flowed in response to the sale of bananas grown by individuals and the larger companies. They were not so permanently settled, however, that they could not move to other locations as that seemed desirable. As migrants, they were not burdened with notions of being tied to the land nor by extended kin networks in a given location.

Finally, *settlement* may refer to the kinds of living quarters in which migrants live. Stories from both Palestinians and other Hondurans suggest that the earliest Palestinian immigrants lived humbly, not investing much capital in their own homes. Single men might rent rooms or even beds in the rural areas they visited when peddling. Once they acquired a wife and family, however, they preferred to live in a separate structure, albeit these were sometimes quite rude. Sometimes several brothers and their wives inhabited the same household; often they lived above or in rooms behind their stores.

## Migration and Cultural Change

Migration is important to an understanding of cultural persistence and change. We tend to think of it as disrupting the flow of everyday life at home, sometimes damaging and sometimes improving the health and happiness of those left behind, depending upon the amount and frequency of remittances from absent relatives. Its impact at the homesite also varies according to decisions made about who goes and who stays.

### The Garifuna

The Garifuna of Central America have used several different migration strategies since 1797, when they were forcibly deported from St. Vincent in the Lesser Antilles. After being abandoned on the island of Roatan off the coast of Honduras, they sent small colonies made up of extended families to settle new villages up and down the coastline between Belize and Bluefields (Nicaragua). From these their menfolk moved outward to seek wage-paying labor opportunities. This practice brought about changes in the division of labor and the structure of decision making and religious expression, both at household and community levels. In the absence of the men, the women took on a range of responsibilities not previously assigned to their gender (González 1969, 1988; Kerns 1983).

In more recent times—since about 1960—women also migrate, sometimes as single persons and sometimes with their husbands. Grandmothers, long a major influence in the households headed by women in their husbands' absence, are more often called on to raise children in the absence of both parents. Remittances may be used entirely to support these skeletal households, leaving nothing for savings or investment, or even for the improvement of living quarters or for the maintenance of household or agricultural equipment. Because their sights are set on emigration as the recognition of adult status, children fail to learn traditional lore and ritual, native crafts, or economic activities such as fishing and gardening. Because their parents often send money directly to them, to spend as they please, they also often defy their grandparents' attempts at discipline and end by being prepared to enter neither the traditional Garifuna society nor that of their dreamworld — New York City.

*Palestinians*

Palestinian migration has had an entirely different character, although, like the Garifuna, men from Ephrata have been traveling to find their fortunes for over two hundred years.[5] Palestinians coming to the Americas often started by going to a major European Mediterranean port — Marseilles was commonly used. There, using their wits and/or their cash reserves, they either obtained new passports or identity cards and passage to an American port. Some have said that Haiti was a popular first destination in the early days because that country was not fussy about one's documentation or nationality. Information about potential settlement sites among would-be migrants was sketchy at first, and there was a good bit of trial-and-error settlement. Some stayed in Haiti (or Jamaica or some other Caribbean or United States port). Others traveled on, to Mexico, Honduras, El Salvador, or any one of several South American countries. If they had no luck where they first stopped, they went on to another country, and sometimes to still another. Or they might return to a place they had left previously. And when they returned to Palestine (as most of them did), they relayed, through anecdotes, a great deal of information which helped others to make decisions more efficiently.

Most of those venturing to Honduras, beginning about one hundred years ago and contrary to what Middle Eastern experts might

---

5. As any reader of *Tales from the Arabian Nights* is aware, the idea of traveling to obtain one's fortune has a very long history in the Middle East, and it is very possible that men from Ephrata have been involved in it for a much longer period than two hundred years. The earliest documentary evidence I have found, however, goes back merely to the 1790s.

have predicted, took their wives with them and raised their families there in nuclear households but with strong mutual assistance arrangements, especially between siblings (sisters sometimes intentionally remained unmarried in order to assist their brothers and their families). Patrilineal, patrilocal, and patriarchal (in contrast to Garifuna matrifocality), Palestinians nevertheless depended greatly upon their women to help in their businesses, and sometimes to manage their own. (See chaps. 5 and 6.)

It is significant that I found no evidence whatsoever that this migration strategy has altered domestic relations in Ephrata. Instead, it seems to have strengthened the extended family or clan, members of which may be called upon by migrants to help manage their properties in their absence. The economic benefits of migration are plainly visible in all three towns but especially in Beit Sahur—the youngest and smallest, and formerly the least well off. Any number of fine houses and businesses were pointed out to me as having been built with money from abroad.

As among the Garifuna, young men and women look forward to traveling to distant lands, many of which they already know a good deal about from letters and visits home by migrants. Yet some people from Bethlehem and Beit Sahur stated that Beit Jala had been negatively affected by emigration—that young people from that community tended to be lazy, smoked marijuana, and looked forward only to emigration. Some of this was no doubt the usual kind of pejorative tattling on neighbors with whom one feels some competition, a phenomenon common in the Middle East and elsewhere. But, as is often the case, there may have been some truth to the specific charges. The mayor of Beit Jala informed me during my stay there that large numbers of people were leaving that town every month, with no intention of returning. On the West Bank explanations tend today to be couched in terms of the current political situation, yet this kind of permanent emigration ideology does remind one of the Garifuna and other Caribbean societies (Rubinstein 1983). For whatever reason, if people feel there is little future for them in their home community, they may lose their ambition to prepare for life there, looking forward to other horizons instead.

There are many other reasons why anthropologists are interested in the phenomena of migration. It has always been one of the great forces shaping both the biological and the cultural faces of mankind. Demographic determinants, such as behavior that alters fertility and mortality, may be affected by the movement of people. Even when wives go along, there is bound to be some gene flow between the migrant and host populations. Diseases, whether of genetic or infectious origin, will change morbidity patterns. Language, technology, art, diet — all these and more are subject to modification in both directions. In fact, the documentation and analysis of diffusion, or the transfer of objects and ideas from one culture to another, has long been an important part of our work and is especially important to ethnohistorians.

Finally, the paradox of ethnicity — the tendency for groups of people of different heritages to exaggerate their differences at the same time that they emulate each other's ways, thus creating boundaries between themselves in an otherwise increasingly homogeneous global society — is of major interest to many, and not well understood. I suggest that migration, in that it creates plural, more complex societies, is largely responsible for the rising interest in tradition, in roots, in the symbols of "peoplehood" throughout the world today. Local, or ethnic, identity need not be specially celebrated unless it is threatened. In this it is similar to processes and movements previously labeled "nativistic" because they were thought to occur only or primarily among traditional societies threatened by the onslaught of Western civilization. But migrants, especially when it seems they may not go home again, and when they find themselves clustered together in foreign environments, may behave in similar fashion.

## Conflict Migration

A good bit of migration in history has been stimulated by the immediate or cumulative effects of violent conflict in the home society. Since it is obviously the case that not everyone chooses to abandon a society at war, even when opportunities to do so exist, this alone cannot be adduced as a cause for emigration, for then we have to determine why some leave and others risk death by staying home or even volunteering for combat, why some who don't leave at one time later change their minds, and so forth. Conflict, especially protracted ethnic conflict, may be seen as a determinant, as well as a limiting factor, in certain migration strategies. Governments may both restrict emigration of likely military recruits and foment the departure of those they consider undesirable. Just as the enslavement of Africans, the indenturing of Chinese and Indian workers, and the recruitment of entire European peasant communities to settle in the American Midwest in the late 1800s may be seen as migration strategies, so may we look upon the mass flight of Guatemalan Indians to "El Norte" (whether to Chiapas or to Canada or to somewhere in between) as an institutionalized mechanism for escaping conflict (and its ensuing poverty) at home (Earle 1988; Falla 1988).

In this book some Palestinians may be seen as having used a conflict migration strategy as early as World War I. Formerly exempt from military service under the Ottomans, Christians were threatened by new recruitment policies in 1914.[6] Although many had already left home for purely economic reasons, larger numbers of young men now chose emigration. Some had the decision foisted upon them by their parents, who feared their possible death in battle. After 1948 new emigration strategies developed in response to ongoing conflict with the new state of Israel. Many Palestinians became refugees, fleeing or being deported without documents to Jordan, Lebanon, Syria, and elsewhere (Lesch 1979a, 1979b). Most of those who could manage a passport, or an "identity card" of some sort,[7] sought new homes in other parts of the world, many of them joining

---

6. The Ottoman Empire introduced the principle of universal military service in the 1840s, but non-Muslims easily obtained exemptions by paying a nominal fee (Rustow 1979:71). Christians, more than other non-Muslims, had long presented themselves and generally had been considered by others to be nonaggressive; they were notoriously uninvolved in raiding and feuding patterns (Spyridon 1938:85; Zenner 1972:410). A new policy intended to effect the recruitment of Christians and Jews was announced in 1909, but it was not until 1914 that its effect upon the population was felt, as the Ottomans found themselves embroiled in a world war. Palestinians in Bethlehem and Honduras said that even then some families managed to save their sons from conscription by cutting a designated number of trees to be used as firewood for running locomotives on the Ottoman railways. Those who had no olive or other fruit trees, or who preferred not to cut them for this purpose, sought ways to spirit the young men out of the country.

7. Between 1952 and 1988 Palestinians of the West Bank and Gaza were considered Jordanian citizens and were entitled to carry passports from that nation, while those living within Israel proper have always been eligible for Israeli passports. After 1967, when Israel defeated combined Arab forces and occupied the formerly Jordanian territories, the country issued only *"laissez passer"* papers to people living there enabling them to travel to and from Jordan. From there they might travel to the rest of the world using their Jordanian passports. In order to encourage the permanent emigration of Palestinians, however, the Israelis usually put restrictions on the length of time a person might remain outside and still have the right to return. They also

relatives who had previously emigrated. Many of these retained their Israeli or Jordanian passports, while at the same time seeking to become naturalized citizens of other countries. For many, the subsequent loss of citizenship in any polity whatsoever has necessitated new behavior patterns, as we shall see below.

## Diasporas

Diaspora refers both to the process of dispersion and to the communities formed by the settlers wherever they journey. Few anthropologists have written about diasporas as such, although the term has come into increasingly popular usage, both among scholars and others. Thus, Hendricks (1974) used it in describing Dominican emigration, almost all of which was directed toward New York City; Posnansky (1983) aims at uncovering archaeological evidence for the "Black diaspora"; and Kemper and Foster regularly use the term to refer to Tzintzuntzanos living outside that town, wherever they may be.[8] A new social science journal has recently appeared, simply called *Diaspora.*

Other scholars have used the term in a different sense, as when

---

made it difficult for Palestinians who had become naturalized citizens of other countries to return for any length of time, and almost impossible for them to return permanently.

Since 1988 Jordan has required young male West Bankers living in Jordanian territory to serve in their army or lose their full Jordanian citizenship privileges. If they consent to this order, Israel will never permit their reentry to the West Bank, even as visitors. At the same time Palestinians born in Jordan are now considered strictly Jordanian by the Israeli state and may not freely cross over to the villages of their parents, even in the latter's company. These rules imposed by both Jordan and Israel present severe handicaps for those Palestinians caught between loyalties to their homeland and to their adopted country.

The case of one young Palestinian couple with whom I was friendly in Jordan is illustrative. The man, born on the West Bank and carrying both a Jordanian passport and an Israeli *laissez passer,* had come to Jordan to attend the university, fully expecting to return home. A marriage was arranged with a young woman born in Jordan but whose parents were from his village. Although he was still permitted to travel to and reside in the West Bank, he learned belatedly that he could not bring her with him. At the time of my fieldwork he had been told by the Jordanian government to report for military service or lose his Jordanian citizenship—an option that would have precluded any eventual return to the West Bank. The couple tried to obtain visas so both might emigrate to a European or American country but had not been successful. Clearly, barring separation, they were being forced into adopting some kind of clandestine migration strategy.

8. Personal communication from Robert Van Kemper.

Abner Cohen (1971) refers to "trading diasporas," which could include both temporary (men only) and permanent (family) movements, and which often involve a coming together of different ethnic groups occupying the same economic niche, at the same time that it implies a dispersion of people on an ethnic basis. As we shall see in chapter 5 below, the Palestinians of Honduras, along with Jews, Chinese, and Europeans from several different countries, might be considered as part of a single trading diaspora in Cohen's sense.

William Adams (1981:4) also used the term in discussing the dispersion of different minorities within the Middle Eastern region. Although he only deals with Greeks, Armenians, Jews, Gypsies, Solubba, Chaamba, and Nubians, he points out, following Coon (1965:1–9), that the Middle East has resembled a mosaic of many different minorities for thousands of years. He thus refers to the settlement pattern of any one of these groups as a "minority diaspora."

Obviously, there have been other kinds of diasporas to which we could refer. Prominent among these might be the diasporas of Protestant religious groups such as the Mennonites, who now truly live scattered over the globe and whose case resembles that of the Jews before 1948 in that it is a religion, a life-style, and a set of values which set them apart from others—not loyalty to a nation or a homeland. It might be useful for some analyses to speak of a "slavery diaspora," or an "indentured servant diaspora," thus putting the emphasis not on the race, nationality, or ethnicity of the people but, rather, on the mechanism or structure that impelled the movement.

Armstrong (1976:393) has suggested that those who have studied diasporas often treat them as anomalies, or at least as very transitory phenomena. He believes they may have been more often the norm if one takes a more longitudinal view. I would agree that the dispersion of peoples probably has great antiquity, and at least some archaeologists would concur (Rouse 1986), but whether all of them should be termed diasporas depends on how one defines that term.

*Webster's New Collegiate Dictionary,* 150th anniversary edition (1981) defines *Diaspora* principally in relation to the settling of scattered colonies of Jews outside Palestine after the Babylonian exile. The term refers both to the people and to the areas they settled outside ancient Palestine or modern Israel. The final (and uncapitalized) definition of *diaspora,* however, is simply "migration." That word derives from the Greek term for dispersion, which in turn comes from *dia* + *speirein,* "to sow." All this is significant in relation to its modern popular usage, and it also leaves us quite free to propose a more technical definition.

I suggest that it is useful to distinguish a diaspora from other types of migratory streams and their resulting settlements in several ways. A true diaspora includes persons of both sexes and of all ages, even though family units may not necessarily travel together. Younger individuals sometimes go on ahead to prepare the way for spouses, children, and, very often, older parents.

Second, a diaspora implies that the people become dispersed to many different parts of the world, not simply to a single general location, as in the removal of Bikini islanders or in the exodus of English Puritans, most of whom migrated to America — more specifically, to what became known as New England. Indeed, I would refer to both of these settlements as colonies, which in time cut themselves off from (or were prevented from returning to) their original homelands. In both cases there was the intention of creating a new and better society than that left behind, albeit one that at the household or family level closely duplicated familiar patterns of behavior.

The third, and most difficult, criterion in defining a diaspora is that the people retain a myth of their uniqueness. They value their cultural heritage and others who share it, and they actively maintain an interest in their homeland in the expectation or hope of eventual repatriation. At first blush it might seem a truism that ethnocentrism, tradition, and nostalgia are universal, but there is considerable evidence from sociological and other descriptions, of nineteenth-century immigrants especially, that they wanted primarily to shed their previous ways of life and become "American." If life has been difficult or its existence threatened and little or no spiritual respite from it has been possible, there may simply not be much that people want to remember. To the extent that life does improve, there may be a conscious attempt to erase the past from personal and collective memory.[9]

---

9. Segments of the American black population are now reexamining their African or African-Caribbean heritage, much of which had been denied them but which they also chose to abandon in their quest for a more "comfortable" life. See Paule Marshall's *Praise Song for the Widow* (1984), for a fictional account of a woman who returned to her Caribbean past later in life.

In a world without modern communication technology the last mentioned characteristic has been difficult or impossible to achieve. Until recently, as I shall detail below, only the Jews of the world properly fit the model, and then only because their religious beliefs and ritual have over the centuries incorporated an overt emphasis on the return to Jerusalem and to the land they believe their god promised them.[10] In this sense *Webster's* first definition, which associated *diaspora* with the Jews, properly reflects previous reality. The more recent emphasis on remembering what has come to be called the Holocaust has drawn even the more secular and otherwise acculturated Jews to the fold. It is one of the more interesting anthropological observations of our time that a people with no consistently patterned genetic unity, who long ago lost any common vernacular, and whose religious beliefs and practices had diverged in extraordinary ways, resulting in large numbers professing atheism, should have been able, nevertheless, to retain their sense of "peoplehood" for more than two thousand years under the conditions of diaspora. Virginia Domínguez (1989) has described the dilemma this has posed for modern Israel, whose incoming populations find they have little in common except the idea of being Jewish.

I would not insist that only the Jewish case is worthy of the term *diaspora*, but it is difficult to cite other examples that have had such success over such a long period of time. In this book I will present some data on part of what appears to be a Palestinian diaspora, one that has persevered for two or three generations even without a common religion. At this point it is necessary to define our unit of analysis and to determine to what extent it corresponds to some concrete and meaningful social reality in the external world. To illustrate the problem, consider Armstrong's assertion that the "Catholic Levantine" diaspora began in 1453 (1976:404) and Tsimhoni's statement that "Christian emigration" from Palestine began at the turn of the twentieth century (1976:21). We know from a number of sources that the latter date is far too late in regard to either Christian or Muslim Palestinians, but that is beside the point that *Levantine* includes people of

---

10. Davies (1982:84) has recently shown that the concept of a divine territorial bestowal cannot be documented clearly in ancient scriptures and that it is more likely a product of political Zionism during the nineteenth and twentieth centuries.

diverse religions from a very broad region comprising what is today Lebanon, Syria, Israel, and the West Bank, while *Christian* lumps a number of very different identity groups whose only bond is that they believe in the divinity of Jesus Christ. Thus, there is no evidence that Catholic Levantines have maintained their separateness abroad, either in distinction from other Middle Eastern Christians or from Jewish or Muslim Levantines. Indeed, I would argue that the Levantine identity may have superseded or outweighed the religious element in the new world — at least until the turn of the twentieth century, when Zionism and Pan-Arab nationalism both were in the process of development.

I am defining the identity group to be discussed in this book as Christian (both Orthodox and Catholic) Palestinians deriving from the small region known as Ephrata, centered on the town of Bethlehem. It may be argued that their diaspora itself has been a primary driver in developing and maintaining their sense of ethnicity. Their reception as pariah entrepreneurs in the American host countries was part of the process of ethnogenesis (see chap. 5), as was the development of the state of Israel.

Today this diaspora, like other transnational migrations, is assisted by radio, satellite television, airplane travel, and telephone and telegraph facilities — all of which make it possible for individuals to remain familiar with ongoing events in their homelands and to keep interpersonal relationships strong. In the Palestinian case institutions such as "the media" and various formal and informal political entities use this modern technology to reinforce on a daily basis what is increasingly seen as a distinctive Palestinian ethnicity on a larger scale and to unify the people professing it.

It may be that a diaspora entails, as part of the symbol system that binds its members together, reference to some deep injustice that has befallen its members as a class. Here again not all disadvantaged or persecuted peoples have developed such a symbolic system. Descendants of slaves in the United States may be moving toward such at the present time, but it is not yet clear to what end it will be addressed nor to what extent it will be successful. Certainly, the notion of a return en masse to Africa was long ago abandoned by the majority of American blacks, although at various times in the past this has been a recurring theme, both in the United States and in the Caribbean (Tafari 1989:Foreword).

## Transnationalism

These newer migratory streams often lend themselves to analyses in terms of a continually active and reactive set of relationships between those outside and those who remain at home. Because most migration today involves the crossing of national borders and not merely an encounter with a different social category or ethnic group, the term *transnationalism* has come to be applied to the way of life it has engendered (Glick-Schiller et al. 1991). Not only do individuals tend more often to go back and forth between the host and home countries, but also they stay in touch with relatives and with significant happenings in both areas. Acculturation is not so much to the host society's patterns but to those of the transnational community itself.

The political dimension of migration is largely dependent upon national-level factors — both countries' labor needs; racial, ethnic, and religious composition and prejudices; the type of government and constitution and the protection they give to minorities and to foreigners. Crucial to transnationalism is the individual's sense of belonging simultaneously to two societies that may differ in many respects, but which share enough characteristics so that a life straddling both is possible without the individual suffering too much cognitive dissonance, psychological trauma, or other forms of culture shock. There have always been some individuals who have been able to manage this, even though they may have been somewhat more at home in one society than in another.

But the phenomenon of whole communities whose life-style, worldview, and ethnocommunal identity *depends* upon a national and sociocultural dualism is something rather new. Many such cases are beginning to be documented in the United States; it is not clear how often they occur in other parts of the world. There would seem to be certain predisposing conditions under which they arise.

Bilingualism from early childhood, preferably learned through experience and not merely in school, would seem to be a necessary requisite for successful participation in such a community, as well as for ensuring the community's persistence through time. Children who grow up in such societies learn speech patterns very early in life which work for them in both communities, even though the "purity" of either of the original languages may be called in question by monolingual speakers of either. Total fluency and literacy in both languages may or may not occur, the degree of success in this usually being dependent upon the social class of the individuals concerned and, thus, upon the type and amount of education available. Access to travel facilities, as well as to reliable and affordable means of transmitting information and goods in both directions, must also be present. Finally, a sense of loyalty to both polities, and a desire to continue living in both, is characteristic. Today the United States permits a citizen to hold two passports, and many transnationals do.[11] The majority, however, rely on the passport of the country of their birth or naturalization, using visas or no documents at all, when traveling to the other pole of their existence. It is easier for those born in the United States, of course, since they can almost always secure visas to visit their parents' homeland. But, even for noncitizens, the holding of a "green card" permits travel between the United States and the resident's home with relatively little bureaucratic difficulty.

Eugenia Georges (1990) has recently written about a Dominican transnational community from the perspective of those who continue to reside much of the time in the Dominican Republic. Others have described the same community through the eyes of those living primarily in New York (Hendricks 1974). Mexicans who regularly cross the border into the southwestern part of the United States may also be thought of as transnationals, as increasingly are many American Jews with strong loyalties toward Israel. The affluent Hong Kong Chinese of the San Francisco Bay area have been described as transnationals by Ong (1991), as have elite Indians in the United States by Lessinger (1991).

The question of how to relate *diaspora,* as I am using it, to *transnationalism* must be addressed. It seems clear that members of the Jewish diaspora acculturated very strongly to the many parts of the world in which they sojourned and that in many cases they felt a strong nationalism and identification with their host countries. Certainly, they served their adopted (native) governments in many ways, including

---

11. Not all countries permit citizens to hold more than one passport, although some merely close their eyes to the fact that many of their nationals do so without revealing the existence of the foreign document. The United States has become increasingly less rigid about the matter with the rise in terrorist attacks on persons carrying United States passports in Europe and the Middle East.

as soldiers and public servants. Transnationalism (as opposed to bi-culturalism), however, was not an issue until the creation of the state of Israel in 1948, and even then it only became possible because the founders of that state specifically granted the "right of return" (to Is-rael) to Jews living anywhere in the world.[12] It is not known what per-centage of those who claimed that right elected to live in Israel, and many who did so have since returned either to their birthplace or to another nation. It would be interesting to examine to what extent those who stayed continue to identify with the place from which they emigrated.[13]

Today I know of no American community that depends for its sense of identity upon such close interaction with Israel, although there are probably very many individual American Jews who may be said to fit that pattern. It is possible that some of the more bounded Orthodox communities, such as New York's Lubavitchers, may be true transnationals (Harris 1985:174). Certainly, there is constant communication with Israel by telephone, mail, FAX [facsimile], and radio, and New York religious leaders are known to wield influence in Israeli as well as in American politics. There is a private airline, generally not known to non-Jewish travel agents, which flies nonstop between New York and Tel Aviv for a very low fare. Modern, as well as ancient Hebrew, although not the language of most households, is widely known, and the Hasidic conservative dress patterns, dietary laws, and religious practices are, of course, very similar among Hasi-dim in both the old and new worlds.

The final question is whether the Palestinians of Honduras (or of any other node in the diaspora) might become transnationals should an independent Palestinian state be created. It is obviously too soon to even speculate on such an eventuality, but the following section and chapters may give us some food for thought on the matter.

---

12. The exact definition of who is a Jew has been a matter of continuing controversy and is irrelevant to the discussion at this point.

13. While in Israel in the winter of 1988–89, I met several young women in their mid teens who had been born in Israel of United States parents. They informed me that, although they were moderately conversant in Hebrew, it was not their "primary" tongue and that they spoke only English at home, attended classes in English, and associated primarily with the chil-dren of other "Americans." This suggests the possibility of a true transnational Israeli-American community resident in Israel, but I know of no formal study of such.

## Palestinians in Central America

In the chapters that follow I will outline what began as a Palestinian migration, or trading diaspora—first temporary and then permanent, if we follow Hamilton's (1985:409) view—and has, since 1948, become what I would call a true diaspora. The Palestinians, since they are divided in their religious, or "confessional," allegiances (as religious affiliations are usually termed in the Middle East), are today primarily united by their sense of outrage and frustration over their exclusion from what to them has been their homeland since time immemorial. Even without a recognized state of their own, since this has never existed as such, there has been an enduring attachment to place and to "their own" people.

The Palestine Liberation Organization has become the central sanctioning authority in the absence of a state or any other body capable of mustering the allegiance of those in the diaspora. Made up of loosely affiliated subgroups with differing political and ideological tendencies, its internal disarray has, in one sense, served the cause well, since in the beginning, at least, it was necessary to pull together diverse sectors of the Palestinian people, who, indeed, never had thought of themselves as a single unity in the past. Its various segments served as magnets for these groups. The development of a flag, a logo, a creed, a set of specific goals, a correction of the historical record concerning past Israeli treatment of the Arab population who happened to live in the territory granted to them by the United Nations, and, increasingly, with the intifada, public demonstrations of how Israelis treat those who still remain there and in the occupied territories of Gaza and the West Bank—all of these have given the cause the symbolic apparatus it needed to win the minds and hearts of all those whose forebears came from what much of the world continues to call "the Holy Land."

To note that Palestinians have not previously been united within a polity is not to say that there was no ethnic unity among them. Countless travelers, as well as social scientific observers, have attested to the cultural continuities in the area. Throughout much of the Middle East religious confession, village, and kin group have been the three most important elements in an individual's definition of community and of self.[14] Even urban dwellers tended to restrict their most

---

14. This trinity is so commonly assumed, or explicated, that references abound. See especially Eickelman (1981); Patai (1969); Sweet (1970:2v).

intimate contacts to their own residential "quarter." The principle of endogamy applied in all three sectors has reinforced local reputations for certain cultural patterns, but it has hardly erased the underlying substratum from which the cultural variations were fashioned — perhaps as conscious efforts to distinguish themselves in an otherwise amorphous peasant mass. Guatemalan Indian villages, similarly, are distinguished by their clothing styles, handicrafts, languages, and at the time of the Spanish conquest they frequently fought against each other. Yet today they retain a sense of overall ethnic unity in distinguishing themselves from the Ladinos of European culture who have come to dominate their homeland — economically, politically, and socially.

In Palestine feuds between nomads and settlers, between leaders of different villages or regions, and even between families or clans within a village persisted despite the repeated conquests and subsequent occupations — by Jews, Romans, Egyptians, Arabs, Turks, British, and, finally again, by Jews under the banner of Zionism and the Israeli state. But internal dissension has long been part and parcel of the Middle Eastern way of life and should not be misconstrued as a justification for denying Palestinians their essential sense of peoplehood.

At the same time it is important to understand the differences among Palestinians living today under different sets of circumstances. The next chapters will examine the historical roots of both their unity and their diversity.

*Chapter 3*

# The Town of Bethlehem in Historical Perspective

"Oh Come Ye, O Come Ye to Bethlehem"
— Eighteenth-century American hymn

## Pilgrimage

Bethlehem's internal economy today is based upon pilgrimage and tourism, and all the evidence suggests that it has been so for at least one hundred fifty years. Even before then, Bethlehemites benefited from the fact that the faithful, especially Christians, found it uplifting to visit their town and the holy sites it harbored. As early as the fourteenth century, St. Francis of Assisi opened a school in Bethlehem to train local children to become guides and interpreters (Musallam 1981:41).

Topolotry, as the adoration of sites was aptly termed long ago (Clermont-Ganneau 1875:206), and pilgrimage seem to be ancient phenomena, although they were not at first prominent in the Judeo-Christian tradition. The earliest Jews and Christians were far more concerned with the spiritual and interpersonal precepts and demands of their religions and did not require visitations in order to prove or bolster their faith (Benzinger 1903:582; Schick 1987:17; Trimingham 1979:240). It may be that preexisting polytheistic religious traditions perpetuated a folk fetishism for certain local spots, many of which later became identified with biblical happenings (Clermont-Ganneau 1875:209). As both Christians and Jews became more widely dispersed in the world, the first through active proselytization and the latter through banishment and subsequent intermarriage, the magico-symbolic aspects of their religions became more salient, including the reverence for certain geographic locations where their founding ancestors had lived and worshipped.

By the time of Muhammad topolotropic patterns had been well

established in the Christian world—going back at least to the time of Constantine the Great (A.D. 323–337), the first Christian Roman emperor, to whose mother, Queen (later Saint) Helena, were divinely revealed the locations of many of the sites associated with the life of Christ. Her campaign to build monuments on many of them was the model followed for centuries by Roman, Byzantine, and, much later, European monks (Clermont-Ganneau 1875:206). It is of more than passing interest that many of these holy places were caves (Maundrell 1963:153; McGarvey 1881:219–20), and several of them had previously been dedicated to other deities. The Church of the Nativity (originally St. Mary's), for example, was built over a grotto sacred to Adonis (Trimingham 1979:239), and it is coincidental, but fitting, that Greeks, both Orthodox and Catholic, came to dominate later Christian worship there. There is little objective evidence that people in this area have lived in or used caves for thousands of years. Yet even today, in both Jordan and the West Bank, one hears stories about "the poor" living in caves. The people of Beit Sahur, e.g., were said by some Bethlehemites to have done so until the Orthodox church purchased lands for them in the eighteenth century. Today caves are definitely considered undesirable as habitations, indicating extreme poverty and/or nomadism. This image fits well with the Christian conceptual linkages among poverty, humility, and sanctity and likely enhances the holiness of such sites.

Pilgrimages to holy sites, especially those where the Virgin Mary reputedly had appeared, were common in Europe during medieval times. For the especially devout or the repentant English sinner the "Jerusalem voyage" from Yarmouth to Venice, and thence to Jerusalem, provided a means of furthering one's chances for salvation from purgatory. Some travel guides listed indulgences to be gained at the different holy places (Duff, cited by Prescott 1950:10). The fourteenth and fifteenth centuries witnessed a steady traffic between Europe and Palestine composed of men and women from all walks of life, enduring what today would seem to be considerable hardship. The rewards were not only spiritual—the trip marked one forever as a devout Christian—but the opportunities for picking up bargains in silk, rugs, precious stones, spices, and more petty souvenirs seem to have been major attractions as well (Prescott 1950: 221). European men of noble birth, for a suitable donation, might be made Knights of the Holy Sepulcher during their stay in Jerusalem.

The records of the earliest of these European travelers mention Bethlehem only in passing—usually referring to St. Mary's as an impressive and venerable building.[1] In early Christian theology the death of Christ was considered a far more significant event than his birth. This relates to the essential and unique existential mystery of whether he was god, man, or god/man. His suffering before and during his crucifixion was deemed evidence of his humanity and of his great self-sacrifice, while the apparent miracle of his resurrection affirmed his status as deity. Therefore, Jerusalem, with its Calvary, Garden of Gethsemane, Mount of Olives, Via Dolorosa, Tomb of the Virgin, and other sites overshadowed Bethlehem and Nazareth for many centuries as a destination for Christian pilgrims.

The Protestant Reformation of the sixteenth century and the ensuing bloodshed throughout Europe significantly decreased the pilgrim traffic to the Holy Land. It was only in the late eighteenth and early nineteenth centuries that such travel again became popular with large numbers of nonclergy, including for the first time Americans (Stookey 1976:353). The timing of this new interest in pilgrimage coincided with the end of the Crimean War and a set of general Ottoman social and economic reforms intended to stave off what increasingly appeared to be the inevitable decline and fall of that empire. From the middle of the nineteenth century onward Bethlehem and Nazareth, places associated with the birth and life of Christ, came into their own, and new symbols, mostly born in Europe, began to permeate the local ambience. Christmas, with its emphasis on the Star, the Manger, Shepherds' Field, and the Visit of the Wise Men, became a truly international event of great importance and made Bethlehem the crossroads of the world during the last weeks of December. Streets were named or renamed for these symbols, and "Manger Square" (the center of the old city) became internationally famous. Local craftsmen and souvenir hawkers expanded their cottage industries into factories for manufacturing religious wares and opened permanent shops for selling them.[2]

But it is not only Christian pilgrims who flock to Bethlehem. The

---

1. Wright (1969) has provided a useful summary of the accounts of the earliest pilgrims, starting with Bishop Arcult in 700 A.D. and ending with Maundeville in 1322. All mention a cave or grotto and the church built above it.

2. Rand (1963) describes the Christmas celebrations in Bethlehem in detail for the period before the Israeli occupation. He carefully documents the ritual differences among the different

Western Christian world often overlooks or forgets the doctrinal con-
tinuity that underlies religious expression in the Holy Land. Bethlehem was also the place where Ruth went to glean the fields following
harvest, where Rachel was buried, and, most important perhaps, was
the birthplace, and therefore the "city," of the Jewish King David.
Since Muslims also revere the Old Testament personalities, as well
as Jesus and his mother, they too find it meaningful to tour the truly
ancient church where Greek and Armenian Orthodox services alter-
nate and go in tandem with those of the Roman (there termed "Latin")
Catholics, held in an adjoining sanctuary (Le Strange 1892:300).[3]

Over the years Bethlehemites not only became more accustomed to the presence of increasing numbers of visitors, but they
became more and more dependent upon them in several ways. In order to serve them better they became sophisticated in the ways of
foreigners, especially Europeans, since the majority of Christian visitors came from France, Italy, Germany, Spain, and England. They
learned and often adopted their languages, dress patterns, foods and
wines, and their tastes in artwork. Pilgrimage, it can be argued, was
an important instrument of acculturation for the local people, at the
same time that it helped preserve the town, its inhabitants, and its
Christian faith against the Islamic tide that began to rise all around
it after A.D. 634.

Despite the oft repeated assertion that conquering Islam tolerated the continued presence of so-called People of the Book in the territories it won,[4] there is considerable evidence that Christians were
especially vulnerable, not only to attacks by ordinary townsmen but
also to inequitable treatment by both locally appointed and foreign
authorities. Even when they were not in danger of losing their lives
and property, Christians and Jews were subject to sumptuary laws;
they paid higher taxes; they could not ride horses — only donkeys; and

---

churches as well as some of the local folklore concerning their observances and doctrinal and
political disputes.

   3. The Franciscans have built a newer adjoining church known as St. Catherine's, situated on the spot formerly occupied by the Crusaders' cloister (Benvenisti 1972:160). The two
sanctuaries may be entered separately, but there is also a connecting passageway, and both give
access to the manger grotto.

   4. The term is generally held to refer to Jews and Christians, both of whom revered the
Bible. According to Khadduri, however, in the earliest centuries it included various others as
well, including both Zoroastrians and Samaritans (1955:80). Monotheism, plus the possession
of some scriptural record, seems to have been the defining criterion. (See also chap. 7.)

during some periods they were required to hand over some of their male children to be raised as soldiers and as Muslims. The specific indignities and burdens laid upon them changed down through the centuries; some periods were far more lenient than others (Khadduri 1955:196–99).

During the Arab, Egyptian, and Ottoman occupations of the Holy Land Christians from abroad served as a conduit of information back to their several countries concerning conditions in Palestine.[5] Their reports gave impetus to pious Christian concerns for the welfare of the people and of the holy sites in the area, concerns which were usually combined with economic interests. The Crusades, as one example of such foreign interference, were a bloody, cruel, extremely unpleasant experience for local Christians as well as Muslims, but they did serve to establish a permanent European linkage that has never been completely severed (Atiya 1962). The Roman (Latin) Catholic church was established in Jerusalem in 1099 and in Bethlehem in 1100, creating a foothold that became an important element in the local balance of power. (See chaps. 7 and 8.)

In spiritual matters pilgrims from abroad provided the local Christians with a continual revalidation and reinforcement of their own faith. In A.D. 600 the bulk of the population of perhaps two million in Palestine was Orthodox Christian, only some 10 to 15 percent persisting in their earlier allegiance, whether Jewish or pagan (Schick 1987:13); this situation continued despite the often violent persuasion accompanying the original Islamic conquests, until the latter part of the eleventh century, when Turkish invasions began a new era that even the Crusades could not halt (Runciman 1968:9–10). By the sixteenth century Christians constituted only about 30 percent of the total, the majority having converted to Islam (Tsimhoni 1976:12). In

---

5. By "occupation" I refer to political control by foreign powers, not necessarily to a large influx of foreign settlers. Most serious scholars today believe that the present-day local "Arab" population is largely descended from people inhabiting the region "from time immemorial." (See Clermont-Ganneau [1875:204] for an early statement of this view.) Religious and linguistic changes have occurred repeatedly, without significant accompanying changes in the gene pool. This is not to say that there was no intermarriage between resident foreigners and locals but, rather, that it was relatively insignificant from a population genetics point of view.

Trimingham (1979:1), on the other hand, believes that some Arabic-speaking peoples (therefore, true Arabs) inhabited Syria, Palestine, Mesopotamia, and Babylonia from early times, intermingled with the Aramaic-speaking peoples of these regions. (See also Mendenhall 1985.)

1922 that percentage had been reduced to eleven (Census of Palestine 1922); by 1942 to eight (Hassan 1981:32); in 1978 to four (Tsimhoni 1983:59); and in 1986 to two (Tabash 1985:6). (See table 3.1.)[6] Furthermore, that tiny percentage is hopelessly fragmented into some fifteen different sects, ranging from the several eastern Orthodox groups through the various Catholics of both eastern and western tradition to the more recently formed fundamentalist Protestant sects. (See chap. 7.) Given the steadily diminishing local Christian presence in the land considered holy by three major religions, pilgrimage by foreign Christians must be seen as having been far more complex and significant than may be thought by those who concentrate only upon its economic aspect. Still, the latter is an important component, even now.

## Tourism

Tourism, as we know it today, which coexists with and sometimes replaces pilgrimage, seems to have had its origin in Bethlehem and the Holy Land generally after the middle of the nineteenth century. The distinction between pilgrimage and tourism is largely intuitive for most people, the problem being that different motivations are usually thought to underlie each. The pilgrim is assumed to be a true believer, whose travels are primarily (if not solely) undertaken in order to reinforce one's faith, improve one's reputation in heaven, instruct one in the history of one's religion, and ameliorate one's condition on earth. Perhaps the last is and has long been the single most important motive for pilgrims, for the world abounds with sites at which the faithful seek miraculous cures or other intercessions in their lives.[7]

---

6. Smith (1984:84) says the percentage of Christians in Palestine rose between 1895 and 1914, from 10 percent to 16 percent. She attributes this to increased urbanization and the consequent success of Christian merchants in cities such as Jerusalem, Jaffa, Haifa, and Acre. Although it is easy to see how Christians might have profited, it is more difficult to understand how greater wealth was related to such a large increase in their proportional representation in the population. It is possible that Christians from other Arab states were attracted to Palestine because of the opportunities offered to them by the British.

7. Pilgrimage has not been a major research interest among anthropologists until recently. Turner and Turner (1978) explored the symbolism of Christian pilgrimage in Europe, which is the geographic area that has been best researched by Western historians. In 1988 the topic was discussed at a conference in Jerusalem attended by theologians, religious function-

TABLE 3.1.    Percentage of Christian Population
in Palestine

| Time Period | Percentage | Source |
|---|---|---|
| 600 | 85 – 90 | Schick 1987:13 |
| 1500 | 30 | Tsimhoni 1976:12 |
| 1922 | 11 | Census of Palestine |
| 1942 | 8 | Hassan 1981:32 |
| 1978 | 4 | Tsimhoni 1983:59 |
| 1987 | 2 | Lahem 1987:6 |

*Note:* The definition and delimitation of *Palestine* has varied somewhat over the centuries. The last two dates refer to the West Bank; earlier ones included a larger area, comprising what is now Israel and the West Bank.

Tourists, on the other hand, may be interested in aesthetics (scenery, art, architecture), history, science, or even religion as a secular topic, but for them getting there is half the fun, while pilgrims may suffer hardships on their journey (and thus, perhaps, enhance the significance of what they have done both among men and among angels). For both pilgrims and tourists the home audience is a necessary component of the trip, for one's prestige rises in response to the telling, or the writing if one's audience is dispersed and literate. To impress those at home even further it is important to bring back souvenirs for display and for prestation.

Modern Bethlehem, even with the intifada, experiences a flood of pilgrims and tourists in its center each day, where they visit the Church of the Nativity and other shrines defined through the ages as places where various events important to Christians, Jews, and Muslims were said to have occurred. For Christians most sacred and/or interesting is the site of Christ's birth, where a sterling silver star marks the very spot, but there is also Shepherds' Field as well as the grotto in which the holy family was said to have lived for a time and where Mary's abundant milk overflowed, permanently staining the limestone floor. Lactating women of many faiths believe their own

---

aries, historians, geographers, and anthropologists. It was reported that the anthropologists had views so different from the others that they had difficulty communicating with those in other fields (Bowman 1988:20–23). In November 1989 there was a session entitled "Pilgrimage in the European Tradition" at the meetings of the American Anthropological Association in Washington, D.C. Perhaps this is a harbinger of greater anthropological interest in the subject in the future.

performance may be enhanced by visiting the site, many offering prayers there to the Virgin.

As they emerge from the Church of the Nativity, visitors will be approached in Manger Square by purveyors of religious paraphernalia, including tiny bottles of (extremely polluted) water from the Jordan River and small plastic bags containing dried flowers or soil from the Holy Land. Or they may be invited to visit the many shops where items made of mother-of-pearl and olivewood are sold. These include jewelry and other secular souvenirs as well as rosaries, crucifixes, and manger sets, Muslim prayer beads, Jewish menorahs, and countless other items.[8] Not all of these wares are today manufactured in Bethlehem, although the mother-of-pearl and olivewood carvings are still important local crafts. Hebron enamel and ceramic ware is becoming more and more popular, much of it now made locally by Muslims who have moved to Bethlehem from the city of Hebron, where, I was told, the tourist trade has been drastically reduced in recent years because of local disturbances brought about by Arab resistance to extensive Jewish settlement there. For sale throughout Israel, and also in Jordan, the manufacturers of this distinctive ware appeal to all three religious groups in the scenes, symbols, and holy words inscribed on the different pieces.[9]

If one dares to venture past the Israeli soldiers on guard throughout the square, one may walk up Star Street, which, in spite of its name, is one of the oldest streets in Bethlehem, lined with deteriorating houses in late Ottoman style but with foundations certainly dating from much earlier periods. On the way one may purchase handmade

---

8. It is hard to refrain from cynicism about the economic importance of tourism today. A shopkeeper, a relative of a friend in Honduras, tried to convince me that a menorah I thought beautiful was actually a Christian symbol and that I should buy it. He knew that I was returning to Jordan and that, if found in my baggage, it would have been confiscated, since nothing Jewish is permitted to enter that country. Other local Christians were aghast at his duplicity, saying they had never heard of a menorah as being anything but Jewish. The incident reminded me forcefully of the old adage, *caveat emptor,* "let the buyer beware." It is likely that everywhere in the world business interests come before friendship, truth, and religious dogma.

9. Clermont-Ganneau (1875:211) suggests the glassware industry used ancient Phoenician techniques. At the ceramic factory opposite the U.S. consulate in East Jerusalem I was told that the characteristic tableware bearing flower and animal designs had been introduced by Armenians in the nineteenth century. Similar wares continue to be made throughout the area once controlled by the Ottomans. The making of ceramic tiles, of course, was a well-known "moorish" art in medieval and early modern Spain. Clearly, there have been many inputs into the modern ceramic and glass industry on the West Bank.

gold jewelry or visit the Bethlehem Folklore Museum, a tiny but exquisite display of former dress and household items, including two rooms set up as they might have been a century ago. The museum also sells embroidered pieces with designs copied from old patterns preserved in photos and old clothing. These today are the basis of a cottage industry for poor Muslim women, the enterprise being directed and managed by female members of the Christian elite.

The more dedicated pilgrims and tourists may have arranged a special mass or other ritual to be held privately in one of the several chapels or other sacred places. They may also stay for a time in one of the hostels run by several different religious orders. There is a handful of private hotels owned by local Arabs, but these have declined and are apparently less attractive to foreigners now than formerly.

Christmas in Bethlehem still has an almost irresistible romantic lure for both pilgrims and tourists, even those who are not particularly devout Christians, and Bethlehemites have strived to make it a fulfilling event, both spiritually and touristically. There are colorful yet solemn processions, masses and services in Shepherds' Field and at the church. Manger Square is strung with lights and other western decorations, including a Christmas tree, and there have in the recent past been massive crowds of visitors in the streets and in the square. The municipal government does its part with speeches and parades and the honoring of special guests—often important religious functionaries from Rome, Greece, or other parts of the world. Israeli restrictions have virtually ended these events since the intifada began, and the number of persons arriving has declined precipitously, even though they have not stopped the most faithful from making their pilgrimage at this special time of the year.

In addition to the sale of handicrafts the town's inhabitants may earn money by acting as guides, by begging,[10] and by selling food and drink, although the latter has come almost to a standstill since the start of the intifada. Not only have Arab merchants and restaurateurs defied the Israeli authorities by closing their businesses each day at noon, but the tour buses, almost without exception run by Jews,

---

10. Small children have learned to beg for coins or to hawk chewing gum in both Hebrew and English (and perhaps in other tongues). My Christian friends said these were, without exception, Muslims—that Christian children would not be permitted to do such. Knowing how children imitate their peers, I am not so sure.

prefer to take their clients to other, perhaps safer, surroundings for lunch.

### Foreign Settlements

Various European powers had been accustomed since at least the fifteenth century to sending both mercantile and religious emissaries to Palestine. Some of them established small residential colonies in the cities, and the inhabitants frequented the holy places in the vicinity more as "weekend" tourists than as pilgrims. Their main reasons for being there were to enhance the European presence in trade and to maintain and minister to their own people, for the Islamic authorities, relying on the Koran's explicit instructions, forbade proselytization. The Greek Orthodox church, for example, until recently has reserved its top ecclesiastical offices for Greek nationals, and during the sixteenth and seventeenth centuries it was fashionable for affluent Greeks to visit and to retire to the Holy Land.[11] In the second half of the nineteenth century Bethlehem and its environs was further invaded by large numbers of Russian Orthodox clergy and businessmen and by Protestant religious orders from Germany, Scotland, England, and the United States, all of which founded convents, schools, hospitals, and orphanages, although they were forbidden by Ottoman law to proselytize.

These various foreign resident groups have, nonetheless, had a profound and cumulative effect upon the region, and especially upon its Christians. At the time of the Crusades Bethlehem's inhabitants were primarily engaged in small-scale stock raising and agriculture, especially important being the intensive cultivation of fruits such as olives, almonds, figs, pomegranates, and grapes. Wine making (as opposed to the cultivation of grapes) in Bethlehem is first mentioned by Maundeville in 1322 (Wright 1969:163), but it is not clear that the wines were for local consumption, for in the early nineteenth century one traveler commented that Christian villagers were like the local Muslims in that they did not drink alcohol and that their grape har-

---

11. Although some Greeks intermarried with locals (see chaps. 6 and 7), most held themselves somewhat aloof. This attitude, plus the insistence on retaining Greek as the official language of the church, has disturbed local members of their congregations for centuries. Even now Greek nuns and monks, several of whom I encountered in monasteries, are reluctant to speak Arabic, preferring English if they must speak a foreign tongue.

vest was processed into raisins and a syrup he called *"dipse"* (*dibs*), both traded to Bedouins (Buckingham 1822:52). Wine making is very ancient, frequently mentioned in biblical texts. T. Glick (1979:94) believes that the wide diffusion of the grape in Europe was intimately linked to that of Christian monasticism. Although it is sometimes assumed that both its manufacture and daily use as a beverage in the Holy Land were learned from the Crusaders (Benvenisti 1972:377), it may be that these foreigners merely "modernized" a known but little-used technology, institutionalizing the use of wine through the sacrament of communion and in their own daily consumption. Apparently, it did not become a major beverage for most local Christians at that time — perhaps because it was expensive. Today, however, many Christians in Bethlehem and elsewhere drink spirits (as, for that matter, do some Muslims). Bethlehem's renowned wines (still today monastery products) may be purchased anywhere in Israel and the occupied territories.

### Economic Development

Because Christians and Jews were not permitted to own land until after the Ottoman reforms of the 1850s, both groups were forced to develop their economic strategies in other directions, most of which were related, in one way or another, to the Western (Christian) world. Money lending and trade became their forte. Not only did they set up stalls in city and town markets, but they also carried goods throughout Palestine and across the Jordan River into Syria and Egypt (Buckingham 1822:4–28). In addition local Christians enjoyed certain tax advantages when aligned with Europeans for business purposes, so many of them sought to represent Europeans, engaging in both import and export activities.

By the nineteenth century Bethlehem had developed several items for which it was famous, both at home and abroad. The carving of shell and wooden artifacts may have been known in earlier times, but mass production was probably stimulated by the rapid development of trade with Christian Europe between 1825 and 1855 (Polk and Chambers 1968:10). George Robinson (1837:153) is the first source known to me in which the mother-of-pearl and olivewood manufactures are specifically noted, although Volney, visiting in 1783, says "beads" (rosaries) were the primary Bethlehem handicraft

(1787:322–23, 426). After Robinson virtually all visitors mention the existence of these souvenirs, which by 1925 provided employment for fifteen hundred workers in Bethlehem alone and were valued at seventy thousand pounds sterling (Smith 1984:208).

According to Stillman (1979:9), the major article of commerce throughout the Levant was textiles, and Bethlehem was one of several weaving and embroidery centers. Conder (1879:283), who visited in 1874, said that Bethlehem was a modern, thriving town of traders, but he does not mention their wares.

In addition to pilgrimage/tourism, wine, carvings, and textiles, Bethlehem once had another industry. Many of the men of Bethlehem and Beit Jala, but especially those of Beit Sahur, were skilled stonemasons, not only quarrying the native rock but also fashioning it into building materials of great beauty and long-lasting utility. They were responsible for building the "New Jerusalem" in the late nineteenth century. In 1890 Palmer (1895:95) found that 30 percent of the men of Bethlehem were engaged in some aspect of construction, much of it, no doubt, carried on in nearby Jerusalem but a good bit also in Bethlehem itself, which was rapidly developing, by now with remittances from abroad.

### Emigration

Economic historians tend to agree that things were going poorly for the Ottoman Empire throughout the nineteenth and during much of the last quarter of the eighteenth century (Abir 1970:1; Clarke 1974:65; Karpat 1985:179). The economic reforms of the 1850s, allowing non-Muslims to own land, resulted in many Christians purchasing large tracts for the first time, but in Bethlehem their acquisitions were relatively small, close to town, and used primarily for planting fruit trees and for building houses and stores.[12] As Ma'oz has pointed out, however, these reforms made things more difficult at the same time that they opened up new economic vistas for Christians.

---

12. Tsimhoni notes that only Christians "in the north" owned large tracts of agricultural land in the early 1940s (1976:35–36). Presumably, she is speaking of the Galilee area, or perhaps the plain between there and Haifa. The land near Bethlehem is mountainous and rocky, and most Bethlehemites had long before lost their agricultural interests and skills. Those of Beit Sahur would have been more likely to have purchased lands if they could, but until recently that town was less affluent than either Bethlehem or Beit Jala.

Muslim retaliations for what they saw as Christian arrogance were often unpleasant and sometimes fatal. At the same time law and order were increasingly difficult for the Ottomans to maintain. Bedouins continuously raided Bethlehem in the middle of the nineteenth century, which may have been another reason its inhabitants increasingly refrained from agricultural pursuits (Ma'oz 1968:132).

Christians in the cities especially, but also in Bethlehem, became concerned about increasing Jewish immigration in the 1870s and 1880s—perhaps, as has been said, because Christians were more likely to be in competition with Jews in banking and commerce.[13] The European-dominated Christian churches may have stimulated some of this anxiety. Christians were the first, in June of 1891, to mount an organized protest and a warning of what might lie ahead (Tsimhoni 1976:202). They may or may not have shared the fears of the French archaeologist-explorer who warned as early as 1875 that the basic culture of Palestine was at risk: "A strong current of immigration from Central Europe has for some time set in . . . and a few years will do what centuries have not been able to effect" (Clermont-Ganneau 1875:213). Most of these early settlers, however, were apolitical religious Jews, not Zionists, who settled in Jerusalem, Hebron, Safad, and Tiberias (Muslih 1988:70).[14]

In any case, well before the turn of the twentieth century Bethlehemites had established temporary migration strategies that took them to many countries throughout North, South, and Central America as well as the Caribbean (Migdal 1980:70). The Greek Or-

---

13. This does not accord with the fact that in earlier times many of the Jewish immigrants tilled the soil, purchasing land largely from absentee Muslim landlords. Although this is not the place for such a digression, it seems clear to me that such an explanation is entirely too facile and needs further thought. Briefly, I suggest that the Christians' "insight" was more related to their greater familiarity with and understanding of the European world, which is where most of the Jewish immigrants originated. They feared the European Jew as an interloper, unlike the Jews with whom they had lived for centuries. The religiously oriented Eastern European Jew was culturally and linguistically distinct from his distant collaterals. It may also be true, as is sometimes charged, that Christians disliked or distrusted Jews because their religion taught that these people had killed Christ. There is no doubt that this sentiment was preached overtly and with rancor by most nineteenth-century European Christian sects, both Catholic and Protestant. (See chap. 7 for more discussion.)

14. Parfitt (1987) describes in detail the Jewish communities resident in Palestine prior to the waves of European Jews arriving in the last two decades of the 20th century. Unlike most other historians, he suggests that both groups played a role in the eventual creation of the state of Israel.

thodox church archives in Bethlehem preserve a note to the effect that one of their faithful died in an unspecified part of South America in 1797.[15] The earliest documentary evidence I have found for the presence of Arabs in Honduras is from 1899, when an illegitimate daughter of a Honduran woman and a Palestinian, perhaps from Bethlehem, was baptized in the San Pedro Sula cathedral. A 1936 note in the Israeli National Archives (INA) speaks of a Bethlehemite aged fifty-eight, who had spent thirty years in "America" and returned with sufficient capital—he was worth eight thousand pounds sterling in landed property and goods, it was said—to open a women's apparel shop in Jerusalem (INA, Box 330-N/14/36). By his name I determined that he had spent his time in Honduras.

This early (eighteenth- and nineteenth-century) emigration appears to have been temporary, sporadic, and probably included more men than women. Kimche (1972:63) describes the opening of the Red Sea to European ships and the establishment, as early as 1775, of the British-owned trading operation known as the Levant Company. This company, like others representing other European nations, further stimulated trade throughout the area and must have constituted an additional lure, especially for young Christian men already familiar with Europeans and with trading as a primary occupation. Due to difficulties in transportation and communication as well as to the hardships and diseases of the times, some early migrants probably did not return, like the ill-fated traveler mentioned above. But most did, bearing tales of fortunes to be made overseas—enough to whet the ambitions of the young men, or of their patrilineal clans (hamulas), which made the decisions about who should go.

During the late nineteenth and early twentieth centuries the population of Palestine rose sharply (McCarthy 1990). Smith (1984:25) suggests there was some immigration of Christians (as well as of Jews) into Palestine during that period, although it is not clear from whence they came nor where they settled. Bethlehem was said to have had a population of 1,500 in 1800, rising to 2,500 by 1840, and 4,750 by 1870.[16] By 1922, when the first official census was made

---

15. I owe this piece of information to Dr. Adnan Musallam, of Bethlehem University, who has also been studying the emigration of his people.

16. These are conservative estimates made by Ben-Arie (1970:29), who reviewed the accounts of various European travelers, most of whom, he believed, exaggerated the size of the local population in order to bolster the cause of the Christians. He did not include, however,

TABLE 3.2.  Estimates of Population of
Ephrata Towns

| Date | Bethlehem | Beit Jala | Beit Sahur |
|------|-----------|-----------|------------|
| 1800 | 1,500 | | |
| 1840 | 2,500 | | |
| 1870 | 4,750 | | |
| 1922 | 6,658 | 3,101 | 1,519 |
| 1931 | 6,815 | | |
| 1944 | 8,820 | | |
| 1967 | 16,313 | 6,041 | 5,380 |
| 1975 | 20,969 | 6,965 | 7,164 |
| 1987 | 34,180 | 10,976 | 10,077 |

under the British Mandate, the town had 6,658 inhabitants, of whom 5,838 were Christian. Beit Jala had 3,101, virtually 100 percent Christian, and Beit Sahur was home to 1,519 souls, 1,234 of whom were Christian (Census of Palestine 1922). These figures are shown in summary form in table 3.2.

Probably this rapid rise in population, especially the near doubling in the one generation between 1840 and 1870, can be attributed largely to declines in mortality wrought by the increased attention to education and health care introduced by Europeans. The area of Ephrata, however, must have had a sufficiently solid economic base or potential to sustain such growth, and I believe there were several factors related to achieving that. Its proximity to Jerusalem was certainly an important factor, as was the increasing pilgrimage/tourism described above. At the same time continuing pressure to find their fortunes must have been felt, especially by the younger generation, and when opportunities beckoned to journey abroad it is not surprising that they took advantage of them, especially since overland long-distance trade had been part of the local economic system for several generations. Remittances during this period may well have fueled much of the economic development, drawn population, and further

---

the work of Palmer (1895), who apparently counted the people in Bethlehem, noting their occupations as he did so. Palmer gives a figure of eight thousand for Bethlehem, but that may have included Beit Sahur and Beit Jala as well. I have used Ben-Arie's figures as the most conservative, even though I consider it likely that he was politically motivated, trying to demonstrate that the population of Palestine was insignificant at the end of the nineteenth century, when major Jewish immigration began. (See also McCarthy [1990] for a more balanced view of the situation through time.)

stimulated emigration. Most of the migration literature shows that it is not the poorest of the poor but, rather, those with some education and/or other liquid assets who leave their homes, looking not for greener pastures but for more lucrative trading arrangements (Migdal 1980:59).

Until 1896 the Ottoman Empire forbade emigration, so for those intent upon a foreign journey special strategies had to be found. Passage to a busy European port, such as Marseilles, could be made with only local identification papers. From there it was not difficult to find a ship that would take them, without papers, to some foreign, preferably American, shore. Many of the people with whom I spoke in Honduras said that the first emigrants went wherever they could get a ship to take them. (See also Ammar 1970:3.)

After 1896 there seems to have been a spurt in emigration. Although Karpat states that "only" four thousand left Palestine between the years 1897 and 1907, as we will see in the next chapter, the number of immigrants to Honduras, now including many women, rose sharply around the turn of the century. Karpat (1985:180,188–89) only considered documented emigration, yet, as he himself noted, once the strategy of illegal flight had been institutionalized, it may have been cheaper and simpler than going through regular procedures.[17]

In 1909 a new factor was introduced, for the Ottomans began to subject Christians and Jews, long exempted by paying a nominal fee, to the military draft. Even before the outbreak of World War I the flight began. Hitti (1965:242) says three thousand people left Jerusalem in 1913 — mostly young men, of whom two-thirds were Christian or Jews. These, presumably, since they were documented, were only those who had somehow obtained permission! When Turkey entered World War I in October of 1914, and conscription meant actually going to war, many young men of Bethlehem and its surroundings quickly found brides and hurried off to join their kinsmen in the Americas (Edwards 1983:627). Other Palestinians left as well. Although most were Christian, Karpat estimates that 15 to 20 percent

---

17. In Honduras the people continually refer to the "Turkish" passports that their ancestors carried, yet I was never able to find one for my own inspection. One woman said she remembered having seen one among her father's things, and, though she thought she had preserved it, she was never able to locate it. Undoubtedly, some had Ottoman passports, but by the very nature of the migration I suspect most of the earliest came without papers.

were Muslims who either remained silent about their religion or converted to Christianity (1985:180). All such emigration was clandestine, of course, but flight strategies were well known and the people imaginative.[18]

Tourism was at a standstill during the war (Musallam 1981:34), and trade in the items handled by Bethlehemites was slack. Following the armistice there was a brief period during which hopes of economic recovery kept Bethlehemites at home. Because many of them were better educated than other Palestinians, spoke one or more European languages, and because they exhibited a distinct Western outlook, they were in demand as interpreters and advisors to the British military occupation between 1917 and 1922. When the latter established a local civil administrative corps Christians were initially given 40 percent of the senior and 47 percent of the junior positions (Tsimhoni 1976:167–68, 170). Probably most of these were held by Christians from the cities such as Jerusalem, Jaffa, Haifa, and Acre, but several of my Bethlehemite friends in Honduras recalled having worked for the British as well.

By 1922 the local economy had improved somewhat, but so had opportunities in Honduras and elsewhere in the Americas. For whatever reasons emigration from Bethlehem between 1922 and 1931 was heavy (Tsimhoni 1976:26). Certainly, the rate of population increase slowed dramatically, for the town had only 6,815 in the official 1931 census, and only 8,820 by 1944 (table 3.2). The global depression of the 1930s was felt in both Honduras and in Bethlehem, but by now emigration had become a norm, regardless of the economic news from abroad. Many went simply to join elder brothers or other relatives — still with the hope of returning to Bethlehem with more money in their pockets than they had when they left. Aggravating the general depression, the domination of certain sectors in Palestine by Jews was having an economic as well as political impact. Matiel E. T. Mogannam noted that the "increased use of cement, reinforced concrete and silicate bricks, all manufactured by Jews, is replacing dressed stone for constructional purposes, and so displacing a large number of stonedressers and stonemasons, nearly all of whom are Arabs. The Arab quarrymen are also being displaced" (1937:222–23). As noted

---

18. One man from Jerusalem told me how his parents smuggled him out of the country wearing a nun's habit.

above, many of the local men, especially those of Beit Sahur, were in these occupations. My sample in Honduras included several.

The Arab Rebellion (1936–39), against what was seen as increasing favoritism toward Jews on the part of the British, must also have been a factor. Christians were well-represented in the leadership of the revolt, which some believe was the most effective Arab protest against their impending fate ever launched. Yet these were primarily the urban elite — businessmen and intellectuals — and my data suggest that the majority of persons leaving Bethlehem for Honduras at that time were of the humbler classes, albeit not without resources. (See chap. 5.)

Adnan A. Musallam notes that emigration was generally seen as a way of life from the 1920s through the 1940s, in spite of the fact that many permanently lost their Palestinian citizenship as a result.[19] During World War II some served in the British army, but their numbers and percentages were low (INA: Papers of the British Mandate). More chose to emigrate to the Americas, where business was flourishing in spite of (or because of) the war.

As Jewish agitation for partition of Palestine grew, the Christian Palestinians became more distressed. More than Muslims, they preferred the continuation of the Mandate, but they had also been opposed to many of the British policies, which were largely seen as pro Jewish (even though the Jews thought the British soft on Arabs). In a sense they felt themselves immured between the Muslim elites, among whom they realized they could never hope to achieve political equity, and the increasingly numerous and militant Jewish masses, who continued to enter the country during the early 1940s. The ineffectual British efforts to deter the latter were in part due to the mounting evidence of their persecution by Nazis and the paucity of countries willing to provide them shelter.

Still, for the majority of Christian Palestinians their socioeconomic position was reasonably well established, with emigration now a major strategy for financial improvement. Bethlehemites had a solid base in a number of different overseas locations, and remittances had been good. New businesses and many grand houses had been built,

---

19. Laws were finally passed to grant Palestinian citizenship to emigrants who returned within two years after 6 August 1924. As Musallam (1981:44) notes, however, this information did not circulate well in the diaspora, and many were, in any case, unable to make the trip.

both at home and abroad. Whole families returned to visit, have their babies baptized, and introduce the youngsters born abroad to their homeland. Young men from America came regularly to seek brides from among their *hamula,* or clan (Rosenfeld 1973; see also chap. 6). Bethlehem emigrants could count on having someone in the same kin group in their foreign destination who would provide a job or at least offer shelter, advice, and credit for starting a new business.

### The Impact of the Partition

Notwithstanding more than fifty years of buildup and warning, the catastrophic events of 1947–48 caught many Palestinians by surprise. Despite their fears and protests, many had behaved as though Israel would never come to be. Only twelve kilometers from Jerusalem[20] many Bethlehemites had acquired properties in both cities, usually with capital earned abroad. The initial destruction in Jerusalem and the succeeding war took a great toll, even on those who were out of the country, many of whom lost their property at that time.[21] But life went on, and, according to the Jordanian census conducted in 1961 after the West Bank had been part of that country for more than ten years, the population of Bethlehem had grown to 15,882 (Persson 1979:28). Many of the new inhabitants were refugees from other parts of what is now Israel, and most at first were Christians — from Nazareth, Jaffa, Haifa, Acre, and elsewhere.

In 1967, after the Six Day War, Israel occupied the West Bank and the Gaza Strip and has done so continuously ever since. In that year many Bethlehemites and other Christians, especially young men, left the country. Many chose to remain on the East Bank in Jordan, where they continued to be viewed as citizens, even after their

---

20. Distances given between Jerusalem and Bethlehem by different authors vary from seven to twelve kilometers. Obviously, some of the earlier figures were estimates, and later ones depended upon the road taken as well as upon one's Jerusalem reference point. I will use twelve throughout, as this is the distance my taxi driver informants cited between the Jaffa Gate and Manger Square.

21. Estimates of the number of Arabs who fled in 1948 range from a ridiculously low 30,000 (Peretz et al. 1977:55) to 770,000 (Rubenberg 1989:98). The latter figure is said to include all those leaving between November 1947 and January 1949, while other figures may refer to more limited time periods or may include only those who became documented refugees. For a recent review of the entire controversy, see *Palestine 1948,* a special issue of the *Journal of Palestine Studies* 18 (1) (1988).

attempt to overthrow King Hussein and his government in 1972. Some went abroad to study in Middle Eastern, European, and American high schools and universities; many obtained citizenship in the countries to which they journeyed and have never returned. Others left with their families, selling what properties they owned in Bethlehem — most often, to Muslim refugees from Arab Israel. Some left without selling, thinking they might one day be able to return; in many cases such properties were termed "abandoned" and were subject to confiscation. Among the new emigrants were a few from Bethlehem who were deported by the Israelis as subversives (Lesch 1979b:103).

Today those who remain struggle, and often suffer. Table 3.3 shows the pitifully small number of persons employed in factories in the 1970s. The intifada has given the residents renewed hope and strength, even though their economic situation declined sharply as a result. The PLO helps those whose houses are destroyed by the Israeli efforts to contain the intifada by punishing the entire family of those suspected of participating in violence, and there are local charitable organizations that care for the injured and give food to those in dire

**TABLE 3.3.   Distribution of Modern Bethlehem Firms by Size of Labor Force**

| Type of Business | Number of Laborers | | | | | |
|---|---|---|---|---|---|---|
| | 1–9 | 10–19 | 20–49 | 50–99 | 100 + | Total |
| Sewing | 50 | | 7 | 1 | | 58 |
| Bakery | 6 | | | | | 6 |
| Macaroni | 2 | | | | | 2 |
| Ice cream | 5 | | | | | 5 |
| Pharmaceuticals | | | | 1 | | 1 |
| Plastics | | | 1 | | 1 | 2 |
| Cigarettes | | | 1 | | | 1 |
| Carpentry | 32 | | | | | 32 |
| Olivewood products | 50 | 6 | | | | 56 |
| Mother-of-pearl | 10 | 5 | | | | 15 |
| Metalworking | 32 | 1 | | | | 33 |
| Garages | 27 | | | | | 27 |
| Stone and marble | 22 | | 3 | | | 25 |
| Solar heating units | | 1 | | | | 1 |
| Total | 236 | 13 | 12 | 2 | 1 | 264 |

*Source*: Awartani 1979:20.

circumstances. Numerous neighborhood groups have been formed to help each other as needed. Many families grow foods and keep livestock such as goats, chickens, and rabbits in their small backyards. Others survive almost entirely on money sent from emigrant relatives. But some cannot endure; during the one month of July 1988 fifty-six persons emigrated permanently from Beit Jala alone, according to the city's mayor.[22]

Yet, in spite of this steady outward stream the population of Bethlehem has continued to grow. In 1984 there were nearly thirty thousand people living there, with another seventy-five hundred in Beit Jala and nine thousand in Beit Sahur (Tabash 1985). By 1987 the area had grown by 14 percent (Laham 1987). (See table 3.2.)[23] Two-thirds of those living in Bethlehem today, however, are Muslim. This includes the population of a large refugee camp located there but also reflects the fact that numerous Muslims have purchased property from emigrating Christians.

The now small city of Bethlehem in many ways has become a suburb of Jerusalem. Recently, the city limits of the latter were expanded to include a modern apartment house complex named Giloh, where several thousand Jews live and commute each day to Jerusalem. Situated on the outskirts of Bethlehem, on land once belonging to Beit Jala, Giloh's entrance is guarded, and there is virtually no communication between its residents and those of the old Ephrata — Bethlehem, Beit Jala, and Beit Sahur. To add insult to injury the Israelis have given the name Ephrata to still another such suburban settlement a few kilometers farther along on the Hebron road. Both of these are architecturally European and contrast starkly with both the natural scenery and with the Arab settlements. They serve as a constant reminder of the new power — one that transcends anything the Palestinians have known in previous conquests.[24]

---

22. Field interview with Mayor Larach (Al Araj), 22 September 1988.

23. Both of the latter counts were made by studies carried out on behalf of Christian churches concerned with the decline in the percentage of their parishioners. Given the complexity of the migration situation, with people constantly coming and going, surveys of this sort must have been difficult and, consequently, crude. Nevertheless, the trends seem reasonable in the face of other data, even though the figures may not be so reliable as those of the official censuses.

24. In reporting on the furor over Soviet Jews settling on the West Bank several newspaper articles have mentioned that many Soviets have chosen to live in Giloh. It is not always recognized that the land on which this stands once belonged to Beit Jala and that this strategy in effect allows the Israelis to annex territory from the West Bank that borders on East Jerusalem.

Tourism to what is still touted as a Christian town continues, but a mosque has been erected in Manger Square, and, despite lamentations from Rome and the few remaining local Christians, the town's future is clearly Islamic. Although the old Christian elite families will only privately admit it, their era has passed. One day Christian pilgrims and tourists may be buying their souvenirs from non-Christian shopkeepers, and a Muslim mayor may be trying to deal with the Israeli military government.[25] The Christian charitable institutions supported from the outside will no doubt remain, but their clients are increasingly Muslim, and their major goals are to help the latter achieve educational, health, and skill levels comparable to those of the Christian and Jewish populations of the region. All the Christian clerics (both foreign and local) with whom I spoke agreed that whether Christianity will survive in the Holy Land depends upon Palestinian nationalism achieving its goals. Many feel that Christianity can better survive within what would inevitably be a Muslim Palestinian independent state than in Israel.[26] Of course, much depends also upon whether Christians in the diaspora would return in numbers sufficient to wield any kind of influence. Their decision to return would obviously hinge in part on the social climate in the new state but also on whether they had made successful adjustments in their new homes.

The next chapters will address the latter issue in relation to the Central American cultural, social, and natural environment in which the Palestinian immigrants have found themselves and which they have been instrumental in remodeling over the past several generations.

---

25. After 1967 the Israelis permitted the election of local West Bank authorities but later removed nearly all the mayors who had come to office in this way. Only the mayor of Bethlehem, Elias Freij, has been permitted to stay (Shipler 1986:415). Opinions among Bethlehemites vary as to whether he is a clever, dedicated, and self-sacrificing public official who has managed to confront and placate the Israelis or whether he is in fact an unprincipled, self-serving tool of the enemy. There is no doubt that holding this office has placed him in the world's limelight and that he enjoys the ensuing fame and prestige. On the other hand, his ability to keep the Israeli military relatively at bay has not been without benefits for the populace of Bethlehem.

26. The 1937 Peel Royal Commission established the notion that neither an Arab nor a Jewish state should be entrusted with protecting the Christian holy places of Palestine (Feintuch 1987:10). From this was born the notion of internationalizing Jerusalem and its environs. Most Christian leaders with whom I spoke believe that the Israeli record has borne out the prediction cited.

*Chapter 4*

# The New World of Honduras

You told me, you know, that when a child is brought to a foreign country, it picks up the language in a few weeks, and forgets its own. Well, I am a child in your country.

— George Bernard Shaw, *Pygmalion*

## Choice of Settlement

The reader should keep in mind that Honduras was not the only Central American country to which Palestinians migrated in the early part of this century. In addition to those already mentioned in El Salvador and Guatemala, large numbers settled in Mexico and in Nicaragua. By 1955, however, when the Arab communities in Central America and Mexico were visited separately by two men from Bethlehem collecting money for charities at home,[1] Honduras had by far the largest number of Arabs, the great majority of whom were Palestinians from Ephrata. (See table 4.1; also app. 1.) By that time, also, San Pedro Sula was the home of most of them and, apparently, the primary destination of new immigrants.

Houghton's anecdotal report from the late 1960s tended to confirm the impressions of the 1950s visitors; he noted that the bulk of the Arab population of Costa Rica was from Lebanon, but he believed that most of the immigrants in all the other Central American countries (he did not include Belize, then British Honduras) were from Bethlehem and its surroundings (1969:1). Dawson (1971) and Crowley (1974) did not contradict this view, and my own work fur-

---

1. The only country visited for which they located a larger number was Chile, often said to have been the earliest target country. Because of the timing of these trips, I have always wondered whether there might have been a political motive as well. However, one of these men was my host in Bethlehem, and repeated discussions turned up no evidence of such. Rather, his concern was simply a desire to keep track of emigrants and to remind them of the needs of their fellows at home. Detailed accounts of amounts of money collected from each were kept and preserved.

**TABLE 4.1.   Numbers of Arab Heads of Families Located by Travelers in Central America and the Caribbean in 1955**

| Country | Number of Arab Names | Percentage of Total Recorded in All Countries |
|---|---|---|
| Honduras | 255 | 42 |
| El Salvador | 199 | 32.7 |
| Nicaragua | 25 | 4.1 |
| Guatemala | 23 | 3.8 |
| Total C.A. | 502 | 82.7 |
| Mexico | 69 | 11.4 |
| Haiti | 28 | 4.6 |
| Dominican Republic | 8 | 1.3 |
| Total Mexico and the Caribbean | 105 | 17.3 |
| Grand total | 607 | 100.0 |

*Sources:* Nasri Jacir (1955–57) and Ayoub Musallam (unpublished fieldnotes, seen in Bethlehem, courtesy of Mr. Musallam).

ther confirms it, now with more documentary evidence, as will be shown below.

Because of the conflict situation in the Middle East, however, as well as those in El Salvador and Nicaragua over the past decade, the demographic situation has changed considerably. Not only are there now large numbers of Palestinians, including Muslims, from places other than Ephrata, but the populations have shifted within Central America itself. Table 4.1 shows the numbers of Arabs located by the 1955 visitors in each of the Central American and several of the Caribbean and South American nations,[2] while table 4.2 shows how

---

2. Arab names, when transcribed using Spanish orthography, may be spelled in many different ways. This results from the quite different sound patterns used by the two languages as well as from simple human error. On the other hand, there have been many cases in which different branches of the same family have chosen to distinguish themselves from each other by retaining different spellings of what was actually a single ancestral name. Another problem has arisen from the confusion sometimes generated by the fact that many Arab surnames have only recently derived from what were given names. Thus, the son of Abdala might be named Baniout Abdala, and his son might be Elias Baniout Abdala, and his son Salvador Elias Baniout Abdala, and so on. At some point Baniout may become the surname, especially if a quarrel should arise between Salvador and his brother, Negrib Elias Baniout Abdala. I have seen as many as seven names recorded for one person in early church records.

Girls were also given the names of their male forebears in the same way, although their own name was gender linked. Thus, the sister of the last two examples might be named Farida

**TABLE 4.2. Numbers of Arabs Located in Various Honduran Settlements in 1955 and in 1986, Showing Increasing Concentration in the Larger Cities**

| Town or City | 1955 | 1986 |
|---|---|---|
| San Pedro Sula | 87 | 531 |
| Tegucigalpa | 61 | 476 |
| El Progreso | 28 | 48 |
| La Ceiba | 17 | 45 |
| La Lima | 13 | 9 |
| Choluteca | 11 | 10 |
| Tela | 10 | 9 |
| Puerto Cortés | 6 | 17 |
| Olancho | 5 | |
| Potrerillos | 5 | |
| Villa Nueva | 4 | |
| El Urraco | 3 | |
| Santa Rita | 2 | |
| Comayagua | 1 | |
| Comayaguela | 1 | |
| Santa Rosa de Copán | 1 | 4 |
| Totals | 255 | 1,149 |

*Sources:* Jacir and Musallam.

many they located in each Honduran community in comparison with the numbers listed in the 1986 Honduran phone book.[3]

This book will provide only minimal, background information on the larger Central American and Caribbean area and will concentrate on Honduras, which, since the 1950s at least, has eclipsed the other countries mentioned to become the most important center of

---

Elias Baniout Abdala. These naming customs facilitated the identification of families over the past generation but made it more difficult to determine lineage connections. Sometimes the people themselves have lost track of their ancestors' collaterals. (See chap. 6 on family life.)

3. The figures from 1955 derive from lists made by Ayoub Musallam and Nasri Jacir, who made separate trips to the Caribbean, Mexican, Central American and South American countries where their countrymen were known to have lived. The purpose was to obtain a record, encourage their brethren not to forget their homeland, and to solicit funds, ostensibly for charities at home. Their lists cannot be considered exhaustive, since they failed to visit some of the smaller towns in each country and neglected places such as Jamaica and Belize entirely. The names appear to be mostly those of heads of families, including a number of widows and sometimes adult single women.

Mr. Musallam was a close personal friend and collaborator in the Bethlehem fieldwork

Central American Palestinian settlement (Dawson 1971; Houghton 1969–70; Crowley 1974). Why Central America? Why Honduras, in particular? Were the other countries not equally attractive? If not, why not? These questions plague the minds of serious and casual investigators alike. Oral traditions offered by local residents often assert that the earliest immigrants simply boarded ships without necessarily knowing or caring about their destinations and that some landed in Central America purely serendipitously. Houghton (1969–701:1), who collected some information on the Palestinian population in several of the Central American countries in the late 1960s, appears to have accepted this scenario, supporting his conclusion and extending the point by citing an anecdote related by Hitti concerning a Levantine who allegedly spent two years in Australia before discovering that he was not actually in New York. The naïveté this suggests was certainly not characteristic of the Palestinians I knew, and I suspect the story was an ironic attempt to make fun of a gullible Western interviewer.

Crowley, on the other hand, a geographer who examined immigration and naturalization records and interviewed elderly Palestinians in San Pedro Sula in 1979, believed that "many, and maybe the majority, of the early immigrants headed intentionally for Honduras" (n.d.a:6). Still, he failed to discover how or why the first adven-

---

upon which this book is partially based, and I believe he tried, to the best of his ability, to track down everyone. Errors in recording names were, however, quite often apparent. Some names appeared more than once, and sometimes with slightly different spellings. I have tried to eliminate obvious duplications. Some names also were of sympathetic local non-Palestinians, mostly of Arab descent.

The 1986 figures come from my own compilation of names in the Honduran phone book of that year. Again, it is far from exhaustive and certainly not perfectly comparable with the 1955 lists. Many people do not have phones, either because they cannot afford the costs or because phone lines are difficult to come by. One collaborator said that many people have unlisted numbers for the sake of security, there being a good bit of paranoia among the Honduran population for various reasons (see chap. 6). Finally, phone service is not available in many of the smaller communities. During the fieldwork I visited Potrerillos, Villanueva, La Lima, Yoro, El Progreso, Tela, La Ceiba, Trujillo, Santa Rosa de Copán, and Puerto Cortés, although my base was San Pedro. Working with the phone book was frustrating because there are sometimes duplications, names remain even after their owners have died or moved away, and misspellings are rife. In a very few cases names have changed over the years to the point that they are no longer identifiable as Arab, but this seems to have been quite rare and probably was primarily typical of Muslims, who did not have a local community to perpetuate their sense of ethnic-religious identity (see chap. 8).

turers decided to opt for that country, noting only that, once a nucleus was established, others came to join their relatives and that peddling was their primary occupation.

There is, in fact, considerable reason to believe that the movement was rational — that in the late nineteenth century word of mouth through networks of kin and neighbors had commended the Central American republics, and Honduras in particular, as future boom areas where an entrepreneur with only a small amount of capital might make a "fortune." Indeed, as I shall argue in chapter 5, the high rate of return to capital invested would make peddling in a developing country like Honduras a profitable undertaking, especially if virtually unlimited credit and marketing information were available through local and transnational kin and ethnic networks. That expectation was quite often borne out, as we shall see, even though not all who came succeeded, and not all remained.

There are, of course, no precise immigration records for that period, and family traditions are often vague, usually unwritten.[4] It seems clear, however, that Palestinians and other Middle Easterners had begun their exploratory journeys to both the United States and Canada and to various countries in the Caribbean and South America by the 1860s or before, but, although a few may have visited there, I have not been able to document their presence in Central America before the 1890s. Oral traditions recorded by Ammar (1970:3) and Crowley (n.d.a:5) coincide with one told to me in Guatemala. All three describe efforts by Bethlehemites to sell mother-of-pearl and olivewood curios at one or another trade fair in the United States. Failing to dispose of their wares there, they journeyed on to Guatemala (or El Salvador or Jamaica, depending on the version), where rumor had it that the Christian population would be eager to buy religious articles manufactured in the Holy Land. Although sales of the latter were not encouraging, the travelers soon developed other lines of goods and remained to found their own enter-

---

4. Neither are there good records for more modern times. The Honduran government has become increasingly cautious about allowing anyone to peruse those that do exist. The church records are dependent upon the dedication and good intentions, not to mention the handwriting, of the priests assigned to keep them. Natural disasters have sometimes damaged the books, and improper handling in the course of serving those who request copies has also taken its toll.

prises, later bringing in relatives and friends from Palestine. A 1911 list of established export-import houses in Guatemala (published in New Orleans) lists two with Arabic surnames. Ammar's account from Jamaica was attributed to a man who had personally made this trip in 1893; it contained a further clue concerning their goods—that they had bought items in the United States for sale in their Central American or Caribbean destinations, not depending merely upon Bethlehem handicrafts.

Crowley also cites an unpublished manuscript written by a Salvadoran, claiming that the first Palestinians in Central America landed at the port of Cutuco, in El Salvador, from which they first journeyed to all the towns in that country and then left from the port of Acajutla for the other Central American countries (Crowley n.d.a:5, quoting Monterrosa Sicilia 1967:15). One man from San Pedro told me that his immigrant ancestors had first lived in El Salvador, reaching Honduras overland and finally settling in Santa Rosa de Copán. Since it was not until 1915 that the first public traffic began to flow through the Panama Canal, it is difficult to imagine how they might have reached El Salvador directly from Europe. A journey through the Red Sea and ultimately across the Pacific was possible but unlikely. It seems more probable that they came from the United States via Mexico, perhaps by sea from the latter's Pacific coast. Such a route is conceivable, since we know Palestinians also settled in Texas, New Mexico, and in various parts of Mexico, where their descendants still live today.

As Crowley notes, these stories, whether true or apocryphal, do accord with the general facts concerning the Levantine exodus during the latter years of the Ottoman Empire. It was not unusual for men to leave home on trading expeditions; they did explore new lands and searched for new markets; and many or most did return to their villages or towns, where they passed on information concerning what they had seen in their travels, thus stimulating further emigration. As is generally well known, both short- and long-distance trading have long occupied the populations of the Levant, the crossroads of the civilized world until the opening of the Suez Canal in 1869 changed global trading routes. A Lebanese colleague, born in a humble peasant village, described to me how from early childhood he had heard tales about trading, told in coffeehouses by local men who had returned from successful forays. Buying cheap and selling dear was everyone's goal — and the mark of a clever man on his way up.[5]

None of this oral tradition, however, fully explains the historical and present-day settlement patterns in Central America, nor does it situate the diaspora in either its Middle Eastern or its Central American context. In order to do this I have put together clues elicited from a variety of sources, including baptismal, marriage, and death records of the Roman Catholic church in Honduras, archives of the British Mandate now stored in Israel, and historical materials concerning the establishment of businesses in and around San Pedro Sula, Honduras — today, the Central American city most closely identified with Palestinian entrepreneurship.[6] Crowley's published and unpublished manuscripts from the 1970s have furnished comparative data, including some information on immigration and naturalization (Crowley 1974, n.d.a and b).

Although local oral tradition — especially that preferred by the oldest, most well established families — does not admit it, and previous scholarship has not developed the point, Palestinian prominence in San Pedro business and manufacturing circles can really only be traced to the 1950s, when the city underwent a postwar economic and population boom. This coincided with events surrounding the Partition and the establishment of the state of Israel, with consequent deleterious effects upon the native Palestinians of that area. Emigration of the latter to all parts of the world had already occurred, of course, but its nature was drastically changed after 1948. For the first

---

5. Edward Azar, personal communication.

6. Official vital statistics were unobtainable, despite repeated efforts to gain permission to use them. For reasons that are not entirely clear to me, officials continually put me off, promising that "next week" the required clearance would be granted. Because Honduras, like most Latin American countries, is highly centralized, all such requests must be channeled up to Tegucigalpa, the capital. I made the mistake of depending upon the goodwill of local officials in San Pedro Sula rather than going directly to the appropriate persons in the capital itself. In previous years this tactic had worked well in Trujillo and in La Ceiba, but it may be that political relations were uneasy between the chief of this department in San Pedro and his superiors in Tegucigalpa. Possibly a bribe would have helped, but I was reluctant to engage in this kind of behavior with such a high-level person, especially one to whom I had been recommended by friends. It may also have been that the records of the early 1900s had been misplaced or were in poor condition, such that the director would have been embarrassed if pressed to produce them. I have no reason to believe that the difficulty was in any way related to the materials I was seeking on Arabs. Eventually, stringencies of time precluded my taking a different tack, and the mystery of my failure remains.

time, Palestinians had to face the possibility that the old order had given way to something new and that they had neither the resources nor sufficient moral support from other nations to contain the expansion, much less to destroy the new state. More than ever it was important to succeed in their foreign endeavors, not only economically, so as to support their relatives and to develop their enterprises in their homeland, but also socially, in the event that one day return might become difficult or impossible. Of this was born, I believe, a new commitment to the New World, a new culture, and a new nation.

## The North Coast of Honduras and the Sula Valley, 1900–1950

Palestinian entrepreneurship in the regions surrounding the city of San Pedro Sula was a significant factor both in their own enrichment and in the development of that city and its hinterland during the first half of the twentieth century, although the latter is often either unrecognized or denied by many other Hondurans today. It is important to correct the record and, in doing so, to cast further light on the nature of the activities of the earliest immigrants and the synergistic relationship that developed between them and other actors and events involved in that development.

Before 1950 the northwestern coastal Honduran population was spread out across the fertile plains upon which the "green gold" of bananas had been produced since the 1870s, dominated by large multinational corporations since the 1890s. Not only were the soils there the best in all of Honduras, but the area was well watered by a number of rivers, most of which also served as waterways for small craft. The Sula Valley, straddling both the Ulua and the Chamelecón rivers, was dotted by several small towns or cities, including Puerto Cortés, one of the best harbors on the Atlantic littoral of Central America; El Progreso, the farthest west, situated in the department of Yoro; and La Lima. The United States (especially Southern) presence in this part of Honduras was strong and pervasive, building upon a generation or more of intensive commerce and travel between New Orleans and Mobile and Puerto Cortés. Some families from the devastated American South had chosen to settle in Honduras after the Civil War, preferring not to live in a land controlled by "Yankees," whom they considered foreign and exploitative. Ironically, of course, they themselves became part of the foreign cultural and political intrusion in Honduras (Dawson 1971:10).

At the turn of the century, when Palestinian immigration was just beginning, there were also many other Americans in Central America, ranging from missionaries to adventurers, from unskilled railroad workers to representatives of banks and entrepreneurial firms aiming to cash in on the general global prosperity of the times and, in particular, on the rise of the banana industry. It is no secret that many of these foreigners were influential in Honduran national politics, swaying presidential elections, rewriting constitutions, and determining commercial policy. The north coast was transformed into a largely English-speaking zone, and in time residential colonies of Americans grew up near Trujillo, La Ceiba, Tela, Puerto Cortés, and finally at La Lima, the eventual headquarters of the United Fruit Company, only a few miles from San Pedro Sula.

In the Sula Valley there were also many smaller hamlets, some of which had developed early in response to river traffic and others that sprang up or whose importance was enhanced with the building of a railroad intended primarily to transport bananas from their source to Puerto Cortés. Other railway lines stretched parallel to the coast, connecting Trujillo, La Ceiba, and Tela, all of which were also at one time important banana ports. The southern terminus of these various railroad branches, which once formed an effective local transportation network, was what is today a mere crossroads, a town called Potrerillos. There, as well as in nearby Santa Rita, Pimienta, Villanueva, San Manuel, El Porvenir, Olanchito, El Urraco, Chamelecón, Cofradía, and Choloma did the immigrant Palestinians establish themselves, usually after having served for a time as itinerant peddlers in the same area. (See tables 4.2 and 4.3, as well as map 2.)

Palestinians shared the area's petty commercial and industrial spheres with both native Hondurans and other foreigners (see table 5.4). Many of the latter claimed agricultural land grants and tried to plant bananas; others became directly involved in that industry as employees of one or another of the larger companies. Unlike what Ammar (1970:4) reported for Jamaica, most Palestinians in Honduras seem not to have planted bananas but instead supplied household necessities and tools to those who did, as well as to the city and town dwellers who worked in the trade or who served the banana empire in other capacities.

A frequently mentioned belief among the descendants of the first immigrants is that their ancestors arrived with nothing but the clothes on their backs and began their businesses by peddling small items on foot or by canoe in the hinterlands. This kind of merchandising, as Plattner as shown (1975a:60) is efficient at certain levels of regional economic development but must eventually give way to fixed establishments of different sorts as the target population grows. Chapter 5 will further describe and analyze Palestinian Honduran business affairs, but suffice it here to note that the evidence confirms considerable mobility on the part of these entrepreneurs. Sapper, who traveled in Honduras in the late 1890s, stated that the Arab population "trav-

TABLE 4.3.  Businesses Established in Department of Cortés, 1900–1949, by Nationality and Gender

| Nationality | Number | Percentage | Number of Women | Percentage of Women |
|---|---|---|---|---|
| Palestinian | 153 | 29.5 | 15 | 10 |
| Lebanese | 3 | 0.6 | 0 | 0 |
| Honduran | 240 | 46 | 48 | 20 |
| Guatemalan | 6 | 1 | 0 | 0 |
| Salvadoran | 15 | 3 | 5 | 33 |
| Nicaraguan | 4 | 0.7 | 1 | 25 |
| Total C.A. | 265 | 51.0 | 54 | 20 |
| Mexican | 2 | 0.3 | 0 | 0 |
| Puerto Rican | 2 | 0.4 | 0 | 0 |
| Cuban | 1 | 0.2 | 1 | 100 |
| Jamaican | 2 | 0.4 | 0 | 0 |
| Dominican | 1 | 0.2 | 1 | 100 |
| Total Caribbean | 6 | 0.9 | 2 | 33.3 |
| United States | 12 | 2.3 | 0 | 0 |
| English | 5 | 0.9 | 0 | 0 |
| French | 2 | 0.4 | 0 | 0 |
| German | 2 | 0.4 | 0 | 0 |
| Greek | 1 | 0.2 | 0 | 0 |
| Italian | 2 | 0.4 | 0 | 0 |
| Spanish | 16 | 3.0 | 1 | 6 |
| Rumanian | 1 | 0.2 | 0 | 0 |
| Swiss | 1 | 0.2 | 0 | 0 |
| Total European | 30 | 5.8 | 1 | 3 |
| Chinese | 45 | 8.7 | 0 | 0 |
| Australian | 3 | 0.6 | 1 | 33.3 |
| Grand Total | 519 | 100.0 | 76 | 14 |

eled as itinerant merchants and sold trinkets, belts, and other small articles" (1928:429–30). Not only did many of them peddle, especially at the beginning of their Honduran careers, but those who opened small fixed establishments moved them frequently from town to town, both in response to external vagaries of the marketplace and to help accommodate (and profit from the presence of) new arrivals from Palestine.

Tables 4.3 and 5.4 show the owners' ethnicity and location of businesses established in the Department of Cortés prior to 1949, while table 4.4 gives the data by year and compares the settlement patterns of Arabs and others.[7] It is true that San Pedro Sula, even though still small (table 4.5), was generally considered the most important city in the valley, if not on the entire north coast, during the first half of the century. A visitor in 1920 reported, "San Pedro Sula is the most important center of the northern littoral; one finds there many commercial houses of considerable capitalization" (quoted by Luque 1979:16). While some of these houses were in Arab hands, the majority were not, a fact that contradicts the widely held assumption that there was a "near-vacuum" of disciplined, organized commercial activity in the area—a false idea usually attributed to the notion that the Spanish culture disdained commerce and banking (Crowley 1974:140; Dawson 1971:14; Houghton 1969–70:2).

Nor were the majority of Arab businesses located in San Pedro in the early days (tables 4.4, 4.6, and 4.7). In addition to those located in the smaller towns near San Pedro, a good number of immigrants also went to the capital, Tegucigalpa, where, according to Rosa (1969:85), there were several Arab families by 1905. Some settled in the several north coast ports riding the wave of banana commercialization—Puerto Cortés, Tela, La Ceiba, and Trujillo. A few hardy souls ventured to Yoro and to Santa Rosa de Copán, the latter a tobacco center, and at some unknown date Choluteca and Nacaome near the southern coast were also penetrated by Palestinian entrepreneurs, as was nearly every site of any size or importance. Al-

---

7. The first chamber of commerce in this area was established in 1948, and all businesses were encouraged to register. There is no way to know how many of the total did so, but the form they filled out when registering included the date at which their businesses had been established, the amount of capital invested, and their nationality. The data accord well with evidence from early newspaper accounts, advertisements, and local tradition.

though hardly definitive, it is suggestive that the only towns in the 1986 Honduran telephone book with no Arab phone clients were Amapala (on an island in the gulf of Fonseca) and Catacamas, an outpost close to the jungles of the southeast.

**TABLE 4.4.  Arab and Non-Arab Businesses Registered in the Department of Cortés, 1900–1948**

| Year | Total | Number of Arab Businesses | Total in San Pedro Sula | Number of Arab Businesses, San Pedro Sula |
|------|-------|---------------------------|-------------------------|--------------------------------------------|
| 1900–1919 | 10 | 4 | 2 | 1 |
| 1920 | 6 | 1 | 4 | 0 |
| 1921 | 2 | 0 | 1 | 0 |
| 1922 | 4 | 3 | 1 | 1 |
| 1923 | 6 | 2 | 3 | 0 |
| 1924 | 6 | 2 | 3 | 0 |
| 1925 | 4 | 1 | 1 | 0 |
| 1926 | 6 | 4 | 3 | 1 |
| 1927 | 6 | 5 | 3 | 1 |
| 1928 | 4 | 2 | 1 | 1 |
| 1929 | 4 | 2 | 2 | 0 |
| 1930 | 11 | 3 | 4 | 1 |
| 1931 | 7 | 2 | 3 | 0 |
| 1932 | 11 | 3 | 4 | 1 |
| 1933 | 7 | 6 | 3 | 2 |
| 1934 | 13 | 5 | 4 | 2 |
| 1935 | 11 | 5 | 5 | 3 |
| 1936 | 15 | 6 | 4 | 2 |
| 1937 | 15 | 6 | 4 | 2 |
| 1938 | 18 | 4 | 4 | 0 |
| 1939 | 12 | 1 | 8 | 1 |
| 1940 | 48 | 23 | 14 | 9 |
| 1941 | 21 | 8 | 9 | 4 |
| 1942 | 20 | 6 | 7 | 2 |
| 1943 | 20 | 6 | 10 | 4 |
| 1944 | 28 | 5 | 15 | 3 |
| 1945 | 28 | 5 | 12 | 3 |
| 1946 | 32 | 4 | 10 | 2 |
| 1947 | 50 | 12 | 14 | 4 |
| 1948 | 71 | 21 | 39 | 10 |

## San Pedro Sula, 1950–1980

Said to have been founded by Pedro de Alvarado in 1536, San Pedro
Sula is today a sprawling modern city, at the center of which is a traditional Spanish-American plaza surrounded by a Roman Catholic cathedral, government buildings, shops, and a major hotel that also
serves as a social center for the more affluent members of the city.
Honduras is so different from Bethlehem, both physically and climati-
cally, that it is clear Palestinians did not settle there because they were
reminded of home: The northern coastal plain of Honduras receives
from 70 to 110 inches of rain per year, the least rainy months being
March through June; although some fifteen hundred feet above sea
level, the climate is hot, with a mean annual temperature of 26–28
degrees Centigrade (79–82 F ). The result is a subtropical vista with
bougainvillea, palm trees, yucca, and other such ornamentals in
abundance. The city itself is relatively flat but fringed by low hills that
climb rather steeply to thirty-five hundred feet as one approaches the
capital, Tegucigalpa, a three-hour drive to the south.

A *periférico,* or modest beltway, now surrounds the entire city,
encompassing the large industrial areas and giving rapid access to
newer and more modish commercial and residential zones, where
many Palestinian Hondurans now live and work. At the turn of the
century the city's most prominent residents inhabited the center of
town, and the first Palestinian entrepreneurs bought or built buildings that became both their shops and their homes. Many of these
have now been purchased or rented by Palestinian newcomers.

TABLE 4.5. Population of
San Pedro Sula, 1900–1980

| Year | Population Size |
| --- | --- |
| 1888 | 1,714 |
| 1900 | 5,000 |
| 1920 | 10,000 |
| 1935 | 17,516 |
| 1945 | 22,116 |
| 1950 | 21,139 |
| 1960 | 58,126 |
| 1970 | 130,000 |
| 1980 | 250,000 |

**TABLE 4.6.** Arab Businesses Registered in the Department of Cortés and in San Pedro Sula, 1900–1986

| Year | Number of New Arab Businesses | Number in SPS | Year | Number of New Arab Businesses | Number in SPS |
|------|------|------|------|------|------|
| 1900–19 | 4 | 1 | 1953 | 10 | 6 |
| 1920 | 1 | 0 | 1954 | 10 | 8 |
| 1921 | 0 | 0 | 1955 | 10 | 6 |
| 1922 | 3 | 1 | 1956 | 5 | 3 |
| 1923 | 2 | 0 | 1957 | 2 | 2 |
| 1924 | 2 | 0 | 1958 | 3 | 1 |
| 1925 | 1 | 0 | 1959 | 2 | 2 |
| 1926 | 4 | 1 | 1960 | 3 | 2 |
| 1927 | 5 | 1 | 1961 | 1 | 1 |
| 1928 | 2 | 1 | 1962 | 2 | 2 |
| 1929 | 2 | 0 | 1963 | 8 | 6 |
| 1930 | 3 | 1 | 1964 | 6 | 6 |
| 1931 | 2 | 0 | 1965 | 3 | 2 |
| 1932 | 4 | 1 | 1966 | 14 | 14 |
| 1933 | 6 | 2 | 1967 | 3 | 3 |
| 1934 | 5 | 2 | 1968 | 8 | 7 |
| 1935 | 5 | 3 | 1969 | 9 | 8 |
| 1936 | 4 | 2 | 1970 | 7 | 7 |
| 1937 | 6 | 2 | 1971 | 6 | 6 |
| 1938 | 4 | 0 | 1972 | 5 | 5 |
| 1939 | 1 | 1 | 1973 | 15 | 14 |
| 1940 | 23 | 9 | 1974 | 8 | 8 |
| 1941 | 8 | 4 | 1975 | 16 | 16 |
| 1942 | 6 | 2 | 1976 | 17 | 13 |
| 1943 | 6 | 4 | 1977 | 22 | 21 |
| 1944 | 5 | 3 | 1978 | 15 | 15 |
| 1945 | 5 | 3 | 1979 | 11 | 10 |
| 1946 | 4 | 2 | 1980 | 18 | 15 |
| 1947 | 12 | 4 | 1981 | 16 | 16 |
| 1948 | 21 | 10 | 1982 | 19 | 18 |
| 1949 | 19 | 7 | 1983 | 19 | 18 |
| 1950 | 18 | 10 | 1984 | 19 | 19 |
| 1951 | 18 | 15 | 1985 | 8 | 8 |
| 1952 | 10 | 7 | 1986 | 16 | 15 |

*Source:* Original unpublished records of the Cortés Chamber of Commerce, San Pedro Sula.

Others were expanded and modernized by the second- or third-generation family members and today stand as monuments to the early Arab presence in the city. (See chap. 5.)

It is probably a moot question to ask whether San Pedro Sula drew more Arabs after 1950 because it was developing, or whether the concentration of Arabs, with capital, connections, and capabilities, was the stimulus that initiated and fed the development process. It seems to me that it was a feedback situation: The Palestinians (and other foreigners, as we shall see in chap. 5) had certainly invested wisely and worked hard, and many of them shared in the prosperity experienced by the United States after the end of World War II. The more successful the businessmen in San Pedro Sula became, of course, the more likely were newcomers to try their luck there. The fruit companies had suffered serious setbacks due to the war, labor disputes, and, finally, to banana diseases that ravaged their crops and became embedded in the soils of their holdings. The Palestinian merchants whose fortunes had originally climbed in tandem with those of the banana entrepreneurs, however, now outstripped the latter, as they wisely branched out into new fields. Chapter 5 will describe in greater detail how they moved from peddling to family general stores, to family manufacturing, and, finally, to corporate status, eventually in collaboration with non-Arabs and then non-Hondurans.

As I write, a further migration is underway, with the United States as the primary destination. My research has given me only tantalizing glimpses of what appears to be a very large and growing population of Bethlehemites in that country. Many have immigrated directly from their homeland — some of them as part of the turn-of-the-century movement that also led them to Honduras. In New Mexico, for example, many of those who trade with the various American

TABLE 4.7. Numbers of New Arab Businesses Registered in the Department of Cortés and Percentage Located in San Pedro Sula, 1900–1986

| Time Period | Number of Businesses | Percentage in San Pedro Sula |
| --- | --- | --- |
| Phase I: 1900–39 | 66 | 29 |
| Phase II: 1940–47 | 69 | 45 |
| Phase III: 1948–55 | 116 | 60 |
| Phase IV: 1956–72 | 87 | 89 |
| Phase V: 1973–86 | 239 | 85 |

Indian tribes and pueblos are Christian Palestinians, although they are often not recognized as such by their neighbors. Similarly, Texas and northern Mexico were also settled by Palestinian traders early in this century — some of them related to those in Honduras. I have some evidence, although only of an anecdotal nature, suggesting that there has been and continues to be a considerable amount of traveling back and forth throughout the greater American Southwest, Mexico, and Central America. Some of those who came to Honduras in the 1950s were listed as "Mexicans" in immigration records, presumably because they had been born or naturalized in that country.

Today, the children of many Palestinian-Hondurans are sent to the United States for their higher education. Many stay on, marrying North Americans working in a variety of occupations, and, in time, become difficult to identify as Arabs. Others return to Honduras but are better considered as having adopted a transnational identity as they pursue new avenues of business and industry that link their interests and their futures to both nations. One young man passionately spoke of his hope that Honduras might one day become the fifty-first state! He, like many others, is discouraged by the continuing conflict and violence in Central America and by the increasing economic and political dependence of Honduras upon the United States. He did not perceive his proposal as a form of revolution but, rather, as a logical union with a long-standing cultural and political ally. He had no suggestions, however, as to how such an outcome might be achieved.[8]

## Two-way Acculturation

Throughout Honduras, but especially in San Pedro, a person familiar with that part of the world will see evidence of Middle Eastern culture traits and patterns. Many of the Arab homes are styled like those in the West Bank and elsewhere, with flat roofs and arched windows and doors. The local market sells a variety of Mediterranean produce which differs from that seen in other former Spanish colonies. These

---

8. It should be noted that such suggestions are frequently made — half seriously and half in jest — by persons who have spent a good bit of time in the United States and who would like to have the benefits of both that country and their own. Often they feel depressed by the disparities between the two situations. Whether they would actively support such a movement is not so certain.

items must have been introduced by Palestinians long ago, although today they are grown or sold by farmers and merchants who may be unaware of their origin. Among others one may buy several kinds of leaf lettuce, eggplants, okra, artichokes, figs, and grape leaves; sunflower, squash and other dried seeds; cracked wheat; pine nuts; pistachios; dates; olives; and coffee with cardamom. Sesame "butter," strained yogurt, and many other items, considered exotic elsewhere in Latin America, are sold everywhere, even in small stores. The larger supermarkets have sections clearly marked "Arab Foods." Many of these are imported directly from one or another country in the Middle East, but others are now produced locally — in Honduras or El Salvador. Some items, such as *ful* (*"haba"* in Spanish, "fava beans" in English) and garbanzos, or chick-peas, have long been staples in the New World, presumably introduced by the Spaniards along with other Mediterranean plants such as apricots and peaches, citrus fruits, grapes, and figs.

On even a casual visit to a Palestinian home, in either Bethlehem or Honduras, one is served fruit juice with snacks such as home-pickled vegetables, olives, raw crisp leaf lettuce, humus, and, inevitably, dried sunflower or other seeds. These may be followed by a large tray of fresh fruits, with knives so that each guest may peel them and serve him- or herself. Finally, there will be the heavy, sweet, cardamom-laced Arab coffee, although in Honduras some have taken to instant coffee instead. In Palestine it is said that, when the coffee is served, it is a signal that it is time to go home. In Honduras the coffee is often served shortly after arrival and carries no such message.

Palestinian women in Honduras frequently cook Arab foods for sale to the public as a means of earning money for favorite charities. These are immensely popular with both Arabs and other Hondurans. Several women have catering businesses out of their homes, serving primarily the Arab community for weddings and other special occasions, but many people with large families will also order their Sunday dinners. One local woman has written a cookbook, adapting Middle Eastern recipes for use in the Americas (Nimer de Bendeck 1979).

Arabic music and dance are considered essential at any familial social gathering, whether at peoples' homes or in public places. Weddings, engagement parties, baptisms, birthday parties, anniversaries — all are considered important occasions for celebration. At large functions a professional "belly dancer " may be hired, but, because most of the women born in Palestine are familiar with the movements, they may take turns demonstrating their skills in more intimate gatherings. Small ceramic hourglass-shaped drums are owned by many families, and one of these may be played to urge on the dancers. Recordings of modern Middle Eastern music are also prized possessions.[9]

At one *despedida de soltera* (a "bachelor's party" for the bride) that I attended only Arab women were present, and the ambience of the evening was definitely Middle Eastern. When I inquired of one of my friends who had been born in Palestine, however, how the activities that night differed from what they did at home, she laughingly said they had no such celebrations there. Some Honduran-born friends did not believe this. They were convinced that they were celebrating as had their ancestors.

Some houses have been built in a style quite reminiscent of what I saw in Bethlehem, with flat roofs, arched windows, and second stories. One family showed me pictures of a ritual during which they had killed a goat and spilled its blood in the foundations of their new house as it was being built. Furnishings usually include some wall hangings, tableware, or other ornaments from Palestine — carved olivewood camels and manger sets being favorites. Those I saw had all been purchased during return visits or brought to Honduras by newcomers or guests; no one could show me any real antiques handed down from the original immigrants. I assume either that the latter traveled very lightly or that they had not valued the items they brought enough to want to preserve them for posterity. On the other hand, most of the homes I visited in Bethlehem were also bereft of antiques, which could be seen only in the museums. The concept of "heirloom" depends upon the fashion of the day. When usages are altered, whether due to changing affluence or to new external actors whose values are imitated, "heirlooms" become "white elephants" and may be abandoned or sold. But the continuing interest among Honduran Palestinians in their cultural heritage is shown by their acquisition of the newer artifacts deriving from their homeland.

---

9. By "Middle Eastern" I refer to popular music deriving from various parts of the modern Middle East, primarily Egypt. Most Hondurans recognize the more linear, melodic music based on a five-note, especially minor, scale as being typically oriental, or Middle Eastern. While there are knowledgeable musical connoisseurs among them who are sensitive to regional and historical variations in mode, most Hondurans are not.

Certain traditional occupations have persisted, with some modifications, in the new environment. In Bethlehem woodworking has long meant the manufacture of religious items; one Palestinian-Honduran family has turned to the manufacture of wooden dishes, ornaments, picture frames, and even furniture, since a larger variety of fine woods is available in Honduras. Religious motifs are "out"; Mayan Indian symbols now decorate most of their wares.

Textiles are still important to Palestinians and other Arabs in the New World; in many places they import and market rugs and carpets. In Central America, with its hotter climate and tile floors, these are not widely used. Thus, the immigrants concentrated more on cottons for clothing, imported from both the United States and Europe. As locally grown cotton became more common, they sold it too, along with imported silks. When synthetics such as nylon and various polyesters became available after World War II, the Palestinian textile merchants were quick to stock them. In addition to selling yard goods of all kinds, some of the early immigrants sold ready-made clothing — some imported and some manufactured in small quantities, often by family members. In time these have become larger enterprises, even factories, and today many of them manufacture almost exclusively for export. (See chap. 5.)

Traveling to other countries has become a habit and a custom. Frequent trips "home" to visit relatives, friends, and holy sites have long been common for those who could afford them. Now, however, with Israel and the West Bank less accessible, Palestinian-Hondurans do their business, shop, and vacation in the United States, Europe, and other Latin countries such as Mexico, Chile, Venezuela, Colombia, and Brazil. In this way they maintain their contacts with others from their homeland, strengthening both personal and business ties among themselves in their new environment.

Are they still Palestinians? Most no longer speak Arabic as a language, although they recognize and use many of its words and phrases. Most are Christian, but now Roman Catholicism is probably the dominant sect, although Orthodoxy is still important, especially in Honduras, Chile, and Mexico. Within their own American country most would first label themselves as its citizen, as defined by relevant documents such as birth certificates, passports, and *cedulas,* or identity cards. But the additional Palestinian identification has never ceased to be important as well and, as I shall argue below, seems to have become more salient since 1950. Yasser Arafat and the Palestine Liberation Organization are important symbols of their ethnic heritage, of which they are increasingly proud, and they follow the events in the Middle East with great interest and passion.

In 1985 the Bethlehem Association was established by a group of expatriates living in the Philadelphia area. Very soon they expanded their membership to include persons from Beit Jala and Beit Sahur. The organization publishes a newsletter with items of information on the intifada as well as more intimate news such as births and deaths among their members; conducts national elections for its officers; raises money for charities in the Ephrata region; and holds an annual convention attracting several hundred people. In 1989 they invited Congressman Pete McCloskey to be their keynote speaker in San Francisco, a decision that suggests a move toward political action in this country, no doubt on behalf of the Palestinian cause and also in relation to the treatment of persons of Arab descent in the United States. Several Hondurans, usually because they have been contacted by relatives who are members, belong to this organization, and it seems likely that a chapter may be established in San Pedro Sula in the future. (Chap. 8 will further discuss the meaning of such actions in relation to ethnicity and nationality among Palestinians in diaspora.)

The next three chapters will describe more about the life and times of Palestinians in Honduras since 1900 and will try to distill from the extant documents and literature, as well as from ethnographic observations and interviews, what it means to be a Palestinian Honduran today. That there is no "typical" member of this category will become patently clear as we go along.

## Chapter 5

# Business as Usual

Merchants have no country. The mere spot they stand on does not constitute so strong an attachment as that from which they draw their gains.
— Thomas Jefferson, letter to Horatio G. Spafford, 17 March 1814

Are you a merchant utilizing the need of society for the necessities of life, for monopoly and exorbitant profit? Or a sincere, hard-working and diligent man facilitating the exchange between the weaver and the farmer? Are you charging a reasonable profit as a middleman between supply and demand?
— Khalil Gibran

### The Myth of Peasant Origins

There is a general impression, shared by descendants of immigrants and non-Arab Hondurans alike, that the first Palestinians to arrive in the country had been illiterate, penniless peasant farmers at home. Although Palestine was largely an agricultural society at the turn of the century, there are many reasons to abandon the notion that these pioneers were unsophisticated in the ways of the business world. First, as suggested in chapter 1, it has long been characteristic of peasant farmers in the Middle East to have engaged in trade as a sideline to their farming, leaving their fields and herds in the care of brothers, sons, or fathers during their absences. In addition to those who combined cultivation and trading, large numbers — perhaps the majority — of Christian Palestinians were engaged exclusively in the crafts and commerce from perhaps the last quarter of the eighteenth century (Volney 1787:426).

Second, all the evidence from Honduras, as well as from other parts of the New World where Palestinians and other Levantines arrived, indicates that these people immediately entered commerce at the level of peddling or above and that most profited from it. Arguably, peddling successful enough to lead its practitioner on to bigger and better enterprises requires a certain degree of literacy, not to mention the ability to calculate rapidly in order to bargain in an ad-

81

vantageous manner and to realize significant profits. These skills may be enhanced both by experience and with schooling, and I will argue that both had long been readily available to the Christian Palestinians of the Holy Land.

Third, although data are sketchy, many of the immigrants appear to have brought capital or had the connections (which we may refer to as social capital) to obtain it in Honduras. These connections were important in establishing credit partnerships, an institution known in the Middle East from the early Islamic period. Udovitch (1977:263) quotes an eleventh-century Islamic legal scholar in describing this as a "partnership of the penniless," a system in which people form a partnership without any capital in order to buy on credit and then sell. Sometimes it was designated by the name "partnership of good reputations" because the capital of the partners consists of their status and good reputations. Family, village, and communal, or religious, ties were the basis for forming such partnerships in the early years in Central America, and the ensuing business relationships within the immigrant community further cemented their status as an ethnic group. Thus, economic behavior was largely embedded in the social relations of this market-oriented society (Granovetter 1985:482). I will elaborate on each of these points as I describe and analyze Palestinian business concerns through time in Bethlehem and in Honduras.

### Levantine Commerce Under the Ottomans

Most contemporary observers and modern interpreters of historical materials on Palestine have suggested that Ottoman Christians and Jews were more often engaged in trade and commerce than were their Muslim neighbors and that Christians were most successful, due in part to their more extensive contacts with Europeans made possible by craft and commercial monopolies granted to them (Joseph 1978:23; Ma'oz 1968:193; Maqsud 1968:60; Kirk 1964:164).[1] Vol-

---

1. One reader has suggested that Christians and Jews traded more often *with Europe* but Muslims traded with their coreligionists in other areas, presumably within the Middle East. Because I do not control the massive Arabic literature, I was confined primarily to accounts by visiting Europeans, and they would undoubtedly have been more observant of the role of local Christians. Thus, although there may be some truth in this observation, I have not found evidence of it. Furthermore, the many works cited in this chapter, written by modern Middle East-

ney's account suggests that by the last quarter of the eighteenth century nearly everyone in Bethlehem was engaged in crafts and/or trade (1787:426). He also makes the interesting point that the men of Bethlehem returned to cultivation and to wine making when sales of their handcrafted wooden beads were poor (322–23). It is likely that many of them also ventured out of town, traveling either to foreign parts or to peddle on either side of the Jordan. Buckingham, who spoke Arabic and traveled on both sides of the Jordan, states flatly, "The Christians are more active in trade than the Moslems" (1822: 4). He describes his Christian guide from Nazareth buying and selling goods along the road of their journey, which, from the context of his account, must have been a common practice (28). Zenner states that the peddlers throughout Palestine were mainly Christian prior to World War I (1972:107), and Ashkenasi (1981:18–20) concurs.

Christianity in Bethlehem fostered a European nexus from the time of Constantine, an influence that became conquest in the eleventh and twelfth centuries with the Crusades. Not only did the town host frequent Christian visitors and immigrants from abroad, but the various religious entities these outsiders represented provided formal educational facilities unknown elsewhere in the area. The Franciscans opened an elementary school (for boys) in 1598, and in the second half of the nineteenth century there was a proliferation of primary, secondary, and vocational schools established by Italian, French, German, English, and American religious groups (Musallam 1981:41–42). Nearly all of these used a European language and curriculum as basic tools of instruction, although the Orthodox Christian schools, dominated by Greeks and Russians, conducted their classes in Arabic and promoted regional, as well as European, history (Tsimhoni 1976:33; see also chap. 7). A teacher's college for women was opened in Beit Jala in 1886 by the Russian Orthodox church (Kedourie 1970:328), and it is probably safe to speculate that its graduates served throughout the region, teaching Muslims and Jews, as well as Christians. Even today the more affluent Muslim

---

ern scholars (albeit only in English, or translated from Hebrew), concur with the idea that non-Muslims were more active in trade generally—at least in Palestine. Issawi (1955:118–19) implies the same in discussing the history of Lebanese trade, but see his 1982 economic history of the Middle East and North Africa for documentation of Muslim trading activities elsewhere in the Ottoman Empire. It may be that the situation in Palestine was different precisely because of its larger Christian and Jewish population.

Palestinians flock to Christian schools, whether in Amman, Jordan, Jerusalem, or in the West Bank. In 1925–26 Bethlehem had sixteen schools, although its population was less than seven thousand.[2] By that time formal education had become part of the Christian value system throughout the area, accounting for the observation by British and American investigators in 1946 that almost 100 percent of Christian children in the Mandate area received schooling of some kind (Anglo-American Committee of Inquiry 1946:716). Rosenfeld (1978:378) states that there were forty thousand Christian Arabs in private schools in Palestine in 1946.

This higher level of educational opportunity for Christians found expression in a number of ways. Although figures are unavailable over the years or for specific locations, illiteracy among Christians in Israel was only 24.3 percent in 1948, in comparison with Muslims and Druze, for whom the figures were 62 percent and 50.6 percent, respectively. At that time Christians employed 421 teachers in their private schools, while Muslims had 18 such teachers and Druze none. Jewish teachers in private schools before 1948 totaled only 15 (Ashkenasi 1981:27–28). Of course, the population surveyed excluded the seven hundred thousand or so Palestinians who had fled in 1947–48 and should therefore be viewed only as a rough but interesting guide to the educational differences among the several religious groups.[3] Ashkenasi (1981) and Lindbeck (1979:25) give birth and infant mortality rates for the three groups, and, as is usually the case for the better educated, Christian rates were significantly lower than the others.

Related to the other demographic trends was the increasing urbanization of Christians through time. According to Ashkenasi, "During the Ottoman period, and retained in Zion, much of commerce

---

2. This population figure refers only to the town of Bethlehem itself. If Beit Jala and Beit Sahur are included, the 1925 population would have risen to about ten thousand. Although some residents of the latter towns might have attended schools in Bethlehem, there were probably also schools in their own towns, although Musallam does not address himself to these "suburbs" of Bethlehem. It should be clear that there were many educational opportunities available to the local residents and that these were in addition to schools in nearby Jerusalem, preferred by many of the more affluent Bethlehemites.

3. Estimates of the number of Palestinians who left Israel and the West Bank in that period vary. Most recent scholarship accepts that the figure was probably over seven hundred thousand (Jiryis 1988:91). It is interesting that Ashkenasi gives no figure for Jews, many of whom must also have been illiterate at that time.

was in the hands of one or the other of the Christian sects, and indeed, Christians or better, Christian bourgeois society set the tone in most of the Arab cities" (1981:18–20). Christians were seen as being more successful in gaining material rewards; Zenner (1972:413) attributed this, in part at least, to their urban, European orientation. In 1946 79.8 percent of Palestinian Christians lived in cities and, presumably, did not farm (Ashkenasi 1981:18–20).

Western visitors to the Holy Land throughout the nineteenth century commented on what they saw as the "progressiveness" of Bethlehem and Nazareth in contrast to other towns. Their judgment seemingly was based on evidence of commercial activity, knowledge of European languages, and a general cleanliness and orderliness in the streets, buildings, and gardens as well as in the appearance of the citizens (Buckingham 1822:28; Conder 1879:283; Schumacher 1890:242; Tristram 1866:408). In 1895, when 1,113 Bethlehemites (of a total population estimated at 8,000) with "independent occupations" were surveyed, only 27 percent were engaged in agriculture; 19 percent were artisans; 23 percent were engaged in trade and services; and 30 percent were in construction (Palmer 1895:89–97). Those interviewed must have comprised nearly the totality of adult males, probably heads of households. It is plain that the population did not consist mainly of tillers of the soil and that they were quick to exploit new employment opportunities — in this case construction, which no previous observer had mentioned but which is regularly noted hereafter, especially for Beit Sahur. The proximity to Jerusalem and the existence of stone quarries in the vicinity were no doubt advantages, especially since Jerusalem, as a holy center for all three religions, grew rapidly during the nineteenth century.

It seems likely that most men of Ephrata had multiple skills and that they turned from one to another occupation as conditions changed. We know also that emigration to the Americas as a temporary phenomenon was already underway at the time. Karpat (1985:180) places the beginning date at 1860, although he notes that some would say 1820. Migdal (1980:70) dates the out-migration from the Jerusalem-Ramallah area as beginning in 1876, and Bethlehem, so close to these in distance and religious persuasion, could not have been far behind. In fact, Banoura (1981) specifically cites 1872 as the date of departure of some members of one Bethlehem family.

## An Entrepreneurial Ethnic Minority
## at Home and Abroad

Bethlehem before the Crusades had been heavily influenced by Romans, Byzantines, and finally Greeks, whose foreign clergy staffed
and controlled the Greek Orthodox church above the level of parish
priest. After 1100 the Latin (Roman Catholic) faith was established
there, and its church came to vie with that of the Greek Orthodox. The
Franciscan order, whose monks came from various European countries, has been especially influential. As happened elsewhere, those
professing Christianity became more and more internally fragmented
as time went on, to the point where the different sects were seen by
themselves and others as having little in common with each other. As
we shall see in chapter 7, the several Orthodox faiths in many ways
seem to have retained more of an Eastern orientation, although from
a Muslim perspective all Christians were perceived to be "Western."

In order to organize the considerable diversity within their empire the Ottomans built upon the Arab *dhimmi* system in their newly
conquered territories, many of which already comprised large and
complex societies, long governed by a series of other weak, decentral-
ized foreign states. There are many descriptions of how this, known
as the *millet* system under the Ottomans, operated, but for present
purposes I have found Joseph's (1978) analysis the most enlightening
and valuable. She describes how each sect—distinguishable from
others by clothing, diet, housing, vocabulary, and ceremony and
ritual—was assigned certain rights and obligations within the empire.
The laws governing the sects varied somewhat over time, and their
impact differed in specific locations. Buckingham, for example, noted
that Christians in Jerusalem were recognizable by their prescribed
black or dark blue clothing; yet in nearby Bethlehem they flouted the
ruling with apparent impunity (1822:218). Some observers have referred to these sects as "nations," by which they meant what we would
today call their ethnic component (Runciman 1968:8; Spyridon
1938:24; Volney 1787:489–90. Also see chap. 7).

Among other things the Ottomans granted craft and commercial monopolies to these religious and ethnic minorities; Volney observed that "almost all commerce is in the hands of the Franks,[4]

---

4. *Frank* was the term used to designate Europeans of Latin Catholic orientation and may

Greeks and Armenians." (1787:426). He then described treaties made by the Ottomans with European nations which included lower taxes on imports. The Europeans, in turn, used local Christians as agents, who received the same privileges, including the right to be heard before the relevant European consul instead of local courts in the event of a dispute. The linkages between foreign and local Christians, then, were beneficial both for their respective states and for the individuals involved. As Joseph notes, the system might be thought of as a means of organizing labor for both Ottomans and Europeans (1978:25).

The situation set the stage for what Hamilton (1978) has called "pariah capitalism," in which a triadic relationship is established among a polity, a set of internationally oriented elite capitalists (in this case foreign Christians), and a local pariah group. In such cases it behooves all three parties to retain the boundaries, often established along ethnic lines, between the pariah group and other segments of the society. Although Jews also constituted a pariah group and were governed by different rules than were Muslims, they did not have the advantages offered by the backing of foreign states.

Economic historians agree that the Ottoman Empire began to be adversely affected by the European industrial revolution during the eighteenth and early nineteenth centuries, with consequent outmigration for economic reasons for those able to manage it (Abir 1970:1; Clarke 1974:65; Issawi 1966:242; Ma'oz 1982:92). Although some historians, like Karpat (1985:179), believe Muslim Ottoman oppression has been overrated as a push factor for Christians, there is no denying that some of the emigration must be attributed to conflict of various sorts. Invasions of Ottoman territory by both European and Egyptian armies occurred repeatedly. Resulting violence sometimes led members of Christian communities to flee in family groups, many of them across the Jordan River, as noted by Buckingham (1825:28, 56). In 1834 there was a massacre at Beit Jala by Egyptian invading forces (Spyridon 1938:85).

The general erosion of law and order was accompanied by Bedouin raids on settlements throughout the Judaean hills, and Bethle-

---

have been related to the perceived salience of Franciscans. Although the Franks adopted the tastes and customs of Eastern culture, they did not lose their identity as Europeans (Benvenisti 1972:370–72). The term included French but also many Germans and Italians. *Greek* referred to Greek Orthodox and Greek Catholics, and *Armenian* to Armenian Orthodox.

hem, especially, was under almost constant siege around the middle
of the nineteenth century (Ma'oz 1968:132). The constant conflict
and deteriorating economy led inevitably to intrafamilial strife, and
it is interesting that Banoura (1981), writing from personal memory
and local tradition, cites family feuds as having been responsible for
a good bit of the emigration from Bethlehem and its environs.[5]

Furthermore, as the empire weakened, persecution of Christians in the form of labor levies and extractions of money and goods
increased (Spyridon 1938:19–23). The general climate of discontent
affected all Ottoman citizens, but in their growing distress many
Muslims tended to blame their problems upon their Christian neighbors, often becoming violent toward them. The Turkish-Russian
War in 1828–29, when Turkey lost some of its possessions, led to the
Ottomans imposing severe taxes on all their subjects (Naff 1983:51).
Efforts to equalize the pressures across the sects provoked Muslims in
many communities to express greater prejudice and hostility toward
their Christian neighbors (Ma'oz 1968:26ff.).

But Christians could not count on continued support from any
given European nation. In 1833 Turkey, Russia, and France signed
a treaty against Austria, England, and Prussia, but a few years
later — when Egypt took over the Sinai, Palestine, Lebanon, and Syria
(1839–41) — the British sided with the Turks, momentarily preserving
the Ottoman Empire and its European commercial arrangements and
further consolidating European influence in the Holy Land by establishing a sustained diplomatic and military presence there (Blumberg
1980:19).

Following the Crimean War local conditions continued to
worsen in spite of repeated attempts by a declining Turkish bureaucracy to modernize and to remove restrictions — a process that continued through 1896, when emigration was no longer banned, and
1909, when Christians and Jews for the first time became subject to
the military draft. As suggested in chapter 4, this last development

---

5. His book, published only in Arabic, was first shown to me in Honduras, where I also
was permitted to take notes from a Spanish summary translation that had been commissioned
by a former Honduran consul assigned to several countries in the Middle East. For this reason,
no page numbers appear in my references to it. The information on surnames and their prove-
nance was translated and published in volume 2 of the *Bethlehem Newsletter* (1988), official publication of the Bethlehem Association in the United States.

further increased emigration, which, once having begun, could not be stopped.

Nineteenth-century life outside Palestine took on a different tone. Across the Jordan Christian settlers seeking privacy and peace lived relatively free of the burdensome taxes and the "odious distinctions," as Buckingham termed them, suffered by their brethren in Palestine. Yet, in this relatively isolated area the people seemed very different from those described by other travelers. Buckingham rued the fact that east of the Jordan the Christians did not seem to have "profited" from their relative freedom. He described a way of life for the men that included a good bit of leisure time spent praying, eating, smoking, sleeping, strolling, visiting, and gossiping (1822:57).[6] He also repeatedly expressed his surprise that the Christian and Muslim populations in this marginal area were not distinguishable by their way of life, dress, dietary habits, or any other characteristic he was able to detect (51, 58).[7]

This perception is quite distinct from that of Volney, who visited Jerusalem and Bethlehem in 1783–85. He stated, "It is remarkable that in consequence of the differences in religion there exists between the Christians and Mahometans a marked difference of character as if they were two distinct nations, living under different climates. Greek Christians are in general wicked and deceitful, abject in adversity, insolent in prosperity and especially remarkable for levity and fickleness" (1787:489–90). He goes on, in a cogent analysis, to cast blame for this set of personality characteristics upon the Ottomans, remarking that the Christians had apparently taken on all the faults ascribed to them and had become deceitful and cunning in order to survive.

---

6. Little mention is made of women at all except to note some of their domestic duties and hospitality obligations. Male travelers in the early days were not really permitted close access to the women, other than to those whose primary function was to entertain visitors. Clermont-Ganneau (1875:212–13) remarked that much of the local tradition was preserved by the women and that a study of it ". . . requires a European woman investigator prepared to penetrate [the society], without the aid of an interpreter." Aside from a few casual observations by wives of European missionaries or diplomats (Finn 1882 and 1923; Rogers 1862), there were none until the celebrated ethnographic descriptions of Hilma Granqvist (1931; 1935; 1947; 1950; 1965).

7. Jordan is the only country today with Christian nomads, and it is often stated that they are hardly distinguishable from Muslims, but Buckingham was speaking of settled townsmen in the east, who specifically revealed their origins in towns west of the Jordan.

Of course, he was also describing what many have suggested is the inevitable demeanor of the businessman, especially the face-to-face salesman, and in spite of his defense of the Christians, Volney's vocabulary betrays his own distaste for this ethnic entrepreneurial minority group. Foster (1974:440) suggests that business dealings must often involve deception and that it is better if traders are from outside the ethnic group they serve, since tensions are then shifted from the interpersonal to the interethnic level. (See Granovetter 1990, chap. 4, for the same idea expressed in more positive terms.)

As we shall see, similar attributes were ascribed to the Palestinians when they reached Honduras, where they continued to occupy a pariah capitalist status. Although there was nothing like the official state repression under which they and their ancestors had lived for centuries, there was considerable covert and some overt hostility toward them by a population that was only beginning to adapt to a mercantile basis. There were also restrictive Honduran immigration laws passed in 1929 and 1934, which, following the permissive "open arms" law of 1906, seem extremely harsh. Both of the later laws taxed new immigrants upon arrival and restricted them to agriculture or to the development of new industries (República de Honduras 1929:557; 1934:12). Neither completely stopped the immigrant flow, although, along with world economic and political events, they did stem the tide momentarily during the 1930s, as judged by the slowdown in numbers of births recorded in Honduras during that decade. (See chap. 6.)

Crowley, who had access to immigration records in Honduras, indicates that more Palestinians left than entered the country in 1930–31 and 1931–32. In 1933–34 there were 592 documented Palestinian resident aliens in the country, a figure that rose to 812 in 1936–37 (Crowley n.d.b, quoting *Memoria o Informe Gobernación, Justicia y Sanidad y Beneficiencia,* for the years indicated). The number of Palestinian naturalizations in 1934–35 and 1935–36 (the only years for which these statistics were available to Crowley) was 35, while the total up to 1972 was only 487, with the largest numbers occurring between 1948–54, when they averaged 49.2 per year (Crowley 1974:14).[8] Like Crowley, I would conclude that there was consider-

---

8. A frequently told story is that Pimienta, one of the small towns heavily settled by the earliest Palestinians, lost all its municipal records in a flood in 1934. After that many of the Palestinians who had come clandestinely claimed to have been born there and were issued "replacement" Honduran papers without going through the trouble of naturalization.

able clandestine immigration, but, unlike him, I believe the flow decreased during the 1930s — perhaps in part because of opportunities to work with the British in Palestine. The *Statistical Abstract of Palestine* (Palestine 1944–45) confirms a severe drop in emigration after 1930, so it is likely that factors other than immigration restrictions in the receiving countries were operating. In any case few Palestinian newcomers to Honduras after 1929 went into agriculture; most found the entrepreneurial requirement of the laws more to their taste. All continued to engage in commerce, but increasingly they turned to manufacturing as well.

The failure of the Honduran state to regulate trade effectively in terms of ethnicity, as had both the Ottomans and the Europeans in the Levant (Maqsud 1968:60), probably exacerbated the early Palestinians' tendency to isolate themselves from the general populace, except, of course, when conducting business. As Granovetter (1990) has shown in considerable detail, such a situation would have been likely to enhance the entrepreneurial success of an expatriate minority group, especially one that already had considerable experience in buying and selling and which had been in a similar pariah position before.

That the Palestinians and Hondurans both tended to look down upon the other group and held each other at arms' length in the early days is clear from numerous contemporary accounts and in jokes told by both groups today.[9] Luque (1979:12–16) and Rosa (1978:23–24), who each produced a memoir containing descriptions of turn-of-the-century San Pedro Sula and Tegucigalpa, respectively, are patronizing at best when referring to this population. They do, however, serve to give us a picture of how the Hondurans viewed the "Turcos." In 1967 Rosa said,

It is time for [the Arabs] to forget avarice and for us to forget envy and exclusion. The truth is that we have never opened our hearts to them, for the first immigrants did not deserve it. However, the new generation of well educated Palestinians is different. Recognizing that the Arab colony is aggressive,

---

9. Most of these are so pejorative that I do not care to publish them. One of the least objectionable has already been cited in an earlier article (González 1989:80). See also Rosa (1978:87).

persistent, audacious, and thrifty, that the drawbacks that
kept them separate before are disappearing, and that they are
today a power inside the economic power of Honduras, why
don't we abandon the distrustful and rude barriers we have
maintained between us for so long? (1978:91)

In turn the Arabs disparaged their hosts' country and its people.
The early migrant's view of Honduras was well expressed by a woman
who had first arrived in 1927 to join family members who emigrated
in 1921. She made several trips back and forth between La Ceiba and
Bethlehem until her eventual return to settle in her hometown in
1959. She described La Ceiba in 1949 as "a lawless rundown isolated
village in an undeveloped region. It was at the end of the railroad, and
there were no motor roads." There she opened a store for banana
plantation workers and "managed to achieve a success in a wilderness no other male Turko [*sic*] . . . was able to achieve" (Bandak
1988).[10]

The account was no doubt somewhat exaggerated by the teller
and embellished by the editor, but it is essentially consistent with
descriptions given me by other migrants. From the perspective of the
Bethlehemites they were entering a wild and primitive country, far
less developed than their own. In the early days most of them saw little
to respect and still less to induce them to stay. Rather, the sojourn
abroad as a middleman pariah minority enabled them, as in the case
just described, to send money home to relatives, to start new businesses in Palestine, and to acquire enhanced prestige in their home
community as a result of their exotic experiences and newfound
wealth. They were really quite uninterested in, and many even unaware of, what the Hondurans thought of them.

---

10. I visited La Ceiba in 1956 and would hardly have described it as a wilderness.
Crowley claims that this town was the first center with significant numbers of Palestinians, although he does not document the evidence for this assertion (1974:38). In any case, it was the
most important Caribbean port of the late nineteenth and early twentieth centuries. Its urban
population in 1950 was 16,645, and in 1930 it had been over 10,000, thus exceeding the size
of Bethlehem at that time.

Certainly, law and order there were of a very different sort than what Palestinians had
become accustomed to under the British Mandate, and, in retrospect, I can understand the immigrant's perception. It seems clear, however, that she and her family must have felt an aliena-
tion from the Latin American society they encountered there, a feeling that she translated into
the pejorative characterization published.

## From Peddling to Family Firm

With few exceptions the earliest immigrants were said to have been peddlers. As Williams (1968:15) has noted for both Lebanese Muslims and Jews in Brazil, the experiences of such immigrants may be thought of as comprising three stages: the peddling phase, the small retail store, and the department store, new arrivals often working for a more established relative. The apocryphal story in Honduras is that each man proceeded to move up the commercial ladder of success, abandoning itinerancy with first a small stall, often within the municipal marketplace, and later by establishing a small store. The next step was a larger store with more varied merchandise and, finally, the opening of branches in other towns. Simultaneously, many also founded factories to manufacture some of the items formerly imported or previously unavailable in the country. Luque describes how members of one of the most successful families in San Pedro today "at first sold their goods from suitcases and backpacks, but then they rented and later bought [a wooden house] and established their store" (1979:16).

Middle Easterners were notoriously innovative in the new world, providing goods and services previously unavailable. Luque says, for example, that two Lebanese (some say Syrian) men established the first cigarette factory in San Pedro Sula in 1914. They were also the first to sell ground coffee in the streets from two-wheeled carts. The fullest range of their entrepreneurial imaginations can be seen in the types of businesses summarized in tables 5.1 and 5.2.

A survey of Palestinian-Honduran business practices in 1988 showed that all of these merchant types are still in existence. In some cases they persist because not all of the immigrants have been equally successful. Peddling, in its usual sense of goods being carried on foot or by animal-drawn vehicle, was not observed among Palestinians in this study, although it is still practiced by many poor Hondurans. More sophisticated analyses of peddling, like those of Plattner (1975a and b), speak of "mobile vendors," a term denoting several types of sellers, including street peddlers in urban areas as well as long-distance itinerant vendors, some of whom may be relatively heavily capitalized. Arabs in Honduras have tended to fall into the latter category, although, as Luque has informed us, in earlier days they also sold in the streets of San Pedro. Plattner has described in considerable

**TABLE 5.1.** Unincorporated Arab Businesses Registered in the Department of Cortés, 1948–88

| Type of Service or Merchandise | Number |
| --- | --- |
| General store (clothing, textiles, housewares, staples) | 365 |
| Manufacture and/or sale of textiles and/or clothing | 60 |
| Specialty stores (records, sports, magazines, autos) | 33 |
| Food production, processing, sales, service | 24 |
| Services (repairs, real estate, travel, laundry) | 16 |
| Construction (manufacture and/or sale of materials) | 14 |
| Hardware | 12 |
| Pharmacy (sales and/or manufacture of medicines, etc.) | 9 |
| Transportation | 8 |
| Furniture (manufacture and/or sales) | 6 |
| Other | 5 |
| Total | 552 |

detail how long-distance vendors must carefully calculate the expense of traveling to the customer (thus saving the latter a trip to a central market or store) in relation to both the wholesale cost of and the demand for their goods (1975a:64; 1975b:208–9). The level of transportation technology available in the region or country where it is practiced is a crucial variable. In early nineteenth-century Honduras peddlers traveled on foot, by canoe, by horse or mule back, or by

**TABLE 5.2.** Arab Corporations Registered in the Department of Cortés, 1948–88

| Type of Service or Merchandise | Number |
| --- | --- |
| General import/export | 129 |
| Manufacture and/or sale of textiles and/or clothing | 66 |
| Manufacture and/or sale of furniture | 17 |
| Manufacture and/or sale of hardware and appliances | 23 |
| Manufacture and/or sale of pharmaceuticals | 33 |
| Agribusiness (production and processing of foodstuffs) | 66 |
| Entertainment (radio, television, restaurants, hotels) | 18 |
| Services (computing, accounting, decorating, etc.) | 51 |
| Construction (manufacture and/or sale of materials) | 44 |
| Transportation | 6 |
| Finance (loans, investments, banking, etc.) | 17 |
| Indeterminate or duplicates | 28 |
| Total | 580 |

train. More advanced technology enlarges the marketing area that can be covered but also increases the vendors' expenses.

In San Pedro in 1988 there were Palestinians working as mobile vendors of the type the public today calls "traveling salesmen." They carry samples of goods in automobiles to outlying towns and districts, taking orders to be delivered on the next trip and offering credit to their customers — practices that were said also to have characterized the earliest Palestinian vendors in Honduras. In one sense traveling salesmen may be thought of as peddlers utilizing modern transport facilities. Usually they are not self-employed but, instead, represent a fixed industrial or commercial establishment in the city, a situation not unlike that practiced by some of their early forebears. In some cases these modern salesmen are recent immigrants, often relatives of owners of successful stores in San Pedro. Sometimes they are merely less successful, poorer relatives — often younger brothers of younger brothers — who, although born in Honduras, had not managed to prosper. A possible step upward for them might have been to open a store in a smaller town, but the attractions of living in the city of San Pedro Sula today are strong enough that they may have continued this "mechanized peddling" by preference. In either case those I observed were dependent upon the larger family enterprise, which extended credit for merchandise and made cash advances when necessary to cover travel and living expenses.

As noted above, many types of credit arrangements were known and practiced in the medieval Islamic Levant, made necessary by the region's importance as an international commercial crossroads. Udovitch quotes an eleventh-century Islamic legal scholar as follows: "We hold that selling for credit is part of the practice of merchants and that it is the most conducive means for the achievement of the investors' goal which is profit. In most cases, profit can only be achieved by selling for credit and not selling for cash" (1977:262). Thus, the Palestinian entrepreneurs, because they themselves had access to credit facilities both in Honduras and in the exterior, may have been more able to extend credit to customers, which in turn enhanced their success over that of their competitors.

Market stalls owned by Palestinians in Honduras are still to be found, although they are less common than the independent small store. Christians asserted that today only Muslims owned and operated such enterprises, but this could not be confirmed. The only two examined during the fieldwork did happen to be in Muslim hands, but this is hardly definitive. Other Muslims are represented in the registry of businesses summarized in tables 5.1 and 5.2, but their numbers are few. In several cases they appear to have been sponsored or assisted by local Palestinians who invested in their businesses rather than loaning them the necessary capital, as they might more readily have done for relatives.

Although the idea will be further developed in chapter 7, I believe it is crucial to the discussion here to point out that Muslims in Honduras are effectively outside of the cohesive social group formed by the Christians — especially today, by the (Greek) Orthodox Christians. When a local committee was formed to collect money for Palestinian intifada victims, it was considered essential to include at least one Muslim, but during the initial meeting of the group no one could think of any names, although they all knew there were some in San Pedro Sula.[11] This bespeaks the social distance between the two groups.

Although many Palestinians have gone on to bigger and better businesses, small stores still abound in San Pedro Sula. These typically consist of one room partitioned to include a storage area and opening directly to the sidewalk. Some have been started by newcomers, but many are novelty shops opened by wives or other relatives of businessmen successful in other enterprises. The amount of capital required to open such a store seems remarkably low (see tables 5.3 and 5.4) until one recalls again the undeclared credit made available to such entrepreneurs by other Palestinians, especially by members of their own patrilineage. Many small shops sell clothing, often specializing by age and/or gender; some include dressmaking, tailoring, and alteration services as well. Others stock "gifts," which may

---

11. One of Houghton's informants declared that there were seventeen Muslims among the Palestinian population of Honduras in 1968, and more than three hundred in Nicaragua (1969:1). Yet Houghton was unable to confirm or refute the claim. Since there is no mosque or other public institution in which they regularly congregate, it was difficult to find them, especially since the Christians with whom I worked were unable or unwilling to help me. The two whom I met in the marketplace spoke Spanish only haltingly and seemed quite reticent to talk about anything other than the intifada. They are aware of suspicions held by North Americans and many Hondurans about possible connections between recent immigrants and the PLO. There is no doubt that some of the early immigrants were Muslims, but, apparently, most either soon converted to Christianity or left the country.

include any assortment imaginable. A significant number is owned and operated by women. (See table 4.3.)

Finally, there are the large stores, some that legitimately can be called "department" stores in that they contain diverse sorts of goods spatially organized within a relatively ample locale, sometimes comprising two stories. Other large stores are more specialized; many sell household furnishings, ranging from cooking and dining ware to linens, appliances, decorative knickknacks, and the like. Hardware has been a very popular and successful line, as have medicines and other items usually sold in pharmacies. Several families not only own pharmacies but also manufacture and package medicines, surgical cotton, sanitary napkins, soaps, perfumes, shampoos, and cosmetics.

Another erroneous but ubiquitous assumption is that most Middle Easterners in the Americas still specialize in the import, manufacture and sale of textiles. As suggested in chapter 4, this once may have been true, since Stillman (1979:9) states that in many towns throughout the Levant the major industry and article of commerce was textiles, and it is natural that emigrants would continue to trade in what they knew best. In Guatemala the modern (as opposed to the traditional Indian) textile industry has long been dominated by Middle Easterners — some Palestinians, some Lebanese, and some Jews (Poitevin 1977: app.). Importing and manufacturing by modern Arab Hondurans, however, runs the gamut of the possible, as shown in tables 5.1 and 5.2. The products are sold through stores connected to the factories themselves as well as in family-owned and other outlets

**TABLE 5.3.   Investments in Stores and Firms by Ethnicity and Amount of Capital, in Thousands (K) of Lempiras, Department of Cortés, 1900–1988**

| | Number of Investors with Capital in Amounts Indicated | | | | | | | |
| --- | --- | --- | --- | --- | --- | --- | --- | --- |
| Ethnicity of Owner | < 1K | > 1K <5K | > 5K <10K | > 10K <25K | > 25K <50K | > 50K <75K | > 75K <100K | > 100K |
| P Stores, 1900–1949 | 10 | 48 | 35 | 38 | 16 | 10 | 4 | 14 |
| H Stores, 1900–1949 | 21 | 127 | 44 | 28 | 12 | 1 | 2 | 4 |
| O Stores, 1900–1949 | 19 | 46 | 38 | 2 | 10 | 1 | 1 | 4 |
| P Stores, 1950–86 | 11 | 115 | 70 | 75 | 52 | 17 | 14 | 28 |
| P Firms, 1949–88 | 0 | 78 | 46 | 120 | 69 | 23 | 64 | 180 |

P = Palestinian
H = Honduran
O = All others

throughout the country. In several cases these firms have contracts to produce goods for direct export, bearing labels of United States products. Sometimes they are partially owned by these foreign companies or their representatives. Some of these products also appear — often only the "seconds" — on the local market. A variety of other items is also manufactured, primarily for local sale as import substitutions, including umbrellas, leather goods, nails, plastics, shoes, and concrete blocks. One young man, a recent graduate of an engineering college in the United States, was contemplating the manufacture of satellite dishes for cable television reception at the time of the fieldwork.

Finally, today there are many Arab businesses selling products with international reputations, manufactured elsewhere, either in the

TABLE 5.4.  Capital Invested in Department of Cortés, 1900–1949, by Nationality and Location of Business

| Nationality | Number | Total Capital, in Lempiras | Average Capital | Number in San Pedro Sula |
|---|---|---|---|---|
| Hondurans | 239 | 3,277,167 | 13,828 | 105 |
| Palestinians | 175 | 5,331,940 | 31,365 | 69 |
| North Americans | 11 | 432,352 | 39,304 | 6 |
| Chinese | 45 | 198,947 | 4,626 | 8 |
| Spanish | 16 | 158,984 | 9,937 | 9 |
| Salvadorans | 15 | 59,351 | 3,956 | 4 |
| Germans | 2 | 10,000 | 5,000 | 1 |
| British | 5 | 3,235,430 | 539,238 | 4 |
| Italians | 2 | 38,000 | 19,000 | 2 |
| Guatemalans | 6 | 24,000 | 4,000 | 3 |
| Nicaraguans | 4 | 91,500 | 22,875 | 2 |
| Mexicans | 2 | 149,967 | 74,983 | 1 |
| French | 1 | 5,000 | 5,000 | 1 |
| Bulgarians | 1 | 17,000 | 17,000 | 0 |
| Greeks | 1 | 45,000 | 45,000 | 0 |
| Puerto Ricans | 2 | 76,570 | 38,285 | 1 |
| Rumanians | 1 | 3,000 | 3,000 | 0 |
| Dominicans | 1 | 1,500 | 1,500 | 0 |
| Jamaicans | 1 | 21,484 | 21,484 | 1 |
| Cubans | 1 | 10,000 | 10,000 | 0 |
| Swiss | 1 | 2,600 | 2,600 | 1 |
| Australians | 3 | 25,000 | 8,334 | 3 |
| Total | 565 | | | 221 |

exterior or locally under license or franchise. These range from pizza and soft drinks, men's shirts and women's lingerie,[12] to paints, fertilizers, large appliances, and automobiles.

In the analyses presented in this chapter I was fortunate in having some comparative information collected by Crowley, a cultural geographer interested in the development of the city of San Pedro Sula.[13] He surveyed the Central Business District (CBD) in 1979 and concluded that Palestinians owned 75 percent of the storefronts in the six busiest blocks (n.d.a:42). He estimated that they owned 27 percent of the nine hundred stores in the entire CBD, as defined by the city of San Pedro Sula and as identified by him in municipal records. His investigation showed that Palestinians owned 50 percent of the hardware stores in the CBD in 1979, with declared annual sales averaging U.S. $600,000. The non-Arab-owned hardware stores averaged only U.S. $109,000 (n.d.a:443).

It is unfortunate that Crowley did not include some mention of the newer, more fashionable commercial areas in the city, where I suspect the concentration of Palestinians may be as high today as in the center. Many stores have opened branches in more outlying districts; others have simply moved out, often leaving their locale in the hands of newcomers. He did note that properties in the core of the CBD were less likely to be owned by Palestinians but that beyond the core, where land was more easily acquired as the city grew, Palestinians own more land than businesses, having purchased properties where values were likely to increase (Crowley n.d.a:43). Many of these have since been developed and now house newer Palestinian ventures.

Although our sources of information differed, and neither study can claim to have a perfect data base, the general outlines of Crowley's and my conclusions are similar. My data confirm his conclusion that Palestinian enterprises dominate commerce and manufacturing in San Pedro Sula and that they influence the economy of the entire country disproportionately to their numbers. I disagree with his analy-

---

12. One of the most wealthy and prominent businessmen, a post-1948 immigrant, has been given the nickname "Lovable" because his firm manufactures lingerie under that brand name, primarily for export.

13. Crowley, in turn, used for comparative purposes information from a brief study by Shirey (1971) which, unfortunately, to my knowledge has not been published.

sis of some of the patterns of Arab-Honduran economic development over time but suspect that some of his conclusions were in error because he relied too heavily upon anecdotal accounts. Much of the historical and documentary information here presented was unavailable to him during the short period of his investigation.

The purpose of this chapter has been to describe the structure and organization of Palestinian-Honduran business as it has evolved through time. This could not have been done merely through recall by selected respondents, most of whom rely only upon personal memories and oral histories handed down in their families. Such interviews were carried out with numerous business men and women, and the resulting data have provided context and correction (a kind of "ground truthing") to the more precise information contained in records of the Cortés Chamber of Commerce, located in San Pedro Sula.[14] With few exceptions the early stores were named for their owners and were said to be engaged in "buying and selling" (*compra y venta*), which I have listed under "General Stores" (table 5.1). Other frequent glosses for their activities included "general merchandise" (*mercaderias en general*) and "merchant" (*comerciante*).

## Patrimonial Management

The chamber of commerce data, taken as a whole, are beautifully illustrative of what has been called "patrimonial management" (Harbison and Myers 1959:69). This consists of business management in which ownership, major policy-making positions, and a significant proportion of other jobs in the hierarchy are held by members of an extended family. Furthermore, the Honduran data, when viewed chronologically, suggest that organizational patterns changed in response to the modernization of Palestinian businesses over time. It might be argued that patrimonial management began in village Palestine when families or lineages made decisions about emigration

---

14. I was accorded full access to all the record books compiled over the years by the Cortés Chamber of Commerce. A good bit of my time was spent in its offices with my laptop computer, entering data into various database files from more than five thousand records of both individual businesses and legal corporations formed since 1948 when the chamber of commerce was created. Thanks are due to the director and the other people in that office who not only tolerated my presence but answered my many questions and took a real interest in my research.

strategies and provided resources for some of their members in Honduras.[15]

As we have seen, the earliest Honduran enterprises were usually registered under one man's name, presumably the founder. His informal connections, of course, were not documented, nor were there listed other members of his immediate family who assisted him in various ways. In succeeding years, as businesses were reorganized — which occurred frequently as they increased their capital outlay or named new (usually family) co-owners — the registration process was repeated. When incorporation became popular, starting in the mid-1950s, many of the businesses changed their names, and, had it not been for the necessity of listing the stockholders, their identification as Arab-owned would have not have been possible.

Khalaf and Shwayri (1966:59) have described how traditional norms in general and family firms in particular may exert a supportive influence on industrial growth, particularly for societies in transition. Their data from Lebanon, collected in the early 1960s and including historical information for ten such firms, is remarkably consistent with what I found in San Pedro Sula, with a few dramatic exceptions. Kocka (1971:155) draws similar conclusions concerning the importance of family traditions in facilitating the transition to industrial management in nineteenth-century Germany. Both studies emphasize that, without some change, traditional patrimonial management techniques may hinder business success in the industrial world but that, when the decision is made to modernize, family firms may have an advantage over others. Let us examine how patrimonial management operated over time in Honduras.

The eldest son in each generation was in charge of all the family enterprises after his father's death. Depending upon his age, strength of character, and business acumen, he might remain in this position until his own death. Younger brothers, as well as their wives and children, were all dependent for their own livelihoods, including all the cash they might need for whatever purpose, upon the judgment of the eldest. He decided which family member should work at which job, and how much he or she should take home at the end of the week.

---

15. Although they do not use this term, Friedl (1976) and Tannous (1942) provide other interesting examples of how families and local communities manage emigration strategies in similar ways.

Even trifling extras, such as money to buy school books or to support church raffles, had to be requested from him. He could refuse to send a nephew or niece to college if he did not approve the intended course of study, and his advice and opinion were sought in all family matters. Many younger brothers and their families remained throughout their lives virtually enthralled by this system. If they were competent, the eldest brother-manager would have been eager to retain their services, for reliable labor was an asset, and the hiring of outsiders was nearly unthinkable.

Following traditional Middle Eastern norms, most men respected both the system in general and their elder brother in particular and lived quite well and happily. Sons of these younger brothers had to compete with their higher-status cousins for jobs within the system or leave it to strike out on their own. In Honduras these young men were sent off to college to become trained in a profession, such as pharmacy or engineering. Sometimes they might be taken in by still another uncle who had previously broken away. In time some of the more enterprising and capable younger brothers and nephews might be given greater responsibilities in expanding or extending the operation or in beginning a new one — still on behalf of the whole.

Other men, however, became restless under such a yoke and, sometimes prodded by their wives, found ways to break away. The major problem was in obtaining sufficient capital to start a new business without dismantling the old. Since the eldest brother generally kept the books under lock and key, other members often did not really know how much they were jointly worth. At some point the frictions often became intolerable and fissions occurred, usually so painful for all concerned that the memory is retained for generations. In such cases a lump sum might be given to the dissident as his portion, upon which he abandoned all other claims. In no case that came to my attention did this process lead to the demise of the original business, although there may have been some such. Rather, the result was still another Arab-owned enterprise that started a similar life cycle — the new owner retaining control until his death (no matter how old), followed by the assumption of power by his eldest son, and so on. It is interesting to speculate that such disputes among brothers may have led one or several to emigrate to the Americas in times past. More often, however, the emigrants probably took with them the family blessings and monetary support. Many accounts tell of men coming to

Honduras to join a brother or an uncle; frequently, a man returned to Palestine to recruit new helpers (including a wife) from among his patrilineage.

Table 5.5 can best be interpreted in light of this patrimonial management cycle. The single largest category, "siblings plus children," constitutes the norm: Several brothers (and sometimes sisters with their husbands) plus their adult sons (and increasingly, daughters) are jointly inscribed as stockholders (#6). A man alone is rare (#1); rather, a newcomer (or dissident brother) today is likely to incorporate with his son or daughter (#4) or, more often, with his wife (#2). As their children approach maturity, their names will be added, and they will be given responsibilities and, later, paying jobs (#3). When the original owner dies his widow and their children remain (#5), but when she dies the siblings and their families continue the family firm. In a few cases grandchildren may be incorporated into the group before the patriarch's death, but this is exceedingly rare (#7).

The table also suggests the increasing tendency to engage in business with Arabs who are not kin as well as with non-Arabs. In many of these instances, however, the families have been joined through intermarriage, as ethnic exogamy is increasing rapidly. (See chap. 6.)

Thus, it can easily be argued that patrimonial management

**TABLE 5.5　Ownership Patterns for Firms Registered in the Department of Cortés, 1949–88**

| Partnership Type | Number of Firms | | |
| --- | --- | --- | --- |
| | Family | Arab Nonfamily | Non-Arab |
| 1. Man alone | 5 | | |
| 2. Husband-wife | 56 | | |
| 3. Husband-wife + children | 27 | | |
| 4. Father-son/daughter | 10 | | |
| 5. Mother-son/daughter | 9 | | |
| 6. Two or more Siblings + children | 179 | | |
| 7. 3 generations | 2 | | |
| 8. Arab (nonfamily) | | 60 | |
| 9. Non-Arab partners | | | 215 |
| Totals | 289 | 60 | 215 |
| | (51 percent) | (10.6 percent) | (38 percent) |

leads to the expansion of the *family* (or, in this case, *ethnic*) holdings, regardless of whether a set of brothers remains together or splits up. Khalaf and Shwayri found that patrimonial managers in Lebanon displayed a readiness to abandon old ways and emulate the new as change occurred in the larger society. Although they do not describe these details, it may be that similar forces operated there as well. In all fields except marketing Lebanese family enterprises were characterized as being animated by a propensity for adaptive innovation (1966:68).

Honduran-Palestinian patrimonial managers, unlike those studied in Lebanon, were far from timid in facing the market, perhaps in part because good family management required them to find something for their younger brothers and nephews to do to prevent their flight and in part because they began to realize, following the creation of the state of Israel, that they were no longer temporary, but permanent, migrants and that greater risk taking might be necessary to make up for what they had lost at home. I believe my data, presented below, will show that, although generally it had positive results, their innovativeness may have sometimes been excessive and damaging to their interests. In general, however, for Palestinian Hondurans the patrimonial system predated the immigration, was a crucial element in fomenting and maintaining the emigration, and was of vital importance in increasing the wealth of Palestinians both at home and abroad. It persists today, although it seems to be in decline.

### Business and Ethnicity in Honduras

As shown in tables 4.3 and 5.3, it is not true that Hondurans were uninterested in business enterprises during the first half of this century and that this left a "vacuum" into which the Palestinians flowed. Two-thirds of all businesses between 1900 and 1949 were in native hands. Of the many foreigners who came hoping to make their fortunes on the banana coast, however, Palestinians made up by far the largest number. Furthermore, the amount of capital they invested was, on the average, twice that invested by the average Honduran and several times that brought by members of other ethnic groups or nationalities, including Europeans, Chinese, and other Latins from Central American countries. Only North Americans, Germans, and

British entrepreneurs invested more, and their numbers were so small that they never formed ethnic enclaves and in no way behaved as "middleman minorities."[16]

Where did Palestinians get the capital invested? Many brought some with them, but much more probably derived from profits earned and reinvested, both in Palestine and in Honduras. In addition to the capital amounts noted it is important to remember the major contribution to success made by Palestinian familiarity with the concept and operation of credit; their "clannishness," which provided a means of establishing linkages and enforcing "proper" behavior; and their connections with other Palestinian businessmen in various parts of the world. It would seem that Central Americans had the will, but neither the capital nor the organization, and perhaps not the know-how, to succeed as well as many of the foreigners. Chinese came in relatively large numbers during the same period, and, although their heritage is still apparent in the area, for the most part they did not prosper as did the Palestinians.[17]

It is clear from tables 5.3 and 5.4 that many of even the earlier Palestinian immigrants had access to fairly large amounts of capital and that their investments were at all times greater than those of other foreigners. Forty percent of the total capital invested in the Depart-

16. The registration included only nationalities, so we have no way of knowing how many of the newcomers were Jews, another group frequently cast in the role of pariah capitalists and "middleman" minorities. There was and is an identifiable Jewish segment in the San Pedro Sula population, which in earlier days was often merged with the Palestinians in the eyes of native Hondurans. The Israeli situation, and the suspicion held by many of the Palestinians that I was a Jew, made it difficult for me to investigate this issue systematically. (Chap. 8 again touches on this issue.)

It is significant that no one was labeled "Turkish" in the written records, despite the fact that in the early years "Ottoman" was their legal nationality.

17. There is a fenced-off section of the municipal cemetery devoted entirely to the Chinese community. The grave markers are written in Chinese characters, so I was unable to gather data from them. From ethnographic questioning, I concluded that the immigrants were nearly all male, that they came with little capital, and that, after fathering families with native Honduran women, they either died or returned to China to their primary families, on whose behalf they had made the sacrifice of emigration—in their cases, a kind of exile. See Coughlin (1960), Fong (1959), Lind (1958), C. E. Glick (1980), and Willmott (1966) for more detailed descriptions of how the Chinese middleman diaspora has functioned in different parts of the world. In Honduras there has been some more recent immigration from China, as there has been to other Central American countries. In addition, there remain many descendants of the earlier men and Honduran women.

ment of Cortés between 1900 and 1950 was furnished by Palestinians, even though their numbers constituted only 33 percent of the total businesses registered. In contrast, Hondurans made up 45 percent of the total number of registrations, but they provided only 25 percent of the capital invested.

For the period between 1950 and April of 1988 I do not have comparative figures for Hondurans. Due to the sheer volume of registrations as the population and business activity expanded, I was not able to monitor all and chose to concentrate on those with at least some Palestinian ownership. But the number of registered businesses and firms with Palestinian stockholders which reported capital exceeding 100,000 lempiras between 1950 and 1988 amounted to 208: 28 in unincorporated businesses and 180 in corporations, or *sociedades anónimas,* as they are called in Spanish. Only 14 had fallen into this category during the earlier time period (table 5.3).[18] These figures are remarkably similar to those presented by Belisle (1988) for immigrants to Ecuador in the first half of this century. In 1909 39.9 percent of the total liquid capital in that country was in the hands of immigrants. Although we do not know how many were Middle Easterners, Belisle reports that the British consul in 1906 referred to the immigration of Chinese and "Turks" as an "invasion."

## Palestinian Women in Business

Nearly all collaborators spontaneously offered the opinion that Palestinians prospered because their wives, from earliest times, devoted much of their time and energy to minding the customers, the books, and the merchandise while their husbands traveled — either on buying or selling trips or to tend business in branch locations. The early figures do not reveal this female participation, largely because neither of the male-dominated cultures from which the immigrants came and in which they found themselves encouraged the coregistration of properties with wives.[19] In Honduras widows and single women did

---

18. No attempt has been made to correct for constant dollars, inflation, or exchange rates. The lempira remained at 50 percent of the dollar from the 1930s through the fieldwork period in 1988. It began to fall in 1990.

19. In relation to this, it would be interesting to compare the roles of early Christian Palestinian women with those of women in fifteenth-century Nuremberg, as described by Wood

**TABLE 5.6.**   Comparisons of Businesses Registered in San Pedro Sula between 1948–86, by Ethnicity and Gender of Owner

| Gender/Ethnic Category | Number | Percentage of Ethnic Group | Percentage of Total |
|---|---|---|---|
| Arab women | 98 | 17.5 | 10.7 |
| Arab men | 459 | 82.4 | 50.0 |
| Honduran women | 52 | 21.6 | 5.7 |
| Honduran men | 188 | 78.3 | 20.4 |
| Other (foreign) women | 10 | 8.2 | 1.1 |
| Other (foreign) men | 111 | 91.7 | 12.1 |
| Total | 918 | na | 100.0 |

make up nearly 10 percent of the Palestinian registrations before 1950, but it is interesting to note that their involvement in business did not equal that among native Central American women, whose enterprises constituted 20 percent of the total Central American activity during the same period. (See table 4.3.) European and Chinese women are virtually not represented.

The combined figures for 1900–1987 show a similar pattern but with enhancements in the same direction. The percentage of registrations by Palestinian women rises to nearly 18 percent of all Palestinian businesses, while that of Central American women is now 27 percent (table 5.6). In my opinion this is an expectable result of the involvement in their husbands' businesses by women in previous generations.

Finally, the educational advantages to which both Palestinian men and women had long been accustomed pushed the women — whether married or single — into many professional and business paths. In addition to those who increasingly own and manage their own businesses today, there are pharmacists, medical doctors, professors, lawyers, journalists, and other professionals — including one woman who has been elected to the national congress of Honduras. Another owned and managed the only television station in San Pedro Sula. Nearly every family firm registered (summarized in table 5.5)

---

(1981:3). I suspect the former may have been, like their European coreligionists, more involved in markets and other sorts of retail trade than is generally recognized. Muslim women, rather than Christians, sell agricultural produce in the present-day Bethlehem market, but Christian women are active in other kinds of retailing.

includes the name of at least one woman. At times she will be the wife, other times the mother or sister of the principal stockholder, but frequently she will herself be the first name mentioned. Nonfamily firms also frequently include women among the directors. Today recent immigrants from Palestine seem to be as often represented in these registrations as are those born in Honduras.

## International Connections

We have seen how the Christians exploited their pariah status in the Ottoman Empire through their connections with European merchants, by means of which they too were extended certain privileges. Interestingly, Rosa describes a situation in Honduras which is reminiscent of the earlier Ottoman system. After 1917 and the defeat of "Turkey," Palestinians were under the "protection" of the British, while the Lebanese were administered by France. In Honduras, as is often the case elsewhere, the consuls representing these European countries were usually expatriate businessmen. Rosa (1967:89) suggests that Middle Easterners in Honduras in the years after 1917 benefited from laws allowing disputes related to foreign commerce to be handled by these consuls, which nearly always resulted in decisions in favor of the "Turcos." He further claims that the laws of Honduras at that time were designed to encourage foreign business investments, even at the expense of local business.

Specific international connections between Honduran Arabs and others are difficult to document due to the reserve that people often tend to have in regard to such matters.[20] Both historical and modern anecdotal evidence, however, attests to the importance of connections between the Palestinian Honduran community and their brethren in other parts of the world. Table 5.7 shows how many immigrants came not directly from Palestine but via some other New World country. Even today visitors in San Pedro from Chile, Colombia, Venezuela, Mexico, Guatemala, and elsewhere come to seek

---

20. It is notorious that money management aimed at maximizing profits—including investments, payment of taxes, and the accumulation of foreign currency—verges on the illegal. Naturally, company directors are reluctant to reveal these and other trade secrets, although many owners of businesses are willing to describe how "other people" handle their affairs—but, even then, usually only on an informal, casual basis and without names, dates, or other details.

wives, to share impressions, and to do business with other Palestinians — often their relatives. Headstones in the local cemeteries often mention that the deceased had been born in another American country. Several local women have married in from other Palestinian-American communities, and San Pedro women have been sought after and taken away as brides.

The nearness of the United States has been important from the beginning of the Palestinian-Honduran experience. Most of the products sold from backpacks or store counters came from that country. According to Platt (1972:122), by the middle of the first decade of the twentieth century, the United States had a near monopoly on textiles imported into Central America. These consisted principally of cheap grey and white shirting, printed ducks and drills and hosiery — exactly the items most likely to have been sold to the new working class and townspeople in Honduras. Later, in the 1930s,

**TABLE 5.7.** Origin of Palestinians in Business in Department of Cortés, 1900–1987

| Nationality | | Number |
|---|---|---|
| Palestinian Hondurans (born in Honduras) | | 315 |
| Born in and coming directly from Palestine | | 170 |
| Naturalized Palestinian Hondurans | | 11 |
| Palestinians arriving via other countries | | |
| Bolivia | 5 | |
| Chile | 5 | |
| Cuba | 2 | |
| El Salvador | 3 | |
| France | 1 | |
| Great Britain | 1 | |
| Guatemala | 1 | |
| Haiti | 5 | |
| Israel | 1 | |
| Jordan | 13 | |
| Lebanon* | 18 | |
| Mexico | 3 | |
| Nicaragua | 1 | |
| Syria** | 2 | 61 |
| Wives of Palestinians, nationality unknown | | 15 |
| Total | | 572 |

*Some of these claimed Lebanese ethnicity.
**One of these declared himself Syrian, the other Palestinian.

Japan became an important supplier of silks and rayons, imported by Palestinian merchants for sale to a more affluent class. Several with whom I spoke stated that many fortunes were augmented with the outbreak of World War II, when debts owed for textiles purchased on credit were canceled de facto by the Honduran government's declaration of war. Rosa (1967:89) refers to something similar and uses it as an example of Arab avarice, noting that the money should have gone to enrich the coffers of the Honduran state. He also points out that during the war, when imports were difficult, the Arab population invested in Honduran real estate, the value of which skyrocketed after the war.

Imports of other items from the United States immediately resumed after the war and continue to the present. Today the more affluent families regularly send their children to college in the United States, and many maintain second residences in Houston, Miami, New Orleans, or elsewhere. They go on buying trips, both to outfit their stores and to satisfy personal needs and wishes. United States fashions in food, clothing, household furnishings, and entertainment are in great demand among most of coastal Honduras, which has long experienced a heavy American influence (Dawson 1971:14). Anyone with a major illness will be taken to the United States for treatment if at all possible.

All of the major businesspeople have American bank accounts, charge cards, and stockbrokers. They are able to order goods on credit by phone or FAX as needed, and they attend product fairs and other business conventions in order to keep up with changing times. As suggested above, they have been generally quick to perceive new trends and to take advantage of new opportunities. During the 1960s and 1970s, when credit was more freely available in Honduras through loans from international sources, many of the patrimonial businesses greatly expanded, naming one of their younger members manager, while other family members branched out into new enterprises. According to several accounts given to me, this practice sometimes led to disaster, as the manager was unable to survive unless he or she abandoned most of the older management practices, such as paying bills, buying raffle tickets, and giving to charity directly from the till, rather than in a more formal manner. Some import substitutions could not compete in quality or price with imports, especially when the latter were brought in clandestinely, as often happened. Accounting practices often did not satisfy their creditors, and many of the innovative businesses started during those decades no longer exist. Despite the many that went under, however, there were always new ideas floating about, many of which took root and flourished.

Glancing through the lists of firm stockholders and directors, one sees certain surnames over and over again, indicating large and active families and confirming at the same time their success in seeking greater profits through diversity. If one looks back through the early records, the same names appear there as well. Muslih (1988:40, quoting Finn) mentions four families that mainly controlled the manufacture of souvenirs in Bethlehem during the last quarter of the nineteenth century. These same four — Kattan, Hazbun, Kawas, and Bandak — were among the earliest arrivals in Honduras and remain as large and affluent families in the area today. (See chap. 6.)

It is striking how often a business will be registered with only a small amount of capital and ten years later will be augmented ten- or twentyfold, while at the same time the owner reaches out in new directions, often with nonfamily members. It has not been possible to obtain any precise figures on the amounts of capital that have been infused into the Palestinian-Honduran business community directly from Palestine. The figures certainly suggest, however, that newcomers brought something with them. It also seems clear that they were frequently able to secure loans and investment support from among the resident Palestinians and Palestinian Hondurans, whether related by kinship or not. As the situation in their homeland has worsened, their self-identification as Palestinians has deepened. Whereas a century ago they may not have felt much kinship with a Muslim from Hebron, today they are all West Bank émigrés, and world events bind them together in new ways.

Hamilton has contrasted two kinds of pariah capitalism — one in which a despised population group is maintained by the elites because its activities serve their interest, the other in which a middleman minority is able to find a niche within the economy because in some way or another the minority group is unchallenged or at a competitive advantage in this niche (1978:10–11). The Palestinian-Honduran case suggests that these two "types" may not be contrastive but, rather, complementary. In the Ottoman Empire, and somewhat less so in Honduras, the Christian Palestinians were despised at the same time that they were granted certain privileges, and their activities clearly enhanced the economic welfare of both polities and their political elites at the same time that they were denied social and political equality within the system. Yet their experience, capital, management practices, and ethnic cohesion allowed them to capture markets, both in the developing (pre-1950) country of Honduras and in the industrializing (post-1950) cities of San Pedro Sula and Tegucigalpa. Although it cannot be said that the country of Honduras is today a developed industrialized entity, clearly the activities of entrepreneurs like the Palestinians have attached it firmly to the rest of the world, and especially to the United States. Indeed, one might argue that the U.S. influence in the area may be measured by the degree to which American values and artifacts have been adopted locally and that the Palestinian merchants' zeal in marketing both to the masses and to the elites has been instrumental in creating today's highly acculturated setting.

The next chapter will deal with the marriage, family, and kinship patterns that underlie and shape so much of Palestinian life, whether in the Holy Land or in the diaspora.

*Chapter 6*

# The Structuring of
# Interpersonal Relationships

Ye crowd around your neighbor, and have fine words for it. But I say unto you:
your neighbor-love is your bad love of yourselves.
— Friedrich Nietzsche, *Thus Spake Zarathustra*

He who understands you is greater kin to you than your own brother. For even
your own kindred may neither understand you nor know your true worth.
— Khalil Gibran

## Marriage and the Family

Family, residence patterns, and religion have been the primary factors
determining who marries whom in both Palestine and in Honduras,
although in both places social class, as measured by education and
wealth, has increasingly played an important role.[1] Cohen suggests
that two principles underlie successful marriage agreements in the
modern Middle East: (1) a woman should be married within her own
patronymic group (to a real or classificatory father's brother's son
[FBS]); and (2) she should be betrothed only to a man who is of the
same social, political, and economic status as that of her father and her
brothers. During the British Mandate period in Palestine the wealthy
of one patronymic group began to marry the wealthy of others, thus
emphasizing social class over kinship (Cohen 1970:196,203).

In Honduras the patronymic group includes a set of families that
have been traditionally linked patrilineally through sets of brothers
who have chosen to perpetuate their own, rather than their father's,
name. Most surnames have derived from given names, since it was

---

1. It is clumsy and inaccurate to refer constantly to the West Bank, Gaza Strip, and Arab
Israel, when, in fact, in the minds and hearts of my informants the conceptual "place" is Palestine. Just as *Dixie* continues to refer to the American South, and especially to its distinctive cultural heritage, so *Palestine* still has significance today. It is in this sense and spirit that I have
used the term throughout the book.

formerly the custom for both men and women to carry the given names of several generations of their paternal ancestors. This custom did not long survive in Honduras, nor is it found today in Bethlehem. In 1900 both male and female Palestinian children in Honduras received, as their second, or "middle," name, the first name of their father. This was then followed by their father's "surname" — most typically his father's surname — and, finally, the family name of their mother (her father's given name), as in traditional Spanish practice. A few families continue to bestow the father's first name on all their male children in this way, and for a while some began to give the mother's first name to the girls as a middle name, although this practice never really caught on and is rarely seen today. The older naming practice served to differentiate generations and collaterals, while at the same time grouping together sets of siblings.

Among both Muslims and Christians in Palestine there exists a similar linkage of families, but there it is based on both patrilineal kinship and residence. This results in a cooperative unit generally called the *hamula* (Cohen 1965:42–46; Rosenfeld 1973:243). The proliferation of different families within it probably originated as I have described above. Said to have been a dying institution during the nineteenth century (Cohen 1965:8–9), the Israelis tried to revive it as a means of establishing indirect rule in Arab Israeli villages and towns. (See chap. 8.)

In Bethlehem collaborators used the term *quarter* for this group when speaking English, explaining that the different hamulas were once residentially clustered within the town. Only those Palestinian Hondurans born in the Holy Land even knew the term, however, and many of these were unable to list all the family names within their own unit. Formerly the hamula not only regulated marriage but was also instrumental in maintaining order under the *millet,* or *dhimmi,* system. Its leader, called a *mukhtar,* settled disputes among members, and, together with others of the older men, offered advice for the good of the whole. Collectively, the members of the *hamula* were liable for each other's misdeeds, including the payment of blood money in the event of homicide. In Honduras the term *mukhtar* is used by those born in Palestine as a term of respect (or burlesque) for the most senior man of their lineage.

The ideal mate for a Christian Palestinian woman would be her father's father's brother's son's son (patrilateral parallel second cousin), provided his economic status and/or potential were comparable to that of her brothers. Although frowned upon by both the Eastern and Western Christian churches, first-cousin marriage also has been common, even in the recent past—dispensations having been readily available for a price. Today's young people are still strongly influenced, but do not feel bound, by their families' admonitions concerning marriage partners. Parents in Bethlehem, however, seem to have less difficulty enforcing their wishes than do those in Honduras, where the ethnic group, rather than the hamula or patronymic group has become the preferred endogamous unit.[2] As will be demonstrated below, even that is presently breaking down, in part because young people meet outsiders in school and elsewhere as they are given more freedom to move about the city as teenagers, but in some cases also because their parents foster relations with other wealthy Hondurans, regardless of ethnic background. Again, as remarked upon by Cohen (1970:203) for the wealthy in Palestine, social class has come to displace earlier criteria based on kinship and ethnicity as a regulator of marriage in Honduras as well.

Interviews with elderly and middle-aged women in Honduras and Bethlehem suggested a strong tendency toward arranged marriages during the first half of the century in both areas. Often the brides were only thirteen or fourteen years old, and the grooms tended to be in their late teens. Sometimes the unions were arranged and sanctified before leaving the Middle East, the young couple being shipped off together to the New World (Edwards 1983:610). Sexual relations with one's bride were not condoned before her first menstruation, however, so consummation of the union might not occur for some time. Parents feared that, left to their own devices, the men might

---

2. While in Bethlehem, I observed an arranged betrothal in which a young woman of eighteen was promised to a "suitable" man a few years her senior. He had recently returned from studying abroad, and, even though she had dreams of going to the United States, the family decided to accept his family's offer. She was given a gold watch and an 18-karat gold set of jewelry, including a necklace, earrings, and bracelets in filigree work. A few weeks after the engagement party, however, her family decided to break off the arrangement, having had more of an opportunity to observe the man's family customs. They explained to me that their daughter had been raised very differently and could not be happy in her fiancé's household. She was largely indifferent, not having known the man very well, but pleased to find that her hopes of emigration could be revived. All the jewelry was returned, and her family also had to reimburse the man's family for expenses in connection with the engagement party, including the cost of the mother's hairdo.

**TABLE 6.1. Numbers of Marriages Recorded in Selected Catholic Churches\* in Honduras between 1900 and 1985 Involving at Least One Arab Partner**

| Years | Number of Marriages | Number of In-Marrying Women | Number of In-Marrying Men | Percentage Endogamous |
|---|---|---|---|---|
| 1900–1929 | 27 | 2 | 1 | 92.5 |
| 1930–39 | 39 | 10 | 2 | 69.2 |
| 1940–49 | 50 | 12 | 13 | 50.0 |
| 1950–59 | 92 | 26 | 17 | 53.2 |
| 1960–69\*\* | 42 | 14 | 7 | 50.0 |
| 1970–79 | 38 | 18 | 12 | 26.6 |
| 1980–85 | 17 | 7 | 8 | 11.8 |
| Totals | 305 | 89 | 50 | |

\*Archives consulted included those of San Pedro Sula, El Progreso, Santa Rosa de Copán, Puerto Cortés, and Yoro.
\*\*The Orthodox church was established in San Pedro Sula in 1963; see the text for a fuller discussion.

marry native (non-Arab, Honduran) women and be lost to their families. General promiscuousness on the part of the men was expected, whether they were married or not, and tolerated so long as it did not result in an unapproved legal union or otherwise prevent them from fulfilling the obligations of their family-arranged marriages.

As feared, however, some marriages with Hondurans did occur, although not many in the first decades (although illegitimate unions also occurred, resulting in children who were recognized by their fathers and baptised.) (See tables 6.1 and 6.2.) After an initial period during which her mother-in-law might publicly vent her anger and distress, the foreign woman could be accepted by her Arab in-laws and in time become incorporated into their family circle.[3] Some of these in-marrying spouses, particularly if of high status, pulled their own relatives into closer relationships with their new families, including the development of *compadrazgo* (godparent) and business ties. Less affluent Honduran families were less acceptable to the Arabs, and it is my impression that in such cases the durable ties proliferated among the woman's kin (see the discussion below). One woman told me that the only thing Arabic about herself was her father's surname!

---

3. One non-Arab wife related how her mother-in-law had resorted to professional magical incantations to try to prevent the marriage and refused to attend the wedding. In time, however, after heroic efforts to adapt herself to her husband's life-style, she became one of the family.

TABLE 6.2. Baptisms of Children with at Least One Arab Parent, Showing Legitimacy and Exogamy

| Years | Total | Endogamous | | Exogamous | |
|---|---|---|---|---|---|
| | | Number Legimate | Number Illegimate | Number Legitimate | Number Illegimate |
| 1897–1909 | 23 | 18 | 0 | 0 | 5 |
| 1910–19 | 97 | 76 | 0 | 7 | 14 |
| 1920–29 | 150 | 122 | 1 | 15 | 12 |
| 1930–39 | 111 | 93 | 1 | 9 | 8 |
| 1940–49 | 22 | 9 | 2 | 1 | 10 |
| 1950–59 | 44 | 23 | 0 | 12 | 9 |
| 1960 (1 year) | 18 | 7 | 0 | 8 | 3 |
| Totals | 465 | 348 | 4 | 52 | 61 |

*Summary:* Of all babies whose baptisms were recorded (465), 75 percent had two Arab parents, and of these couples 98.8 percent were legitimately married (see text for discussion).

He had completely abandoned his people and his culture in favor of her mother's.

Arab women marrying Honduran men was a less common phenomenon, but the same set of conditions governed its outcome. After initial objections, which often included years of ostracism, and depending upon the affluence of the two families, the union might be accepted by one or both. If only one family relented, then the children and future generations were likely to ignore and forget the other heritage.

If accepted by both families, there might be continuing interactions of various sorts, followed by further unions between the two in later generations. A number of such cases can be identified among the stockholders of the various firms described in chapter 5 as well as in the endogamy/exogamy patterns shown in table 6.3.

In addition to those contracting marriages with Palestinians, numerous children were born to Honduran women and Palestinian men out of wedlock, only a few of which were recognized by their fathers. In some of those cases the man apparently settled down and had several children by the same woman, and in time some of these couples married. In one case an Arab woman had several children by a Honduran man, and they were finally married when both were in their fifties. Unfortunately for this study, most of the latter retained only their mother's (Spanish) surname and are thus not identifiable. Other such children were sometimes raised by their fathers' Palestinian wives as though they were their own. One man revealed that his father's brother had sired thirty-six children by three different women, although the church records I examined showed only seven for him, with two women. The others had no doubt been registered in some other parish. The same man's maternal grandfather, in addition to his Arab family, had two "outside" daughters.

A contrivance sometimes used by a man was to marry a Honduran woman legally but not in church. His argument later, when proposing to a Palestinian (assuming she and/or her family were aware of the first union), was that the first marriage was not real or permanent, since Honduras was in many minds a primitive country whose laws need not be heeded, especially since the law under both the Ottomans and the British specified that the validity of Palestinian mar-

**TABLE 6.3.   Types of Endogamy/Exogamy in 302 Honduran Marriages Involving Persons of Arab Descent, 1900–1985**

| Type of Marriage | | Number | Percentage of Total |
| --- | --- | --- | --- |
| 100 percent endogamous AAAA | | 148 | 49 |
| 75 percent endogamous | | | |
| AAAN | 9 | | |
| AANA | 3 | | |
| ANAA | 5 | | |
| NAAA | 1 | 18 | 6 |
| 50 percent endogamous | | | |
| AANN | 51 | | |
| ANAN | 2 | | |
| NAAN | 2 | | |
| NNAA | 19 | | |
| NANA | 0 | 72 | 24 |
| 25 percent endogamous | | | |
| ANNN | 25 | | |
| NANN | 7 | | |
| NNAN | 26 | | |
| NNNA | 4 | 62 | 21 |
| Totals | | 302 | 100 |

A = Arab
N = non-Arab
Positions significant as follows: groom's father, groom's mother, bride's father, bride's mother.

riages depended upon "the observance of a religious ceremony in accordance with the rites of the religious community to which the Palestinian citizen belongs."[4] So long as he remarried in Palestine, his bigamy might go unnoticed or unremarked, inasmuch as his Honduran marriage was not legally recognized there; the new marriage might even be accepted by his first wife so long as he provided for her and her children. In effect, she would be relegated to secondary status in a *"casa chica,"* a situation not without some advantages. When this happens today, however — as it sometimes does — both women are likely to make things difficult for the man.[5]

In most cases a man first came to Honduras alone and then either brought his wife, if already married, or returned to Palestine to find a bride. Usually he depended upon his parents and the local hamula to select a few suitable candidates in advance, from whom he made a selection, largely based on their physical attractiveness. The young women had little power to affect the decision, although, ideally, they could refuse.[6] Several told me they had originally objected but were "persuaded" by their relatives, who spoke of the romance of the journey and the glamour of life in "America." The bride wealth offered by such men was also often an attractive feature of their proposals. Still, most of the early brides with whom I spoke had no idea of what lay ahead of them, and almost all said that if they had known, they would have objected more strongly and perhaps have sabotaged the arrangement.[7]

As time went on, however, and the local population grew, more potential marriage partners were available in Honduras itself, and the larger families were even able to maintain endogamy among their linked patronymics to a certain degree. Yet the custom of going out-

---

4. Letter from R. C. Lindsay [to FO, Apr. 19, 1929], Israeli National Archives 2/559/24a.

5. Apocryphal stories of such happenings abound. One involves a man who was returning to Honduras with his new bride. They stopped off briefly in Haiti, where he had lived for some time previously, and to his wife's surprise and horror he was visited by a black woman and several small children, who addressed him as "father."

6. Since I only spoke with those who went through with the marriages, I cannot say with what frequency the men were rejected.

7. One young woman who knew little geography thought that the Philippines, where she and her new husband were bound, was close to Honduras, where her brother lived. When she discovered her error she was thrown into a depression so severe that her husband took her to Honduras instead.

side of Honduras to find a bride persists to the present time. Not only do young men still journey to Ephrata, but they may pursue daughters of their extended family resident in other American countries. Increasingly too, nonmigrant Bethlehem (Beit Jala, Beit Sahur) men seek marriages with Palestinian Americans. Honduran Arabs are suspicious of their intentions, believing they merely want to cash in on the reputed wealth of the Hondurans. One woman told me that, within two days of her arrival in Bethlehem on a 1986 visit, she received five proposals for the hand of the nubile daughter who accompanied her. (All were rejected.) The few instances where such marriages have occurred have been the result of an adult woman going alone to visit the Holy Land, falling in love with a man there, and making her own decision to marry him. Predictably, given the emphasis on family and family-arranged marriages, most of these have ended in scandal of one sort or another. On the other hand, unattached Palestinian men arriving in Honduras today, if well connected and considered competent in business or a profession, are likely to find some local young women amenable to their advances, despite the more generally expressed view of the latter that they would rather die than marry someone from "over there." Such distaste is usually based upon the belief that Middle Eastern men are more demanding of their wives and more likely to keep them at home.[8]

In order to test some of the conclusions suggested by anecdotal ethnographic evidence, I sought marriage records to illustrate changes that appeared to have occurred through time. Unfortunately, the task proved impossible for a number of reasons. First, most of the early marriages were performed and recorded in Palestine. Some, but by no means most, of these were later registered in San Pedro Sula as well. Those immigrants who were Roman (Latin) Catholic before their arrival in Honduras were more likely than were the Greek Orthodox to accept the legality and the sanctity of marriages performed in the local Honduran parish, but some Orthodox immigrants converted to Catholicism rather than do without the

---

8. In fact, Christian women in Bethlehem seemed to me to be exceptionally free to come and go as they pleased. Through the ages, however, visitors have made this remark in contrasting Christians with Muslims. It is also the case that Honduran men say that Palestinian women born in Ephrata make better wives because they are more submissive. As this is a subjective matter, I know of no way to confirm or refute it.

sacrament.[9] For many years, however, probably so long as they still considered themselves temporary migrants, adherents to both religious persuasions preferred to return to Bethlehem for marriages and baptisms, since that is where their primary reference group was to be found, and it was that group's recognition they most desired.

Death records were also examined, but these were even more poorly kept than were those for marriage and baptism. Whole books were simply missing in the archives. Visits to cemeteries provided some data, but tombstones were often missing, defaced, or lacking details, such as place and date of birth.[10]

After 1963, when the first Orthodox church in Central America was built in San Pedro (see chap. 7), weddings performed in Honduras became more acceptable to more people, but, due to the fact that records were not dutifully kept by the earliest priests, we still have an incomplete roster of Palestinian marriages. Older people recalled having been visited before construction of their own church by Orthodox priests from Mexico and from the United States, who performed baptisms and marriages while there. The records of these sacraments apparently are to be found in the home churches of the visiting priests, so they were not available for my inspection.

Nevertheless, in order to get some idea of the marital behavior of the first immigrants, I examined the records of the Roman Catholic parish of San Pedro Sula as well as those in El Progreso, Santa Rosa de Copán, and Yoro for the years between 1900 and the middle of 1985.[11] Because the Catholic church at one time demanded information on where the couple had been born and baptized, these records provide considerable insight into the history of the Arab migration to Honduras.

---

9. See chap. 7 for further explanation of terminology used in reference to religious groups in the Holy Land.

10. When I inquired about these I was told that tombstones were frequently stolen, to be used as lintels, entryways, or in some other manner. Even if true, this does not explain those stones in place but with no information whatever engraved upon them.

11. In attempting to uncover patterns I perused marriage, baptismal, and death records of the Roman Catholic church in Honduras. The data are extremely deficient for a number of reasons. In addition to the problems explained in the text, the records themselves were in many cases illegible, lacking crucial data, lost, or had been allowed to deteriorate to the point where they were unusable. As explained previously, I was unable to obtain permission from the central Honduran government to examine its official records, which would have been a valuable addition to my analysis, which must perforce remain inexact. I am convinced that the general patterns described are valid but deplore the fact that they cannot be supported by better quantitative data.

Of the 305 unions involving at least one partner with at least one Arab parent, 92.5 percent were ethnically endogamous before 1930 (table 6.1). The endogamous rate fell to 69.2 percent in the decade of the 1930s, and again to 50 percent in the 1940s, where it remained until the 1970s, when it dropped to 26.6 percent. Of the 17 marriages recorded between 1980 and 1985, fifteen involved one partner who did not have an Arab surname.

The definition of endogamy used here refers first to the cultural patterns by which the bride and groom have been raised as well as to their genetic heritage, as indicated by surname. In the Honduran community, however, the matronymic is also important, and for many families today it is enough if one of the two is Arab. Thus, depending on whether one is emphasizing the degree of endogamy or of exogamy, these marriages may be categorized in different ways. As shown in table 6.3, I have considered the union to be 100 percent endogamous when the patronymics and the matronymics of both partners are Arabic. This is coded AAAA, there being 148 (of 302 marriages of certain three-generation ancestry) in this category. The apparent rate of endogamy, however, based only on uniformity in the patronymics of the couple, would have reached 163, for the categories ANAN, AAAN and ANAA would all provide this condition (table 6.4). On the other hand, 243, or 80 percent, of the unions would have perpetuated the Arab surname in the next generation, for, in addition to those men whose fathers and mothers were both Palestinian, we must now include all those whose mothers were not, as well as those marrying non-Arab women.

Another way to view the problem of defining endogamy is to count those unions in which 100 percent, 75 percent, 50 percent, and 25 percent of the parents of the bridal couple had Arab surnames. These turn out to be 148, 18, 72, and 62, respectively, as seen in table 6.2. There is no way of knowing how many of those of mixed blood have grown up identifying, in one way or another, with the Palestinian in group, but it may be significant in assessing both their past and future ethnic and family leanings to consider the ethnicity of the marriage sponsors (*padrinos*). In 152 cases both sponsors had Arab surnames. (I have counted in-marrying spouses of primary padrinos as Arab if their names suggest that status — i.e., the first name of the woman followed by her husband's surname, the two separated by the Spanish *de*.) In 51 instances both padrinos were non-Arab, and in 30 cases one was Arab and one non-Arab; in 69 cases no padrinos at all were listed. (See table 6.5.)

It is interesting to note the frequency with which young Palestinian men and women have sought spouses from outside the ancestral identity group, suggesting, of course, that its ethnic unity has indeed broken down or that it depends on something other than surname. Seventy of the 302 union sample (23 percent) involved a "pure" Arab (AA, or someone for whom both parents had Arabic surnames) with a "pure" non-Arab partner (i.e., neither of whose parents had an Arabic surname.) It is also important to consider that for these 70 unions, in only 23 (32.8 percent) were both padrinos of Palestinian ancestry — again, judged by surname. If we break this down by gender, 35 percent of the couples consisting of Arab men and non-Arab women chose Arab padrinos, but when the woman alone was Arab the padrinos were also Arab only 26 percent of the time. Because padrinos are generally drawn from among the closest friends and relatives of the couple, this finding suggests that couples in which the part-

**TABLE 6.4.   Marriage Types Contributing to the Appearance of Endogamy**

| Types of Marriages Perpetuating Arab Surname | |
|---|---|
| Type | Number |
| AANA | 3 |
| ANAA | 5 |
| AAAA | 148 |
| ANNN | 25 |
| AANN | 51 |
| ANAN | 2 |
| AAAN | 9 |
| Total | 243 (80 percent) |

| Types of Marriages in Which Patronymics of Both Bride and Groom are Arabic, despite Mixed Ancestry | |
|---|---|
| AAAA | 148 |
| ANAN | 1 |
| AAAN | 9 |
| ANAA | 5 |
| Total | 163 (54 percent) |

A = Arab
N = non-Arab

ners come from distinct backgrounds are more likely to be drawn into the non-Arab community, regardless of whether the bride or groom is Arab. This might be interpreted in several ways, including an exclusivity on the part of Arabs. It is a fact that traditional Arab parents, especially those born in Palestine, are likely to reject a non-Arab son or daughter-in-law — at least at first — and may not assist in wedding plans or the selection of padrinos. But it is also possible that the practice indicates a tendency toward upward mobility, a kind of "passing" into the dominant sociocultural group.

All of these figures must be approached and used cautiously, however, for the existence of the Orthodox church, to which only Arabs belong, confounds any statistical analysis. Because its members include most of the newer immigrants, as well as those whose self-identification is most strongly Arab, it is probable that the endogamy rate among the observant Orthodox is very high, approaching 100 percent. In fact, I identified only two non-Arabs, both in-marrying women, among the membership, and neither one of them attended any service or function where I was present during the entire fieldwork period.

**TABLE 6.5.** Incidence of Arab *Padrinos* in Different Types of Marriages Involving Arabs

| Ethnicity of Bridal Couple | | Ethnicity of *Padrinos* | | | |
|---|---|---|---|---|---|
| | | Arab | Non-Arab | Mixed | None |
| AAAA | (148) | 101 | 5 | 6 | 36 |
| AAAN | (9) | 6 | 2 | 0 | 1 |
| AANA | (3) | 0 | 0 | 1 | 2 |
| ANAA | (5) | 2 | 1 | 0 | 2 |
| NAAA | (1) | 1 | 0 | 0 | 0 |
| AANN | (51) | 18 | 13 | 8 | 12 |
| ANAN | (2) | 2 | 0 | 0 | 0 |
| NAAN | (2) | 1 | 0 | 1 | 0 |
| NANA | (0) | 0 | 0 | 0 | 0 |
| ANNN | (25) | 6 | 12 | 1 | 6 |
| NANN | (7) | 2 | 4 | 0 | 1 |
| NNAN | (26) | 8 | 7 | 8 | 3 |
| NNNA | (4) | 0 | 4 | 0 | 0 |
| NNAA | (19) | 5 | 3 | 5 | 6 |
| Totals | (302) | 152 | 51 | 30 | 69 |

A = Arab
N = non-Arab

The church has more social than religious implications for most Palestinian-Hondurans, for the theological differences between the Greeks and the Latins do not seem to evoke much interest, even when they are understood. Newcomers gravitate to the church because it reminds them of home with its icons, distribution of homemade bread at communion, Greek prayers, and after-service coffee hour. The priest, fluent in both Spanish and Arabic, was born in Chile of Bethlehemite ancestry, while his wife is a Honduran-born Palestinian. His patronymic is one of the more prominent in town, and he and his wife both have close relatives there.

Many members of the Arab colony find it expedient to support both the Roman Catholic and the Orthodox churches in San Pedro with financial contributions and at least occasional attendance. These include both those whose ancestry was Catholic in Palestine and those whose ancestors were Orthodox at home but converted to Catholicism in Honduras. Masses marking the anniversaries of deceased Orthodox relatives are as likely to be held, for example, at one or another of the local Catholic churches as at the Orthodox church.

New Greek Orthodox immigrants, of course, flock to the church, which is the only purely Arab religious institution in Honduras, and I suspect, although I cannot confirm, that new Catholic immigrants may also feel more at ease there than in the local parish of that faith. The members and directors of the church include nearly the entire gamut of Arabic patronymics in Honduras, even though some insisted that their "family" was entirely Catholic. A wedding performed during my Honduran fieldwork was jointly officiated by the local Orthodox priest and a Latin Catholic priest resident in Jordan, who made the special trip because he was a relative of the groom. Some relatives suggested that having both an Orthodox and a Catholic priest was not unusual, and this was confirmed by both Catholic and Orthodox priests in San Pedro.

It does not seem sensible, given the population increase over the years, that the total number of marriages should have declined so precipitously as seen in table 6.1.[12] Several possible explanatory factors suggest themselves. First, more young people may be abandoning their Arab heritage in a cultural and ethnic sense and choosing

---

12. In three cases I was not able to identify the ethnicity of one of the four parents, so in tables 6.2 and 6.3 the total number of marriages is 302 rather than 305.

marriage partners on the basis of other personal and social characteristics. After two generations, the Arab surname of an outmarrying
woman would be lost to her descendants, although legitimate children
of Arab men should still be identifiable.[13]

Another possibility is that more people are turning to the Protestant churches, whose records were not examined. Despite the rise of
a strong Christian fundamentalist ethic among many of the Palestinian Hondurans, they are still overwhelmingly attached to Catholicism or Orthodoxy.[14] Third, as suggested above, more may be turning to Orthodoxy and thus are not marrying in the Catholic church.
Finally, and I believe most important, more of the young people may
be leaving San Pedro Sula, going either to Tegucigalpa or to the
United States. I have no specific data on such emigration, but it is apparent that more are seeking university educations, in the course of
which they are likely to meet and marry non-Arabs.

Baptismal records of the Catholic churches in Honduras also
shed considerable light on marital behavior, for unmarried parents
are identified as such and by name, so long as the father recognizes
the child. Most of these involved non-Arab women.[15] Again, the
records are imperfect for all the reasons given above, but they do
give us some indication of trends through time. It is clear that Arab
men who fathered children by Honduran women usually did not
marry them, even if they formally recognized their paternity. As
shown in table 6.2, of the four hundred sixty-five baptisms recorded
between 1897 and 1960, four hundred (86 percent) were of children
born to married parents. Three hundred and fifty-two (75.6 percent)
were born to Arab-endogamous unions, and of those 98.8 percent
were legitimate. Arab men fathered children with non-Arab women

---

13. Only three cases have come to my attention in which Arabs changed their name
after coming to Honduras, and none of them was from the Ephrata region. In all three cases
the explanation was that the Arabic was too difficult to pronounce or spell or, as related by
Rosa (1978:89), because an English name (Brooks) "sounded better" than his own.

14. Charismatic movements are strong in Honduras among Palestinians and others,
including resident Americans. One of the latter introduced the movement known as the
"Sword of the Spirit" to San Pedro. This was said by informants to have begun in 1967 at
Notre Dame University, when four students locked themselves into a sanctuary, vowing to
remain until they had a sign from God. (See chap. 7.)

15. Extralegal pregnancies among Arab women no doubt quickly forced the principals
to the altar. In a few cases where I have had both marriage and baptismal records for the
same family, they suggest that this had happened.

in ninety-six cases, only forty-five of which (47 percent) were legitimate.

If we further break down the data by decade, we find some interesting trends. As may be seen in tables 6.2 and 6.6, the endogamous rate (combining legal and common-law unions) hovered around 80 percent during the first thirty years for which we have records, contradicting the idea that the earliest immigrants did not bring women from home. In the next decade, when births soared as the number of young immigrants increased, endogamy actually increased. Not until the 1940s did it begin what has become a continuing decline. In all periods unions between Arab men and non-Arab women greatly exceeded the reverse. Arranged marriages at very early ages, coupled with the fear of parental punishment and/or virtual banishment from the family seem to have kept most Arab women within the fold, at least during the early years.

## Place of Origin

In addition to family connections another element of importance in establishing identity in the Middle East is the village or town where one was born, or, in the case of emigrants, whence one's ancestors derived. The three communities of Ephrata—Bethlehem, Beit Jala, and Beit Sahur—are ranked in that order in both Palestine and Honduras, although the rivalry of the latter two with Bethlehem is well known (Plascov 1981:111). The prestige of Bethlehem as the place of

**TABLE 6.6  Baptisms Showing Endogamous/Exogamous Trends, 1897–1960**

| Years | Number of Baptisms | Number of Couples | AA | AN | NA |
|---|---|---|---|---|---|
| 1897–1909 | 23 | 19 | 18 | 4 | 1 |
| 1910–19 | 97 | 56 | 76 | 19 | 2 |
| 1920–29 | 150 | 93 | 123 | 25 | 2 |
| 1930–39 | 111 | 76 | 94 | 13 | 4 |
| 1940–49 | 22 | 16 | 10 | 11 | 1 |
| 1950–59 | 44 | 38 | 23 | 15 | 6 |
| 1960 (1 year) | 18 | 18 | 7 | 9 | 2 |

AA = Arab father and mother
AN = Arab father, non-Arab mother
NA = Non-Arab father, Arab mother

Jesus' birth, as well as its antiquity and greater size, place it at the pinnacle. It has long been the destination of pilgrims and tourists, most of whom know nothing of Beit Jala or Beit Sahur.

Beit Jala runs a close second to Bethlehem in many ways, however, and in Honduras is so often touted by its emigrant sons and daughters that many non-Arabs there know more about it than they do about Bethlehem.[16] The town includes the site of Shepherds' Field, where according to legend angels announced the birth of Christ. Rauwolff, who traveled in the area in 1573, mentions passing Beit Jala on the way to Bethlehem from Jerusalem (Macalister 1909:216). In the nineteenth century another traveler described the town as "belonging to" the Tekiyeh, a charitable establishment in Jerusalem, and as containing three Greek Orthodox convents. The villagers were protected by that church, to which they paid tribute (Robinson 1874: vol. 2, 3).

Even today Beit Jala has the highest percentage of Christians among the three in Ephrata, and nearly all are Greek Orthodox. (See chap. 7.) One of the largest and wealthiest families of San Pedro Sula comes from there, and one of their kinsmen was Beit Jala's mayor at the time of the fieldwork. An interview with him in 1988 revealed that Beit Jala was then undergoing a strong out-migration as a result of the intifada. He said that during the previous month twenty-six families had left permanently, having disposed of their property and abandoned their rights to return.

Bethlehemites disparaged the town of Beit Jala in my conversations with them, as they did, to a lesser extent, the third village, Beit Sahur. Among other things it was said that the people of Beit Jala were lazy, inclined toward drug use and alcohol consumption, and willing to sell out their lands and properties to either Israelis or to immigrant Muslim villagers. Ironically, there is more evidence for the latter in Bethlehem itself, although not in Beit Sahur.

In many ways Beit Sahur is the most interesting. During the intifada it has repeatedly been mentioned in international press accounts for its rebellious spirit. Its citizens, in an impressive demonstration, burned their Israeli-issued identity cards and have led their

---

16. A prominent scholar whose son had married a Palestinian-Honduran insisted that most Arabs in San Pedro Sula were from Beit Jala. Perhaps the evidence presented here will persuade him otherwise.

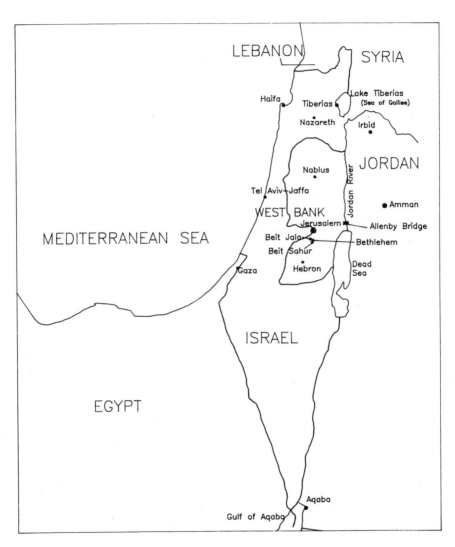

Map of Israel and the Occupied Territories of Palestine

Map of Central America

View of modern Bethlehem, taken from village of Beit Sahur

View of modern San Pedro Sula

A street scene in modern Bethlehem

A street scene in San Pedro Sula

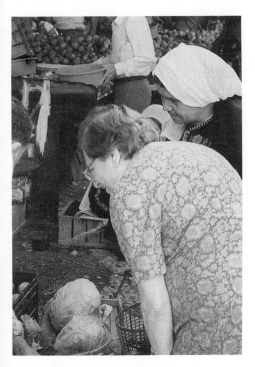

A Christian woman buying
cabbages from a Muslim woman in
the Bethlehem market

A San Pedro Sula supermarket
interior, showing sign indicating
display of Arab foods ("Alimentos
Arabes")

Interior of Greek Orthodox
church in Jordan

Honduran Orthodox priest in procession with two altar boys

Jordanian Greek Orthodox priest
officiating at wedding

Tomb of a Palestinian-Honduran
(in Spanish and Arabic)

Group of Palestinian-Honduran men relaxing

Palestinian-Honduran woman playing
traditional drum

Palestinian-Honduran woman dancing in
Middle Eastern style

Masked youths running from Israeli soldiers, Bethlehem

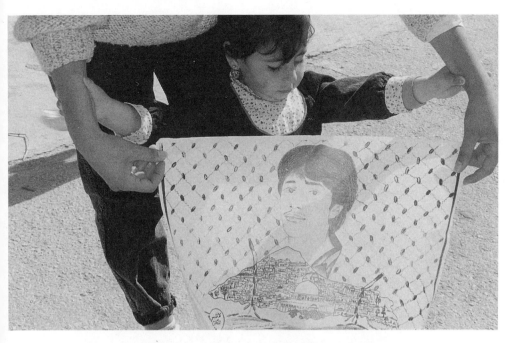

Beit Sahur child holding commemorative drawing of a fallen brother

Palestinian-Honduran children holding palm decorations on Palm Sunday in Orthodox church (priest in distant background at altar)

Wedding of Latin Catholic couple, Bethlehem

fellows in the West Bank and in Gaza in refusals to pay taxes, renew car license plates, and the like. Cooperative neighborhood units were formed early in 1988 to grow produce and raise animals such as chickens and goats so as to become more self-sufficient. (See chap. 8.) Several of their men have been killed or jailed, and the women and children frequently demonstrate in the streets, taunting the Israeli soldiers. The village has become an important symbol of Palestinian resistance, not only throughout the West Bank but also in the diaspora.

In addition to the pride generated by these recent activities Beit Sahur also exhibits an entrepreneurial spirit not seen in Bethlehem or Beit Jala. In part because it is smaller and more rural, with available undeveloped spaces, a good bit of new building has occurred over the past few years. According to one source, its built-up area grew between 1969 and 1979 by 267 percent, in comparison with Beit Jala's increase of 55 percent and Bethlehem's of 125 percent (Shinar 1987:27). I was told by local collaborators in Beit Sahur that much of this had been paid for by remittances sent by relatives in the diaspora. One of the largest enterprises in the West Bank, a plastics manufacturing company, is situated there as well (Benvenisti 1987:26). Even during the strife of the rebellion people were enlarging and furnishing their homes in as luxurious a style as they could afford. One gets the impression that emigration from Beit Sahur is still thought of as a temporary phenomenon, even though most families count numerous relatives in the exterior, many of whom have been away for generations.

Nevertheless, despite its recent prosperity and growth and its fame for fierce resistance in the intifada, in Honduras Beit Sahur is distinctly less prestigious, and the evidence suggests that emigrants from that village came later and in fewer numbers than those from Bethlehem and Beit Jala. The people from Beit Sahur are said to be "more rough," with poor manners, and not so good-looking as those from their neighboring towns.[17] Although many of them are among

---

17. Early European travelers often commented upon the beauty of the Bethlehem women, saying that they looked very much like Europeans and comparing them favorably with other Arabs of the area. It has commonly been supposed that considerable admixture occurred during the Crusade period, and a few families in Bethlehem are said to be directly descended from, and bearing the surnames of, Crusaders. These include, according to Banoura (1981): Abujaber, Abukhalil, Batarse, Dabdoub, Daoud, Deik, Fleifel, Giacaman, Gabrie, Mikel,

the most wealthy in San Pedro Sula, they are not included in the most elite Arab social circles, to say nothing of Honduran ones. There is a sense that they are considered *nouveau riche* and social climbers by other Arabs, who in turn receive those epithets from other Hondurans.

The number of Arabs in Honduras who do not come from one of these three villages is quite small. (See table 6.7.) A few are from Jerusalem, which is always accorded respect, and a handful are from Ramallah, another Christian town. Still another set derives from Lebanon or Syria, and, although today its members are thoroughly integrated into the Palestinian community in most respects and have intermarried with them for several decades, they and the others are quick to point out their different origin.

As mentioned above, there are some Muslim Palestinians in Honduras, but they are completely set apart from all others. Not only do they not share family and village origins, but they are of a different religion, and, as in their homeland, it is unthinkable to marry outside the faith. Only in the secondary diaspora, i.e., of Palestinian Hondurans who emigrate to the United States, does one occasionally find such a marriage.

Marriage with Jews is similarly rare. I learned of only three such cases in Honduras. Two of these were Palestinian-Honduran women living in the United States, who did not expect to return to reside in Honduras. In the third case, involving a high-status local man and an American (nonpracticing) Jew, the couple lives in Honduras, and, although now she is finally (after more than twenty years) accepted by her husband's family, the rest of the community has never forgotten her background. She and her husband interact socially more with non-Arabs than with Arabs and live according to a basically American-Honduran life-style. Their teenaged children, although baptized in the Orthodox church, think of themselves as Hondurans or Americans, rather than as either Jews or Arabs.

Many of the social distinctions important in Palestine have continued in the diaspora. The Bethlehem Association, headquartered near Philadelphia, makes a point in its editorializing that it wishes to

---

Marcos, Mubarak, Sabat, Suwadi, Tabash, Talamas, and Tarud. It is not clear on what basis he has made this judgment. In Honduras the family most often said to have been of Crusader origin, based both on its members' very light coloring and their name, was Handal.

**TABLE 6.7.** Arabic Surnames Present in Honduras, 1988

| Name | Alternates | Origin |
|---|---|---|
| Abbassy | Abassi, Abassi | Acre |
| Abboud | Abud, Aboud | Syria |
| Abdalah | Abdullah, Abdala, Abdalla | |
| Abdelnur | | BL |
| Abedrabo | Abdrabo, Abedrabbo, Abed Rabo | BJ |
| Abou-nehra | | |
| Aboumohor | Abumohor, Abumojor | BJ |
| Abraham | Ibrahim | BS |
| Abudeye | | BJ |
| Abudoj | Abdo | BL |
| Abufele | Abufhela | BL |
| Abugattas | | BJ |
| Abuid | | BJ |
| Abujerjes | Abugiries | BJ |
| Abullarade | Abuyarade | |
| Abumojor | Abumohor | BJ |
| Abureyes | | |
| Aburuman | Aburoman | BJ |
| Abuyiries | Abujiries, Abugiries | BJ |
| Affif | | |
| Aljobhan | | |
| Amad | Ahmad, Ahmed | |
| Amer | | |
| Andonie | Andony | BL |
| Asfura | Asfourah, Asfuras, Asfoura | BL |
| Assaf | | BL |
| Atallah | Atala | |
| Atti | Atiq | BL |
| Atuan | Atwan | BL |
| Awad | | BL |
| Azar | | Lebanon |
| Azize | | BL |
| Azzad | | |
| Bader | Badr, Padra | BJ, BS |
| Bamar | | |
| Banayotti | Panayotti | BL (Greek)? |
| Bandak | Bendek, Bendeck | BL |

BL = Bethlehem
BJ = Beit Jala
BS = Beit Sahur
  No entry under "origin" indicates contradictory information received, despite
identification of the surname as "Arab."

| Name | Alternates | Origin |
|---|---|---|
| Bandy | Bandi, Bandes | BJ |
| Baracat | Barakat | |
| Barhum | Barhoum, Barjum, Barjun | BS |
| Barjun | Barjum | BL |
| Batarse | Batarseh | BL |
| Bedran | Badra? | |
| Bichara | Bishara | BJ |
| Boadla | Boadli | |
| Botto | Boto, Butto | BL |
| Burbura | Burbara | BL |
| Busmail | | |
| Canahuati | Canahwati, Canavati, Canawati | BL |
| Cassis | Kassis, Caseese | BL, BJ, BS |
| Chahin | Shahin, Chain | BL |
| Chehadeh | Shehadeh | BJ |
| Comandari | Kamandari | BL |
| Cronfel | Kronfel | BL |
| Cury | Kury, Curi, Kuri, Khoury, | BJ |
| Dabdoub | | BL |
| Dacarett | Dacaret, Daccaret | BL |
| David | Daoud | BL |
| Dieck | Diek | BL |
| Dip | Dipp (Diab?) | Ramallah |
| Dogadher | | |
| Duaje | | Lebanon |
| El Hayek | Al Hayek | Syria |
| Elias | | Lebanon |
| Ennabe | | Ramallah |
| Facusse | Facouse | BL |
| Fanous | | Lebanon, Egypt? |
| Faraj | Farage, Farah | BS, BJ |
| Fattaleh | | Jerusalem |
| Fayad | | |
| Flefil | Flefile, Fleifel, Flefel | BL |
| Frech | Freij, Freich | BL |
| Fuadi | | |
| Gabrieh | Gabrie | BL |
| Ganem | | BS |
| Gattas | Gataz, Gattis | BL |
| Gawy | | |
| Giacoman | Yacaman, Jacman, Jacaman | BL |
| Hamis | Jamis | BJ |
| Hanania | Janania | BL |
| Handal | | BL |
| Hasbun | | BL |
| Hassim | Hassin, Hazim | BL |
| Hawit | | Jerusalem |

| Name | Alternates | Origin |
|------|-----------|--------|
| Hiaczi | | |
| Hilsaca | | |
| Hoch | Joch | BL |
| Hode | Odeh | BJ |
| Hreizi | Herezi | BL |
| Ibrahim | | BJ |
| Ictech | Iktaish, Ectech | BL |
| Isabrin | | |
| Jaar | Iga | BL |
| Jacaman | Giacoman, Yacaman, Jackman | BL |
| Jalal | | |
| Jamal | | |
| Jarufe | Kharufa, Kafie? | BJ |
| Jibrin | Yibrin | |
| Jorge | | Lebanon |
| Kafati | Kaffati, Kaffaty | BJ |
| Kafie | | |
| Kaled | | |
| Kamandari | Comandari | BL |
| Kamar | | Jerusalem |
| Kattan | | BL, BJ |
| Kawas | Cauas | BL |
| Khoury | Cury, Kury, Khuri | BJ |
| Konkar | | BJ |
| Ladat | Laadeh? Lado? | BL |
| Lama | | BL |
| Larach | Larage | BJ |
| Mahchi | Machi, Mahshi | BL, Jerusalem |
| Mahomar | Mohamar, Mouamar, Mouammar | BL |
| Maloff | Maalof, Malof, Malouf | Lebanon |
| Mansur | Mansour, Manzur | BL, BJ |
| Marcos | Marcuse | BL |
| Marzouka | Marzuka | BL |
| Massou | | BL, BJ |
| Michel | Mikel, Miguel | BL |
| Miguel | Michel, Mikel | BL |
| Miladeh | Milady | BL |
| Miselem | Michalen, Musallam, Musallem | BL |
| Misleh | Musleh | BL |
| Mitri | | BL, BJ |
| Mukaquer | Makaker | BJ |
| Murra | Mourra, Moura | BL |
| Musleh | Misleh | BS |
| Nacir | Nasser | BL |
| Nafky | | |
| Nahomed | | |
| Nahum | | |

| Name | Alternates | Origin |
|---|---|---|
| Nassad | | |
| Nasser | Nassar, Nacir, Nazar | BL |
| Nastas | Anastas, Nustas, Noustas | BL |
| Nazrala | Nasralla | BJ |
| Nicoli | | BL |
| Nimer | | Ramallah |
| Numman | | Ramallah |
| Nusthas | Nasthas | BL |
| Odeh | Hode | BL |
| Paranky | Baranky | BL |
| Rabat | Rabbad, Rabhah | |
| Rafeq | | |
| Richmawy | Rishmawy, Rachmaoui | BS |
| Rock | Rok | BL |
| Roman | Rumman | BJ |
| Saade | Saadeh, Sadi, Saad | BL |
| Sabat | Zabath | BL |
| Saca | | BL |
| Sacaan | | BL |
| Safie | | BL |
| Sahury | | BL |
| Said | Zaid | |
| Sakhel | | |
| Salame | Salameh, Salomeh, Saloumi | BL, BJ, BS |
| Salem | | BL |
| Salman | Soliman, Soloman, Selman? | BL, BJ |
| Salomon | | BL |
| Salty | Salti | BL |
| Samara | Samour, Samoura | BL |
| Samra | Saamra | BL |
| Sansur | | BL, BJ |
| Saybe | | BL |
| Segebre | | BJ |
| Sikaffy | | BL |
| Simaan | Siman | BJ |
| Simon | | |
| Sirene | Zurene, Zarini | BJ |
| Siwady | Siwadi, Souadi, Suwadi | BL |
| Soliman | Suleiman | BL |
| Stefan | Estefan | BL |
| Talhami | | BL |
| Tanios | | Greek |
| Tome | Tueme | BJ, BL |
| Yacoub | | BJ, BS |
| Yaghmur | | |
| Yamani | | |
| Yazbek | | |
| Yibrin | | |

| Name | Alternates | Origin |
|------|-----------|--------|
| Yones | | BL |
| Yuja | | BL |
| Zablah | Zableh | BL |
| Zacarias | Zacaria | BS |
| Zakieh | | |
| Zarky | | |
| Zaror | | |
| Zarruck | Zarruk | BL |
| Zarzar | | BL |
| Zoghbi | Zogby, Sogby | BL |
| Zummar | | BS |

include persons from Beit Jala and Beit Sahur in its membership. Indeed, today Bethlehem and Beit Jala do form a continuous settlement, and Beit Sahur appears to be growing so rapidly that the short distance between it and the others may soon disappear. In any case Bethlehem is clearly visible in the near distance, across the olive-studded slopes that still separate the two towns. Yet, it is obvious that the leadership of the Bethlehem Association seems firmly in the hands of Bethlehemites. In a recent election of officers there were eight candidates presented for four offices. Five of them had been born in Bethlehem or in the diaspora of Bethlehem parents, and one was from Beit Jala. The remaining two did not have their origins listed; one of these had a Bethlehem surname, but the other was not listed in Banoura's *Families of Ephrata* at all. Photos of members which appear frequently in the association's newsletter are most often identified as being from Bethlehem or Beit Jala.

## The Families

The question most frequently asked about my findings is: "How many Palestinians are there in Honduras (or Guatemala or Central America) today?" The answer is that it all depends on how one identifies a Palestinian. One starts with the surname, but that is also not so simple as it sounds. Recognizing those that derive from Arabic requires not only some familiarity with that language but also with Spanish orthography. In addition, the long period of Arab domination in Spain left its mark on the language and on Spanish surnames themselves, even though, as T. Glick (1979) suggests, there may not have been much actual intermingling of the races. One must exclude names of possible Arabic origin, like "Medina," which is common among Spanish populations everywhere but is not found in modern-day Ephrata at all.

In the present work the identification of Arabic surnames started with the assistance of a Lebanese colleague and a Palestinian graduate student, who marked what they believed to be Arab surnames in the Honduran telephone book. Unfortunately, since neither was familiar with Spanish, they missed many whose spelling was an exotic attempt to convey the sound of the original surname in that language. Since in many cases there might be several ways to achieve that, the same name might appear in a number of different forms. It required field-work in Honduras and considerable checking with collaborators, however, to create a definitive list.

Arab surnames in the telephone books of the five Central American countries were then entered into a computerized data base, to which were also added surnames encountered elsewhere in the research. The task was continuous, for, as I worked directly with knowledgeable persons in Honduras and Ephrata, I discovered names not in the phone book and learned to recognize others that had not previously occurred to either me or my earlier collaborators. All of this required continual reworking of the original lists. The compilation presented in the appendix is undoubtedly both incomplete and overly ambitious — i.e., it may contain some names that do not belong to persons of known Arab ancestry. Also, due to the fact that errors are frequently made by non-Arab clerks, first and last names are sometimes turned around, which may account for "Affif" being listed as a surname, when it is more generally a given name; yet, since many surnames are also given names (Abdala, Abraham, Bichara, and Mikel, for example), I thought it best to include it.

The complete list contained more than 450 surnames, but when minor spelling variations were removed it was condensed into the 338 presented in the appendix. The names recorded here have appeared at least once in one or more of the following: telephone books from the six countries of Honduras, Guatemala, El Salvador, Nicaragua, Costa Rica, and Belize; baptismal, marriage, and death records in Honduras; the Musallam and Jacir Central American lists from the 1950s; chamber of commerce data from San Pedro Sula, Honduras, and Guatemala. Some names are found in several countries, but most are concentrated in one or two. For this chapter I have further reduced the list to those appearing in Honduras at one time or another (table 6.7.) Of the surnames comprising this list, the largest single group (105) is from Bethlehem and includes names found only in that city (or in a few cases in one of the neighboring towns), according to both my many collaborators and Banoura.[18]

Beit Jala, on the other hand, has contributed only thirty-six, plus another ten shared with Bethlehem and/or Beit Sahur. Finally, only seven names come from Beit Sahur, plus another four the town shares with its neighbors. Sixteen were identified by collaborators, either in Honduras or in Bethlehem, as coming from other Palestinian or Middle Eastern regions, but forty-seven remain in the "origin unknown" category. Aside from the definite identification of them as Arabic, respondents were simply unable to place these names. Most of them, they believe, are recent arrivals. Some, like Barakat and Hilsaca, are said to be recent arrivals; some names are common in Jordan and elsewhere and are not necessarily limited to Palestinians, although the assumption is that their owners in Honduras belong to that group. Others, like Kafie and Boadla, have been in Honduras for at least three generations and are said to be certainly Palestinian, although no one is certain of their exact origin.

Besides the conviction that they derive from Arabic, the other characteristic these names of unknown origin seem to have in common is that respondents all suggested they were originally Muslim, rather than Christian. My interpretation is that this is further evidence of the in-group cohesion among the Christian emigrants from Ephrata. Although it is possible to break into their closed circle, it is usually done both through the demonstration of the possession of wealth and by adhering to either the Catholic or the Orthodox church. As in earlier times, then, it is still family, village, and religion that matter most in the identification of self and the structuring of interpersonal relations, although wealth and mutual business interests can overcome the first three, as they did for many Lebanese, Syr-

---

18. Several of my informants were surprised to find that Banoura's list is incomplete. Having struggled with the effort myself, I can well understand how this may have happened and hope my work will be seen as a friendly correction to his monumental contribution. He was kind enough to take time from his busy schedule to talk with me in Bethlehem, and I have enormous respect for his scholarship. Since his book is taken by many to be "the last word," however, it is important that readers take note of this point.

ians and Jews who came to Honduras at about the same time and entered commerce under the same circumstances as the Palestinians.[19]

## Voluntary Associations

As in most complex societies, another way people have of relating to each other is through their voluntary association with different organized groups, such as clubs. In San Pedro there are a number of these, some in which Arabs and Hondurans come together and others that are exclusively of Arab membership. The first group includes the Rotary Club for men and the Cortés Chamber of Commerce, to which a very few women also belong. There is a traditional social club with restricted membership which has in the past excluded Arabs but now embraces a number of the most prominent and wealthy. The International Club was founded to bring together the more affluent foreigners who have come to visit or settle in San Pedro, and it contains numerous Arab families as well as Europeans and Americans. Finally, among the women there is a very prestigious grouping called the Garden Club. For many years it excluded Arabs, but now it has come to be dominated by them. Membership is still by invitation, and several wealthy Arab matrons have found themselves snubbed even by their co-ethnics, perhaps because they came from the "wrong" family or the "wrong" village.

The second category — associations comprising only or primarily persons of Arab descent — includes three attached to the Orthodox church: the Comité Ortodoxo, the Comité de Damas Ortodoxas, and the Club Juvenil. These will be further discussed in chapter 7. In addition there is a Palestinian Sports Club (Club Deportivo Palestino), the Associación Femenina Hondureña Arabe, the Centro Cultural Hondureño Arabe, FEARAB (Federación de Entidades Americano-Arabe), and an investment group called simply Inversiones, S.A.

Little information was gathered on the sports club or on the sports world of Honduras in general. Soccer, however, is the favorite

---

19. A small book on Guatemalan *modismos,* or idioms, provides identical definitions for *Jew* (*Judío*) and *Turk* (*Turco*) (Rubio 1982). Informants in both Guatemala and Honduras confirmed the fact that these terms denoted a type of person rather than a nationality or ethnicity.

game, as it is in much of Latin America and the Middle East, and this club has a team that plays other amateur teams about the country. Young Arab men who excel in this sport have gained recognition and prestige within the general populace, regardless of their class or ethnic background, much as occurs in the United States and elsewhere.

The Arab Women's Club operates much like such clubs in the United States. It brings together the more affluent for social and charitable purposes and today serves the function as well of helping to integrate non-Arab wives into Arab society and introducing Arab newcomers to Honduras to the local customs. Ostensibly, it supports charitable projects, contributing to orphanages and hospitals and the like, and does not limit itself to serving the Arab population. Any woman, Arab or non-Arab, with a special interest in the Arab population is permitted to join, and it does attract many women with its fashion shows, teas, and other social functions at which Middle Eastern foods are served and Arabic music and dancing presented.

The group known as FEARAB (also meaning "Arab Faith") is overtly political in its purpose. Composed primarily of men, it is sometimes referred to by persons in the category just described as a group of "fanatics" and, many believe, formally connected with one or another faction of the PLO. (More will be said about this in chapter 8.)

The Centro Cultural Hondureño Arabe was conceived as a social club for Arab men, women, and children with a large locale for meetings, dances, picnics, and general recreational activities. Tegucigalpa has long had such a club, among others that were founded and are used by immigrants from different countries. In San Pedro Sula, however, despite the donation of a lot and some funds collected from the membership, the club has never succeeded in constructing a building. The Orthodox members tend to cluster at their church, which has a large meeting place attached to the sanctuary itself. This auditorium is generally made available to the Arab community for various secular purposes.

Another reason for their failure to secure sufficient funding is that many of the most affluent members of the community prefer now to further their connections with the traditional Honduran elites as well as with individuals and families descended from other immigrant groups such as Jews and Americans. Although interested in the events in Palestine and willing to help maintain a spirit of brotherhood with other Palestinians in Honduras, they do not wish to continue to cut themselves off from the rest of the country. They have no notion of returning to Palestine, except as tourists; some state that they no longer even have relatives there, all of them now living somewhere in the diaspora.

## Life in the Diaspora

The picture of life in the diaspora suggested by the information presented in the above sections is one of general order—a harmony based on the "togetherness" of family and kin group with a morality and worldview taught and continually reinforced by a firm commitment to Christianity. The verbal accounts of events and traditions, the rules of life as set forth eloquently by the older men and women, and even the written records used in this study all suggest a rather straightforward, romantic, and idyllic tableau, albeit one that entailed many physical and emotional hardships requiring sacrifice and hard work to overcome.

Analysis of the qualitative information gathered through ethnographic interviews and participant observation suggests to me a quite different view of the past and present Palestinian presence in Honduras, and probably elsewhere. The exodus from their homeland must have posed an extreme trauma for most of them, and it resulted in a life without stability, filled with passions that often led to violence, deceit, and calumnies directed within the ethnic group and even within the family circle. Their precarious position as a foreign, pariah group made it difficult to engage in overt actions against the natives, so their frustrations were diverted in some cases toward clandestine cheating of their clients and toward those with whom they lived on closest terms.

My field notes include an enormous amount of gossip about scandals including murder, beatings, theft, smuggling, deliberate burning of businesses to collect insurance, adultery, bigamy, abandonment of wives and children by men and of husbands and children by women, abuse of alcohol and drugs, and the swindling of unsuspecting relatives in a marvelous variety of ways. Although it is undoubtedly true that many of these accounts were simply malicious gossip, most of them are truly believed by many people to have happened. Sometimes I heard the same story told in different ways by the opposing principals, each of whom exaggerated the other's guilt in his or her own vilification.

Frustrating in the extreme for the anthropologist is the tendency toward creative reinterpretation of seemingly trivial matters. Women constantly misrepresent their age, even in official places such as marriage records. Their relatives sometimes perpetuate the misrepresentation on their tombstones. Sometimes many years are subtracted, probably for the sake of vanity. On the other hand, especially in the early part of the century, young girls were sometimes presented to the Catholic church as being older than they were, presumably because the priest would have frowned on such early marriages. As Ata (1986:48) has pointed out, early age at marriage has long been a culturally rooted norm within the Palestinian society. He suggests that parents' fears for their daughters' possible involvement in sexual, emotional relationships led them to arrange marriages before puberty whenever possible. One of my Honduran friends told me that his Palestinian grandmother had eloped with a Honduran man at the age of fifteen. Consequently, her parents quickly married off her younger sisters to prevent the same "disaster."

Other individualized truths are also common. One woman of eighty-four years, in relating her life story, remarked that her husband, a prominent member of the first generation born in Honduras, had been one of only two children, despite the fact that five male siblings are mentioned for that family in Luque's account (1979:39), some of whom show up in church records. I can only conclude that, for one or another reason, she and/or her husband had had some serious dispute with the others, that they had died and been deleted from memory, or that they had moved away years before and had lost contact with them.

Indeed, turning the other cheek is not a primary behavioral or philosophical value of these people. Many stories were told of men and women going to their graves without consenting to see or talk with estranged spouses, siblings, children, or parents. Others refer to still remembered and unforgiven transgressions by certain individuals or families which occurred years or generations before. As mentioned above, Banoura alludes to such family feuds as one impetus for emigration. Indeed, flight to or from Palestine is frequently described in Honduras as the action taken by either the transgressor or the victim. Humiliated spouses of either sex have been said to have taken flight rather than suffer the inevitable gossip. Some have gone to the United States or another country instead, not wishing to face the Palestinian community in either Honduras or the Holy Land.

Palestinian personal security in Honduras, especially for members of the more prominent families, has sometimes been threatened from sources outside the ethnic group. Kidnappings are constantly feared, for at least two daughters of wealthy Arabs have been taken in the past — one never to be seen again, the other recovered in a daring assault on the house in which she was held captive for several weeks. Another man, son of perhaps the wealthiest Arab in Honduras at the time, was killed while apparently resisting capture by unknown assailants. These assaults have presumably been motivated by the hope to gain a ransom, although in the first case mentioned no ransom request was ever received. In all three cases the other members of the immediate family were immediately sent elsewhere, either to Mexico or to the United States.

The Arab community continues to refer to these events as evidence of their failure to be accepted by the dominant society. In fact, there are other reasons to support that view which are more persuasive. In the last presidential election one of the candidates was the son of a Honduran man and an Arab woman. The opposition often referred to his ancestry in their propaganda, suggesting that the president should be a "real" Honduran and that this particular candidate was not, despite the fact that the first immigrant bearing the surname of the candidate's mother had arrived early in this century and had quickly developed a reputation as a respectable businessman. Today the name is one of the most highly respected in the Arab community. A favorite ploy was to refer to the candidate by his matronymic, rather than by both, or only by the patronymic, as is usually done.

Prominent Hondurans, even when generally friendly, at least toward selected Arabs, often harbor reservations about the ethnic category in general. One non-Arab woman said she thought it would be difficult to get most Hondurans to admit it but that a new bank advertising itself as "by Hondurans, for Hondurans," really intended to exclude Arabs, who were thought to have too much influence in the most popular local bank. Indeed, a Palestinian-Honduran was the manager of the San Pedro branch, and there were many Palestinians in positions of considerable importance within it. Her comment, of course, revealed her own bias, but I feel sure she had heard similar thoughts from others.

Another prominent non-Arab businessman and politician said that he feared one day there would be an outbreak of violence against the Arab population and suggested that it would come largely from the nationalistic Left. The fact that the most desirable residential neighborhood in San Pedro Sula is inhabited almost exclusively by Arabs, many of whom have built palatial homes and gardens that overlook, yet symbolically exclude, the rest of the city, leads many to believe that this group is still foreign, exclusive, arrogant, and, above all, extravagantly rich. Many believe they acquired this wealth solely in Honduras and at the expense of Hondurans, despite the fact, as we have seen in chapter 5, that many of the earliest Palestinians invested capital and took considerable financial and personal risks in amassing their fortunes at the same time that they helped develop the entire north coast of Honduras.

As intermarriage becomes more frequent, some of the above prejudices will no doubt change. One non-Arab told me, however, that among her friends the gossip about Arabs continued, even from the lips of those who had Arab in-laws. She said they commonly began their stories by saying, "I shouldn't be saying this, now that I have 'Turcos' in the family, but . . . . " No other immigrant or local ethnic category in Honduras is targeted in this way, probably because the others are either very small in number and/or are nonthreatening in the larger economic and political world that includes, but is not limited to, Honduras. As the Palestinian-Israeli conflict becomes more prominent (and its progress is seen regularly on the Cable News Network (CNN), there is an increasing tension between the local Palestinians and others, especially Jews. One Jewish man said he actually feared for his life at times, for, even though he had many close friends among the Arab population, he also "knew their tendencies toward sudden violence when angry." A Palestinian-Honduran woman told me that she found it more and more difficult to intermingle with her former Jewish friends because she was continually angry over what she saw on television and found it impossible to discuss the issues with them. At the same time, for the Arab community itself the news serves to strengthen its sense of ethnic pride and many of its members are deeply concerned. One woman said that her husband had died three years ago of a heart attack while watching a newscast about the West Bank.

Despite some internal differences in viewpoint, today a sense of pan-Palestinian sensitivity, whether new or renewed, is beginning to arise as an ethnic marker in Honduras. This development not only tends to divide the Arabs from the Jews but exacerbates their problems with other Hondurans as well. This will be further discussed in chapter 8. First, however, in the chapter that follows we will look more closely at the role of organized religion in the Palestinians' personal lives and their cultural setting and also in the sociopolitical process in the Middle East and in Honduras.

*Chapter 7*

# Palestinian Christianity
# and Politics

Christians in the Holy Land are in a state of mind which presses them to despair and to mass exodus . . . the state of war in which the country finds itself is not conducive to remaining in the country.

— Archbishop Joseph M. Raya

## Church and State

It is often difficult for Westerners — Europeans and Americans alike — to understand how deeply religious persuasion enters into all aspects of everyday life in the Middle East. Identification with a specific religion, even when its belief, ritual, and ceremonial are ignored or abandoned, remains an important way of defining oneself and one's community. Middle Eastern pluralism over the millennia, under many different governments, has depended upon religion and its symbolism as a means of social organization and political control.

The three major faiths in the area today — Judaism, Christianity, and Islam — have derived from the same fundamental set of ideas and still share many things, such as their moral codes, their belief in a single, all-powerful god, and their explanations of causality and order in the universe. The Muslim Ottomans, following a governing practice going back to Roman times, recognized these similarities and respected both Christians and Jews as being "People of the Book," referring to the Hebrew Bible, which Christians call the Old Testament. This was in contrast to most other religious persuasions in the area, whose adherents were considered pagans, without access to "truth" and not eligible for salvation either in this world or the next.[1]

---

*Epigraph:* Archbishop Joseph M. Raya, in a 1969 message to his Greek Catholic superiors, quoted in Alexander 1973:183.
1. But see chap. 3, n. 4.

145

Yet, aside from the clergy and scholars of each faith, most people then, as now, probably understood little and cared less about the finer philosophical points that divided them, not only into these three major divisions but each one of them into numerous minor sects deriving from centuries of disagreement and consequent fissioning. Some of these developed as protests against established religious and secular regimes (Runciman 1968:3), as some believe Jesus Christ led or provoked. At the same time the historical record shows that both pagans and people of the book have had a remarkable tendency to change their religious persuasion — often as whole communities — when faced with powerful pressures to do so.[2] What is even more remarkable in the face of both of these tendencies toward change is the stubborn adherence to older faiths by many others. The fact that both of these processes have occurred suggests a certain conceptual separation of civil and religious loyalties at the popular level at the same time that it demonstrates the power of strong governments to achieve either compliance with or exclusion from the official religion, as its leaders see fit.

Separation of church and state is often thought by both Middle Easterners and Westerners to be a distinctly Western phenomenon, usually associated with Christianity (Rekhess 1979:136), as is implicit in the use of the word *church,* a term usually reserved for Christian sanctuaries. At the same time, however, Christianity is sometimes asserted to be an instrument of imperialism (Kedourie 1970:324). How can it be both ways? The Holy Roman Empire, the conquest of the Americas, the establishment of the Church of England by Henry VIII, the Lutheran church in modern Norway, and other such pieces of evidence suggest the latter more than the former, at least in earlier times.

Most social analysts, following Tawney (1926) and Weber (1958), relate increasing secularization of governments in Europe to the rise of capitalism, industrialism, and the Protestant Reformation, the latter itself a reflection of the first two. It is true, of course, that the Middle East was largely underdeveloped industrially until after

---

2. Most of these conversions were from Christianity to Islam, sometimes whole villages being forced into submission (Runciman 1968:12). Also, at least some Christians converted to Judaism after the Sassanid conquest in A.D. 614, including one priest from Acre who was tortured into submission by Jews assisting the invaders (Schick 1987:68).

World War II. After that some countries began to industrialize with the help of international loans and technical assistance programs, others from a fuller exploitation of their own oil wealth. The creation of the state of Israel and the tensions this produced throughout the area stimulated a greater dependence on industrial armaments, either imported or manufactured at home. With few exceptions, however, the governments have not become increasingly secular as a result of these changes.

Neither has the Middle East harbored many Protestants, often considered to represent the epitome of the modern commercial, capitalist spirit. Their large numbers in the Western world, however, have certainly been influential due to the fact that many of the more fundamentalist sects consider Israel to be the fulfillment of the first of several biblical prophecies concerning the Second Coming of Christ.[3] Despite increasing secularization in the more industrialized Western nations, therefore, Christianity is still seen as a potential threat to established Middle Eastern governments; certainly, the behavior of the British and the French during the mandates following World War I were seen as such by many.[4] In fact, and ironically, in the case of Palestine, a foreign, basically Christian regime fostered the climate by which much of that region was to become dominated by Judaism (Hassan 1981:30–34). Nevertheless, the subsequent and continuing alignment of Israel with Europe and the United States has been portrayed primarily as a cultural and political phenomenon, and as such, it seems to reflect the so-called Western separation of religion and government.

Freedom to practice one's own religion, even when it differs from that of the majority or of the dominant faction, was and is found in many countries, including many of those in the Middle East, and

---

3. It has been suggested that Lord Palmerston, British foreign secretary during the Mandate, had links to the evangelicals in Britain, who believed in the restoration of the Jews to Zion as part of the messianic plan of biblical prophecy. They thought the British should help them, and, apparently, so did he (Blumberg 1980:25).

4. Until recently, of course, the population of Lebanon had a Christian majority — clearly a legacy of the French occupation. The reasons for the political, economic, and military "fall" of Lebanon and its increasingly Muslim leadership are complicated and beyond the scope of this book. The demographic shift has certainly been in part a result of the exodus of Christians, most of whom left because of the economic perils resulting from the protracted civil war, itself influenced by events in Israel as well as elsewhere in the Middle East. Both intra- and inter-communal jealousies have been prominent in the ongoing conflict.

is only one of several elements associated with the separation of civil and religious authority, which may be thought of as a continuum of decreasing governmental control over religious expression and clerical organization. Other characteristics of governmental control relate to the way in which civil and religious hierarchies are constituted; the use of religious symbolism in civil ceremonies; the incorporation of religious holidays into official calendars, and, thus, into secular life; differential taxation of citizens belonging to nonofficial religions; the enforced use of different colors or types of apparel (sumptuary laws); and so on. It is difficult to think of any country today where all of these practices have been abolished, while at the same time all manner of religious expression is permitted. Among others, the United States and the Soviet Union, in different ways, have aspired to achieve total separation of church and state, yet both have had difficulty with the concept in actual practice. A few, like Saudi Arabia, forbid all but the official religion—in this case, Islam. Israel continues to debate the issue, many of its citizens opting for a nation with an all-Jewish citizenry; so far, however, other religions are still free to practice there, although the state religion is Judaism, and the country largely operates secularly in terms of that tradition (Domínguez 1989).

## History of Christianity in the Middle East

Historically, the Middle East has been relatively tolerant, despite periodic waves of violence and persecutions by different invaders of all three faiths. Both the dhimmi system of the first conquering Arabs and its successor, the Ottoman millet system, institutionalized religious differences within the state, which in both cases was officially Muslim. In Palestine, however, the Ottomans recognized only three indigenous millets—Greek Orthodox, Armenian Orthodox, and Judaism (Tsimhoni 1976:110). The Latin Catholics had a unique position, for they were not regarded as a local indigenous community. As discussed above in chapter 5, their members had special rights and were placed under European protection—still a different way of managing religious diversity within the larger community but one with important implications both for politics and for the economic system, as we have seen.

Christian religious pluralism of some sort has even deeper roots. Schick (1987:13) has pointed out that during Byzantine times small towns and cities throughout the Jordan Valley contained a very large number of what can only be interpreted as places of worship, although he was unable to discern any features that differentiated one from another in the archaeological record; nor did he find evidence suggesting ethnic differentiation within these communities. Schick speculates that each church practiced a different rite, but it seems also possible that early Christian teaching, which emphasized love and brotherhood, might have led each family or neighborhood to worship together, thus keeping congregations small and otherwise undifferentiated in belief.

The segmentation process within all of the major religious systems through history can usually be shown to have had political ramifications and from another point of view seems to have been related to an effort to maintain or create ethnic separateness, religious identification being part of the symbolic code by which each group establishes or emphasizes its uniqueness but which can also be used by the state as a means of control. Thus, a people's desire to cluster with others of its own kind can become a means for its own repression, as has happened with Jews throughout the world.

In this regard it is interesting to note that, although many Palestinians converted to Islam during and after the Arab invasions in A.D. 634–39, Palestine was still largely an Orthodox Christian country until the Turkish invasions of the latter part of the eleventh century (Runciman 1968:9). The Crusades, ostensibly intended to "reestablish" Christianity in the Holy Land, led to massacres of natives of all three faiths. In addition many local Christian churches were taken over to serve the needs of the invaders, their liturgies and clergy transformed from Greek to Latin (Runciman 1968:10). Thus, the Europeans only succeeded in further dividing the local Christian community, setting a precedent for the bitter intra-Christian rivalry that continues to the present day, and opening the door to Western Christian influence via the Roman Catholic church.

In 1099, when Germanic crusaders took Jerusalem and then Bethlehem, the Latin Catholic church was established, and, although it has had some setbacks from time to time, it has remained a strong force, becoming especially effective at the national level during the nineteenth century. Indeed, even though Europeans respected the other Christian faiths more than they did Islam it was the Latin Catholic church and its adherents with which they felt most comfortable.

It is clear from table 7.1 that they were most successful in Bethlehem itself, where Latin Catholics still outnumber the others. Beit Jala and Beit Sahur, in contrast, have always been and remain heavily Greek Orthodox, as does the rest of the Christian population throughout the region. Members of the latter faith are proud of the fact that theirs is the older of the two, many believing it to have been founded by Jesus himself. Banoura even lists the five "original" families of Bethlehem which he claims were among the first converts during the time of Christ.[5]

In Ottoman Palestine, Christian missionaries were free to proselytize only among other Christians and Jews, but, in part because the available pool was continually growing smaller as a percentage of the total population, the established churches increasingly resented intruders, especially Protestants. Spyridon (1938:24) relates that in 1822, when Calvinists brought Bibles written in Arabic, the Franciscans told their flock they must not touch them on pain of damnation, but relatively few seem to have been tempted, whether for that or other reasons.

### Christianity in Modern Ephrata

The Christians of the Bethlehem area are today divided into many sects, as shown in table 7.1. The details upon which Christian fissioning has occurred over the centuries are out of place here, particularly since none of my friends, either in Honduras or in Bethlehem, was able to tell me precisely how their faith differed theologically from the others. Indeed, in Honduras I was often told that there was no difference at all and that it mattered not whether one attended mass with the Orthodox or the Catholics. The priest of the Orthodox church told me sadly that his congregation was woefully ignorant of such matters, even those who had recently arrived from the Holy Land. Trimingham says, "The history of Christian interpretation hangs on the question, unique in religious history, of how to represent Christ as God-Man, *one* person; and all interpretation whether in terms of life or of dialectics has failed to achieve a true balance" (1979:208). No wonder, then, that the average Christian of whatever persuasion re-

---

5. These were Asfoura (Asfura), Dweiri (Dwery), Fakkousseh (Facusse), Salibi, and Shihadeh (Chehade).

**TABLE 7.1.** Religious Affiliations, Bethlehem Metropolitan Area, 1984

| Sect | Bethlehem | Beit Jala | Beit Sahur | Total |
|------|-----------|-----------|------------|-------|
| Latin Catholics | 4,800 | 809 | 670 | 6,279 |
| Greek Orthodox | 3,500 | 5,330 | 6,000 | 14,830 |
| Syrian Orthodox | 2,000 | – | – | 2,000 |
| Armenian Orthodox | 130 | – | – | 130 |
| Greek Catholic | 150 | – | 500 | 650 |
| Syrian Catholic | 150 | – | – | 150 |
| Armenian Catholic | 10 | – | – | 10 |
| Maronites | 10 | – | – | 10 |
| Protestants | 200 | 140 | 150 | 490 |
| Total Christian | 10,950 | 6,279 | 7,320 | 24,549 |
| Muslim | 19,000 | 1,300 | 1,700 | 22,000 |
| Total | 29,950 | 7,579 | 9,020 | 46,549 |

*Source:* Tabash 1985.

mains confused. All those with whom I discussed the matter knew that allegiance to Rome and the pope was characteristic of the Catholics, whether Latin, Greek, or Armenian, but they did not think of this as a political fact.

Bethlehem University was founded by the Vatican, and its faculty and administration are largely made up of foreign and local Roman (Latin) Catholic religious personnel.[6] All Christian sects, however, as well as Islam, are represented among the students. Although in principle the university does not proselytize or teach Christianity as such, masses are held on campus, and its presence serves to underscore the historical importance of Christianity in the area.[7]

---

6. In the Middle East the term *Roman Catholic* refers to the Greek Catholics, indigenous Orthodox Christians who accepted the Catholic Rite established by Rome in 1724. The *Roman* reflects their allegiance to Constantinople, whose Greek inhabitants continued to call themselves Romans. They are also still sometimes known as Melkites (Betts 1978:45). *Latin Catholic* is the proper term for those churches that practice the rite known elsewhere in the world as Roman.

7. The terminology used in the Middle East derives from the intricacies of Christian fissioning over the centuries. I cannot do better than to quote Betts:

Heirs to the New Testament Church of Antioch, the Greek Orthodox communities in the Arab East are those which adhered steadfastly to the political authority of the Byzantine Emperor in Constantinople, and maintained a Greek liturgy though their ethnic stock and mother tongue was Aramaic or Hamitic, and later Arabic. Following the Christological controversies of the 5th century by which Orthodoxy lost the loyalties of most Christians to the south and east of the Cili-

Bethlehemites spoke also of a continuing strong Greek influence in the Greek Orthodox church, clearly manifested by the presence of native Greek priests, nuns, and monks and especially by the fact that until modern times only Greeks served in the higher religious positions, such as bishop. In the late fifteenth and sixteenth centuries — after the Ottoman Sultan Selim I conquered Syria, Palestine, and Egypt — Greek hegemony reached a peak; many Greeks retired to the Holy Land, where they set the tone in both religious and political affairs (Runciman 1968:13). There was also considerable social interaction between the newcomers and Palestinians; several of the surnames now found in the Ephrata region have possibly Greek derivations.[8]

The Orthodox sects differ considerably from the Catholics in their internal organization. They do not recognize the Pope in Rome but owe allegiance to one of many regional patriarchs, one of whom is located in Jerusalem. Their priests may marry, but, if they do so, they are unable to rise in the clerical hierarchy. At various times in the past Armenians and Russians were permitted to proselytize amongst Christians, and the latter, especially, became a leading force in Orthodoxy and other matters. As shown in table 7.1, however,

---

cian Gates, the few remaining faithful were contemptuously referred to by the heterodox masses as "Emperor's men," or Melkites, and survived only where the military arm of Constantinople was strong enough to protect them. So long as the [latter] held firm against first Arab then Turkish invaders, the Melkites remained loyal to the Empire, but after 1453 they transferred their loyalties to the Ottoman Sultan through whom they achieved immense power and influence. (1978:43).

When Turkish hegemony in the east began its decline Orthodoxy looked once again to a sympathetic force, this time . . . to Moscow, whose power [with the Oecumenical Patriarch in Istanbul] . . . became paramount in the 19th century, spreading its influence into Syria and Palestine as well. When Tsarist Russia [along with the Ottoman Empire], collapsed in 1917, the Orthodox of the Arab East turned to the various Pan-Arab movements, since there were no remaining Orthodox Christian powers among the European nations that now dominated the region politically. (1978:45)

8. Banoura lists several, including Abuz'rur, Anastas, Basil, Gattas, Hoch, Nassar, Neno, Saca, and Samur. Of all of them he says, "Greek or Roman, came during Byzantine times" (1981). It is not clear what evidence he has used, either for his determination of their origin or for the time of their first appearance in the area. Although he does not list it, Panayotti (from Baniyot), found in Honduras, is also generally acknowledged to be Greek in origin.

Russian Orthodoxy no longer exists in the area, and the Armenians, both Catholics and Orthodox, have almost died out. Syrian Orthodoxy still has a significant congregation in Bethlehem but not in Beit Jala or Beit Sahur.[9]

Since the nineteenth century there have also been some small groups of Protestants, largely recruited from the Orthodox community. Never very numerous, they are concentrated in Jerusalem and Nazareth, where they have been economically and intellectually important (Tsimhoni 1976:327). Their entry further fractionated the Christian community, although they have not been prominent in local religious power struggles. During the British Mandate period none of the heads of the Christian communities in Palestine, with the exception of the Greek Catholic bishop, was Arab, and, thus, they could not claim political representation comparable to that provided for Muslims and Jews. This definitely worked to the disadvantage of the Christian community in the Muslim-Christian struggle against Zionism (see the discussion below).

The language used in the mass, the order of worship, the method of receiving communion, the baptismal and marriage ceremonies, and, most prominently perhaps, the form of the cross rising above the sanctuary became the primary symbols by which the different churches were identified. Latin was used until the middle of the twentieth century by the Latin Catholics, and Greek was replaced by Arabic among the Greek Orthodox only toward the end of the nineteenth century.[10]

### East versus West

Most important for present purposes has been the division between Eastern and Western rites, which, because of the foreign locations of clerical power and authority in the several cases, has had serious political implications. Control over the various holy sites in Bethlehem, Nazareth, Jerusalem, along the shores of the Sea of Galilee (presently

---

9. Tsimhoni says that, during the Mandate, the British brought Lebanese and Syrian Christians into Palestine as interpreters and advisors (1976:167–68). That may account for the presence today in Bethlehem of Maronites (prominent in Lebanon) and Syrian Catholics.

10. Parts of the service are still conducted in Greek, both in Honduras and in the West Bank.

Lake Tiberias), and other places where Christ was said to have preached or performed miracles has long preoccupied the different Christian religious establishments. Throughout, however, more than religion was at stake in this competition. European commercial interests have long been recognized as having been as important as faith in fueling the Crusades. The Levant was the crossroads of the civilized world; salvation, fortune, and empire were the potential rewards for journeying there, depending upon one's ambitions, station in life, capital investment, and connections. From the mid nineteenth century markets for various industrial products such as textiles, paper, and glass, became another goal (Stillman 1979:4). Thus, the people of Bethlehem and its surroundings were drawn into the web of foreign Christian centers from many lands — Germany, France, Italy, England, and the United States being the most prominent among the westerners and Greece, Armenia, and Russia representing the East. Each nationality built convents and monasteries, many of which became wealthy through the acquisition of land, the sale of agricultural products, tithes exacted from local parishioners, and donations from foreign visitors. In times past, when there were no hotels (or even inns), most of them provided hostels for pilgrims, and even today some of the major tourist accommodations in the cities mentioned are associated with the different churches.[11]

At the same time concern for the welfare of the local worshipers led to the building of schools, clinics, and orphanages in the manner of European charities of the day. During times of actual or threatened violence the local Christians were given shelter in the convents and monasteries, sometimes along with their domestic animals (Spyridon 1938: 32–34, 86). Christians repeatedly avoided becoming involved in the bloodshed by claiming a spiritual proscription against violence, a kind of conscientious objector stance. Not only was this a reason for many to emigrate just before and during World War I, when the Ottomans began drafting Christians, but Tsimhoni has documented

---

11. In Jerusalem I often stayed at the Hostel of Notre Dame, a very large, modern, and comfortable establishment associated with the Franciscans, just outside the gates of the Old City. Inside the Jaffa Gate may be found numerous other accommodations, including many run by different Orthodox, Catholic, and Protestant groups. In Tiberias I stayed at the hospice run by Scottish missionaries of the Presbyterian church. In all of these the rooms are sparsely furnished and the food is plain, but the cost is very slight when compared with hotels.

the fact that Christians were less often involved in violent crimes (1976:259). The several denominations, their leaders mostly ensconced in Jerusalem, had jurisdiction over matters of marriage, divorce, wills, and disputes between coreligionists, the latter being largely left to the secular community of extended family elders, or mukhtars.

The Westerners self-consciously aimed at cultural as well as spiritual "salvation," instilling European tastes in dress, music and literature, diet, standards of cleanliness, housekeeping and decoration, and more fundamental values regarding marriage, the position of women, honor and shame, and sin. Mass in the Latin Catholic church was held in Latin, which preserved its mystery, but schools were taught in whatever European language the attendant monks and nuns preferred, and the curriculum was basically like that taught in the home country (Tsimhoni 1976:34). Even the history of the Holy Land itself was taught from a European perspective.

The Eastern churches, on the other hand, perhaps because Orthodox Christianity had always been an Eastern religion, tended to teach in Arabic and chose curricula that emphasized Middle Eastern culture and heritage. For whatever reason, they always perceived themselves, and were perceived by others, as being closer in spirit to the Muslim majority, if not to the Ottoman rulers. As Tsimhoni has pointed out, many Christians accept much of the Prophet Muhammad's teachings about everyday life and good manners as well as the fact that all Arabs owe much of their history to him, his ideas, and his ability to gather people around him who subsequently carried his message throughout the Middle East (1978a:75). Thus, it was not surprising that by the middle of the nineteenth century many of the more adventuresome Palestinian Orthodox intellectuals, like their brethren in Lebanon and Syria, were seeking closer ties with the rising Arab nationalist leaders—a connection that has persisted and strengthened up to the present time.

In some ways, then, the Christian population stands both together and apart from Muslims, for in spiritual matters it recognizes its common belief in Christ's divinity and uniqueness—that he was god, not merely prophet. In cultural and political matters, the Orthodox sometimes break with their coreligionists who adhere to the Latin, more Western rite.

## Christian Participation in the
## Anti-Zionist Movement

The impact over the centuries of foreign influence upon the local Christian population has been great, and, as I shall argue in the final chapter, the preservation of Christianity for so long in a basically Muslim sociocultural environment can only be understood in relation to the religious and secular—especially commercial, later industrial—forces that have shaped political behavior in the whole of Europe and the Levant since the twelfth century. Both Christians and Jews played an important role in the slow but inexorable Westernization process, which Middle Eastern leaders have sometimes welcomed and encouraged and at other times resisted.

Jews, however, until the end of the nineteenth century, were largely unobtrusive in any institutionalized way; their contributions to the larger polity were as individuals in commerce, banking, and the professions. Their religious leaders, unlike those of the various Christian sects, were more concerned with theology and the maintenance of ritual than with politics. Although their total numbers were small, [12] they lived in many communities throughout the land alongside Muslims and Christians. As Sephardics, they shared a basic Middle Eastern culture with their neighbors of other faiths. Bethlehem had a dozen Jewish families in the twelfth century, described by the pilgrim Benjamin of Tudela as being dyers (Wright 1969:86). This obviously would have been complementary to the spinning, weaving, and embroidering activities for which the town was known but suggests too that there was some ethnic specialization of labor.

During the last few decades of the nineteenth century many small groups of Ashkenazi Jews came to Palestine from various countries in Eastern Europe. In Russia societies of Jews for the colonization of Palestine were formed in the wake of pogroms following the assassination of Tsar Alexander II in 1881 (Kayyali 1978:14). Some

---

12. On the eve of the seventh-century Arab invasion Palestine was almost entirely Orthodox Christian, Jews making up only 10 to 15 percent of the population of perhaps two million. They must have felt some discontent as a minority, however, for they assisted the Sassanid invaders of 614 A.D. causing more destruction than the foreigners (Schick 1987:17, 37, 44). By 1880 there were only about 35,000 Jews in Palestine, constituting roughly 6 percent of its total population of about 590,000 (Garfinkle 1984:9).

tried farming in the north and on the western plains; others settled in the cities, especially Jerusalem, Hebron, Safed, and Tiberias. By 1883 there were twice as many Jews as Christians resident in Jerusalem, and together they made up more than three-quarters of the total population (Conder and Kitchener 1883:162–63). It has often been pointed out that Jews and Christians in Ottoman Palestine occupied similar pariah positions, although the Christians were generally better off because of their individual and institutional connections with European entities that could intercede for them.

Ironically, the growth of Jewish nationalist or Zionist sentiment in Europe coincided with the rise of Arab nationalism in the various provinces of the Ottoman Empire. At first Arab nationalism was strongest in Egypt and among the Christian minorities of French-dominated Lebanon and Syria (Garfinkle 1984:9), most of whom were quite Westernized in life-style and worldview. Although the masses of peasants and less well-educated townsmen in Palestine had not yet awakened to the nationalist fervor (Finn 1868:68; Garfinkle 1984:10; Ma'oz 1982:103), the more educated—especially Christians who were thrown into the same circles as the Lebanese and Syrian Christians—were fully active even before the first Zionist congress was held in 1897. It was members of the Palestinian Christian community who in June 1891 organized the first Arab protest against Jewish immigration (Tsimhoni 1976:202). By the last decade of the nineteenth century both Jews and Arabs had developed a passionate desire for a homeland; unfortunately, both set their sights on the same territory, with the tragic results we see today.

Many have speculated as to the reasons for such early Christian leadership in the anti-Zionist movement. Some have pointed out that Christian-Jewish relations were always worse than between either group and the local Muslims, perhaps because of Christian sensitivity to the Jewish role in the death of Christ. At the same time, because Jews and Christians shared an economic niche, Christians might well have feared greater competition with the immigration of more Jews. For similar reasons, it has been argued, Christians had long campaigned against land sales to foreign Jews, especially in the north, which was the only part of Palestine where Christians owned large tracts of land (Tsimhoni 1976:35–36). As landowners, contractors, and agents, they were often involved in direct confrontation with Jewish associations wishing to purchase land. However, most of the alienated territory belonged to expatriate Muslim Palestinians resident in Europe (Tsimhoni 1978a:80).

It has also been suggested that Christians, because of their association with Europeans, were more anti-Semitic than were Muslims. The same association, of course, might have made them more aware and fearful of the freely expressed intentions of the Zionist leaders. The British chief administrator in Palestine reported to his foreign office in August 1919: "The great fear of the people is that once Zionist wealth is passed into the land, all territorial and mineral concessions will fall into the hands of the Jews whose intensely clannish instincts prohibit them from dealing with any but those of their own religion, to the detriment of Moslems and Christians. These latter, the natives of the soil, foresee their eventual banishment from the land"[13] The King-Crane Commission, headed by the president of Oberlin College and a Chicago industrialist, also warned of the Zionist threat and recommended the formation of a united Syrian nation composed of Palestine, Syria, and Lebanon, with freedom of religion for all citizens, including Jews (King-Crane 1922).

By the end of World War I and the defeat of the Ottoman Empire Palestinian Muslims and Christians had joined forces to combat the growing specter that seemed to have been given substance by the Balfour Declaration of November 1917. This document, in effect, promised that England would aid and abet the establishment of a homeland for Jews in Palestine. Although well-meaning—it specifically noted that this should not dislodge or disinherit the non-Jewish inhabitants of the region—little thought was given to how both intentions might be accomplished in actuality, and most Palestinians today look upon the document as the death warrant for their people and their land. The *Husayn-McMahon Correspondence* of 1916 outlined British commitments to the Arab Palestinians but failed to provide a specific policy for carrying them out (Hourani 1991:316). Into that vacuum flowed what became an uncontrollable tide of Jewish immigration during and after World War II.

By 1918 not only were Christians largely town or city dwellers and better educated than many of their Muslim brethren, but also the majority of the newspapers were owned and edited by Christians

---

13. PRO.FO 371/4171, quoted in Ingrams 1972:81.

(Lesch 1979c:29; Tsimhoni 1978a:78). Thus, they were intellectually and practically better prepared than the Muslims to mount a campaign both at home and abroad. Also, the British authorities favored the Christians, not necessarily because of their religion but because they more often spoke European languages and generally seemed more Western than the Muslims.[14] Christians published books and pamphlets presenting the Arab case in English, French, and Arabic; they were in a position to appeal to the pope, to the archbishop of Canterbury, and to other influential Christians around the world.

By 1921 there were Muslim-Christian political action associations established in all of the main urban centers, and Muslims had taken the lead in efforts to stop Jewish immigration. In fact, the Palestinian-Arab national movement came to be dominated by the large and leading Muslim families. Since Christians did not have a part in this establishment, it became increasingly difficult for them to exert political leadership. Furthermore, as the perceived danger and the protests became more general among the Arab population, much of the anger was directed against the Mandate and Christian-European imperialism. This must have presented a dilemma for many Christians. As we have seen, Christians were employed disproportionately by the occupation forces, and for the most part were more favorably disposed toward the Mandate than were Muslims. Yet, as time went on, many of them, especially the Greek Orthodox, joined the Muslims in attacking the British. In one sense this was consistent with the long-standing internal rift between Christian Greeks and Latins — the former being on generally better terms with the ruling Muslim establishment. Again, East versus West, or Orthodoxy versus Catholicism, became a prime issue, with the Latins considered hopelessly Western and foreign in their ideas and culture.

Ironically, despite the political and philosophical differences between them and in accordance with Muslim suspicions, there is no concrete evidence that the British favored Catholics over the Orthodox. The Mandate recognized three millets — Christians, Jews, and Muslims — and tried, with only moderate success, to strengthen intra-

---

14. Betts notes, however, that Arab Anglicans are almost exclusively Palestinian and probably the best-educated and most highly Westernized Arab community. Many of them have long been transnationals, with homes and businesses or professions in London as well as in Palestine (1978:214).

communal ties, although in some matters, such as the granting of religious holidays, the authorities finally had to make separate arrangements for the Eastern and Western Christian churches (Tsimhoni 1976:141). Over all, however, the British seem to have perceived a greater kinship between themselves and Christians of either persuasion, all being seen as more European than were the Muslims, or more Christian than Arab.

## Palestinian Christianity in Honduras

The earliest immigrants to Honduras probably included both Muslims and Christians, the latter being divided between Orthodox of one or another persuasion and Catholicism. The record is not entirely clear, but it suggests that the Muslims either left the country for parts unknown or converted to Roman Catholicism, as practiced in the New World. As discussed in chapter 5, many Christians, regardless of their religious membership in Palestine, accepted the local Catholic church in Honduras from the beginning of their residence there. Many of the Orthodox, however, preferred to wait for a visiting Orthodox priest or to return to the Holy Land for occasions such as marriage and baptism. Presumably, attendance at mass was not a primary value (as, in fact, it seems not to be even now).

Given the apparent strength of the Orthodox religious commitment, it might seem odd that no Orthodox church was established in Central America until 1963. The explanation, it seems to me, must take into account the creation of the state of Israel and subsequent changes in the migration strategies of those already in the New World as well as of newcomers.

In the first place the number of Greek Orthodox present in Honduras before the 1960s may not have reached a size sufficient to support a priest and a church building with suitable accoutrements and decorations. As we have seen in chapter 6, the earliest immigrants were largely from Bethlehem, which was predominantly Latin Catholic. Since in financial matters each Orthodox congregation is autonomous, there was no central organization to which they might turn for other than spiritual and organizational help. The first resident Orthodox priest in San Pedro was, in fact, a Lebanese-American who was sent out by the patriarchate of St. Louis, Missouri. He, along with several prominent local Palestinian-Honduran men, is given credit for the successful establishment of what is now clearly a permanent church. I find no consistent patterns among either the founders or those active today in relation to origin. All three of Ephrata's towns are represented, and some members are of families that were Latin Catholic at home. I am inclined to believe that the impetus for many was to create an identifiable Middle Eastern or Arab presence in Honduras — a celebration of their Palestinian ethnicity. But it could not have been a success without the larger number of Palestinian emigrants who arrived after 1948. Newcomers to Central America, and bitter about their recent experiences in Palestine, these immigrants needed a place to congregate and share reminiscences, to speak Arabic, to plan their lives, either in the diaspora or, as many hoped, in a new Palestine.

It seems also likely that for many of those who had arrived before 1948, the possibility of return was increasingly remote, and, as they contemplated permanent residence in Honduras, they might have been comforted by the thought of having a church of their own. The Roman Catholic church in Honduras serves all who seek it, and, although its form is slightly different from that in Bethlehem, it is clearly identifiable by Catholics from any part of the world.

The San Pedro Sula Orthodox church has the form and decoration of similar churches in the Middle East. Icons and hanging lamps adorn the sacristy and the doors separating it from the congregation, while paintings of scenes from the Old and New Testaments adorn the side walls. Even the dome-shaped ceiling is decorated with Middle Eastern motifs.[15] The priest's garments and the cross he holds out for the parishioners to kiss as they leave after mass are of Eastern design. The Julian calendar is in use, and it differs significantly from the Gregorian calendar used by other Christians; Easter, for example, is generally celebrated a week later than among Catholics in both Bethlehem and in Honduras. Finally, the mass is still partially recited in Arabic, with occasional phrases in Greek. As the local parish priest told me, "You cannot really appreciate the Orthodox mass without understanding Arabic." No doubt Greek priests would say the same

---

15. Construction of the church took two years. At the end they brought from Egypt a well-known painter, Jacobo Fanous, brother of one of the founders, to paint the ceiling and the partitions dividing the altar from the congregation. While there, he also did some painting in the San Pedro Roman Catholic cathedral.

about their own language. Although some of his parishioners beg him to conduct mass entirely in Spanish, he refuses, although he is perfectly fluent in that language, having been born in Chile. He continues to hold an Arabic mass at eight A.M. on Sundays, but it is rarely attended except by a few visitors from "over there" and the one or two elderly men who assist in the prayers and chants.

The regular mass, held at ten A.M., is treated quite casually by most of those who attend, in part, perhaps, because they do not fully understand the Greek and Arabic. People come in late, move noisily to their seats as they greet and kiss relatives and friends, chat among themselves throughout, and often leave early. Children run around freely, sometimes even attempting to enter the sacred space behind the lectern. The priest on occasion must admonish the altar boys not to whisper so much among themselves during the service. He insisted that this casualness must be a Honduran custom, since, he said, the Orthodox congregations do not behave that way in either Chile or in Palestine. In Bethlehem, however, I observed similar patterns, which differed considerably from the more solemn, traditional, and isolated Orthodox masses I attended in Al-Husn and Irbid, Jordan.

Each Orthodox church is run by its members, who elect a board of directors, called the "Grey," to serve it each year. These men, traditionally thirteen in number, with the help of the women's and young peoples' clubs, maintain the physical plant and religious paraphernalia, arrange special decorations for holy days, collect and manage dues and contributions, sponsor various social events, select the priest and monitor his behavior, and even make decisions concerning moral issues involving members.[16]

The Orthodox church in San Pedro Sula also involves itself in certain secular affairs and has taken a strong stance on behalf of an independent Palestine. In the salon attached to the church — where regular coffee hours following mass, wedding receptions, church dinners, and the like are held — there is a large map dating from pre-1948 times labeled "Palestine." Meetings to raise money for Palestinian refugees, to hold masses in honor of martyrs of the intifada, or to place advertisements in the local newspapers on behalf of the Palestinian

---

16. They refused, for example, a special dispensation requested by a divorced man who wished to marry again within the church. The petitioner ended by going to Mexico to seek a more lenient Orthodox congregation.

cause are often held at the church. The amount of time and money Palestinian Hondurans are willing to spend on such activities varies greatly. A few, like those of FEARAB, labeled "fanatics" by some of the less committed, make it a priority. Most of these are either recent immigrants or those who have maintained property and kin ties in their hometowns in Ephrata.

But even those who are not activists feel strongly about the present situation on the West Bank. As mentioned previously, one octogenarian, who had lived in Honduras since his early youth, had a heart attack and died while watching a television newscast showing violence in Bethlehem. Almost all will speak up both privately and publicly on behalf of Palestinians and in opposition to "Jews."[17] With every crisis between Arabs and Jews in Israel and the occupied territories, new emigrants arrive in Honduras, where their stories are avidly sought and repeated throughout the Palestinian community, both in San Pedro and elsewhere in the country. Those with relatives in Ephrata make regular phone calls to check on their safety and that of friends. Sometimes they are unable to get through because the lines have been temporarily blocked by Israeli authorities; secret numbers allegedly immune to this problem are carefully shared among friends.

So far, however, neither the Orthodox church nor its members has been effective in creating any awareness of the possibility of Arab-Honduran power or influence in the national politics of Honduras. Those "Turcos" who have exerted influence do it behind the scenes, primarily by contributing large amounts of money to the campaigns of all the likely candidates. There is no evidence, however, that any of these have been able to move the government to take stands favoring Arabs in any of the Middle Eastern crises of recent years, beginning with the original Partition and creation of the state of Israel.

To the contrary, among the wealthiest and most socially prominent Palestinian-Hondurans — most of them second- or third-generation citizens — the whole subject of Palestine seems increasingly embarrassing. Whatever they may say among themselves, it is not

---

17. Most Palestinian-Hondurans tend to lump all Jews together and fail to distinguish between Israel as a nationality and Judaism as a religion or an ethnic heritage. Some have gone so far as to cast aspersions on old Honduran families who they believe were *"conversos,"*—i.e., Jews who converted to Catholicism during the Inquisition. One woman told me that she believed Palestinians were looked down upon in Honduras because most of the original Spanish Hondurans were really Jews!

otherwise voiced, as they avoid taking public stands. Moreover, their financial contributions to the cause are a mere pittance in relation to the amounts they spend on their own homes, businesses, vacations, and general life styles. Most no longer have close relatives in Palestine, and their visits have been more in the form of excursions to an interesting place than a sentimental journey "home."

The participation of this class of Honduran Palestinians in the Orthodox church is very slight, although many of them support it financially, and some were among its founders. Most of them have, in fact, aligned themselves with the local Catholics, and in the past few years they have built a small chapel in the expensive suburban neighborhood many of them inhabit. According to the local Catholic priest who gives mass there each Sunday at five P.M., 95 percent of the parishioners are Palestinian. In this way they have succeeded in creating a smaller, more exclusive Catholic Arab church, thus achieving some of the communal benefits enjoyed by the Orthodox but in a more acculturated setting. This group does not identify, however, with the Latin Catholics of Bethlehem, who increasingly have set aside old barriers to intercommunal communication and are working as one with other sects to counter the Israeli presence in the West Bank and in Gaza. Their "Palestinianness" is more related to their own need to preserve and improve the lot of their immediate families in Honduras, in what many still feel is an essentially hostile foreign environment. I am reminded of Schick's description of what may have been neighborhood or family chapels in many of the early Christian villages in the Jordan Valley. One does not see visible evidence that this "Arab" church differs from other Catholic churches in Honduras. The Roman Catholic church in America has had a long-standing practice of permitting, even fostering, ethnic parishes, an accommodation that nevertheless creates few outward, or physical, symbols of their special character (Liptak 1987). An archaeologist might very likely miss the ethnic component in such sanctuaries, since it is obvious only in the membership, the language spoken, the music, and some of the social activities requiring group action.

The establishment of the Orthodox church in San Pedro Sula as well as the building of the Catholic chapel described above seem to me to be political as well as religious statements.[18] The former is directly

---

18. In San Pedro they do not use the modifier, *Greek*, but refer to their church simply as Orthodox. This usage is consistent with that in other parts of America and reflects a tendency

related to the happenings in the occupied West Bank and to the frustration felt by many Arab Hondurans in their adopted country. The latter seems to be simultaneously an effort to preserve a semblance of Arab ethnic separateness at the same time that it rejects the foreign atmosphere of the very Eastern Orthodox sanctuary, rite, and community. The final chapter will deal with the question of Palestinian ethnicity in both Palestine and in Honduras and will consider the options open to both recent and earlier immigrants for improving their lot as well as the probability of their adopting any one of them.

---

toward ecumenicalism. Furthermore, since it is the only Orthodox church in all of Central America, there seems little point in emphasizing a by now forgotten and long unpopular Greek connection.

# Chapter 8
# Ethnicity, Nationhood, and Citizenship

The decision to partition Palestine by creating the Jewish State is one of the most serious mistakes in contemporary politics. The most surprising consequences are going to result from an apparently small thing. Nor is it offensive to reason to state that this small thing will have its part to play in shaking the world to its foundations.

— anonymous French journalist, 1947

## Ethnic Pride and Prejudice

In this chapter I will try to compare the West Bank and Honduran situations in several dimensions. I will argue that the two are, for better or for worse, bound together by their past, but perhaps even more importantly by contemporary world events and attitudes that have resulted from the Partition.

In the West Bank Christian Palestinians suffer prejudice from two sources — their Israeli occupiers and their Muslim brethren. The first has been well documented, both in journalistic and scholarly publications. The second is less well known. Although the official stance of the PLO is separation of religious and civil hierarchies, there is a good bit of evidence that Christians will not be accorded full and equal status in any future Palestinian state, which will inevitably be Muslim, Middle Eastern, and in opposition to European and American Western ideas and culture.

The evidence for my conclusion is anecdotal, as, of course, it must be. In conversation with a prominent Palestinian scholar-politician in Jerusalem, I asked him what qualities would make for an effective local Palestinian leader. Somewhat to my surprise, since he was aware of the focus of my research, he began by stating emphatically that "he" must be Muslim. Following this, the leader must also

---

*Epigraph:* Chiha 1969:frontispiece, quoting a French journalist's 1947 remarks.

be of a respectable family, have contacts with significant institutions in the larger world through which capital may be raised, and have proved himself individually as a responsible person.

When I asked why the Christian Palestinians should even consider returning to such a state, even if it were officially "secular," he replied that in order to placate them, "one nice clean Christian" would be found and placed in a prominent cabinet-level position. It was his opinion that the Christians would return, nevertheless, primarily to protect their investments but also because of a continuing and growing sense of Palestinian ethnicity, which, in his opinion, would override religious loyalties.

Prejudice against Christians is not officially condoned in any Middle Eastern country today, although most of the Muslim states make it difficult for them to worship, and in some countries, such as Saudi Arabia, they may not do so publicly. Even where formal church structures and worship are permitted,[1] as in Jordan, the national calendric rhythms, as well as expectations concerning "proper" public and private behavior, are based upon the Islamic religious calendar, rites, and codes. Bailey (1966:111) noted that Jordanian army officers were evaluated in part on how often they prayed, it being assumed that religiosity was an essential gauge of loyalty and an indication of a man's susceptibility to radical, often materialistic doctrines.

My observations in Jordan confirmed the Palestinian Christian view that Jordan makes it difficult for Christians. In 1985, in an unusual kind of "hate crime," five dogs were found hung on tombs in the Christian cemetery at Irbid, Jordan's second largest city (Day 1986:66). During my stay in 1988 I rescued a Greek woman stranded at the Jordanian border while seeking to visit her uncle, the bishop of the Greek Orthodox church in Irbid. Since I had not lived there for long, I was not familiar with its location, and we spent five hours trying to locate what turned out to be a large and impressive sanctuary. No one with whom we spoke on the streets could or would tell us where it was.

In Al-Husn, a predominantly Christian town only ten minutes from Irbid, the people told me that to be a Christian was becoming

---

1. Christians are free to practice their rituals, but Jews are not. I am not aware of other organized religions in Jordan.

more and more difficult, despite the immigration of thousands of Christian Palestinians from Israel and the West Bank in recent years. By 1961 Amman had 42,800 Christians, most of them immigrants from Jerusalem and other West Bank towns and cities. The 1967 war brought a second wave of Christian immigration, although smaller than the earlier one. Indeed, Amman became the largest Christian center in the combined West Bank / Jordanian area (Tsimhoni 1983: 57).

Still, emigration to Europe or America was the primary hope for many of the young (and not-so-young) people of Al-Husn. As in Bethlehem, nearly every family had relatives abroad. It is stories like these, as well as a perusal of the statistics showing a steady decline in the number of Christians in the West Bank area and a review of events in Lebanon and Israel, that lead me to question whether a truly secular state is possible in the Middle East at this time. The force of Islam there, like that of Christianity in Europe and America, is likely to dominate, even when formal separation of civil and religious functions is declared.

As economic and political conditions worsen in the Middle East generally and in the West Bank in particular, it seems likely that more and more Palestinians will emigrate, and many of those with connections in Honduras will seek refuge there. As the community in Honduras grows larger, prejudices against them, especially against the newcomers, will increase. Old jealousies, deriving from ethnocentric attitudes of Hondurans forged over a hundred-year period, will be reawakened.[2]

In addition to envying Arab economic success many Hondurans today express other fears — groundless in my opinion — concerning the possible role of Palestinian-Hondurans in the Middle Eastern conflict. These have been generated by stories in the local and United States press about international Palestinian terrorism and the supposed monetary and moral support of the PLO by Palestinians, wherever they may live, as well as by at least one specific incident in 1985

---

2. The Arab merchant in America has been portrayed several times in literary accounts. The attitude has ranged from the extremely vituperative hatred expressed in Jamaica Kincaid's *A Small Place* (1988:58, 62–65) through the harmless but clownish peddler in Rogers and Hammerstein's *Oklahoma* to the peaceful and misunderstood, yet *simpático*, hero in Jorge Amado's *Gabriela, Cloves and Cinnamon* (1962).

in which terrorists were captured carrying Honduran passports.[3] The details of this have never been fully revealed, so, naturally, rumors and speculations abound. Because the Honduran army has several Palestinian Hondurans in its officers' corps, some have thought that perhaps some or one of them had exercised influence in obtaining unauthorized passports, either out of a sense of Palestinian loyalty or for money. It is also possible that some ordinary citizens or residents may have managed such a fraud, since the illegal immigration of Hondurans to the United States has spawned numerous counterfeiting enterprises in the country.

The matter is complicated by the fact that the majority of Palestinians Hondurans do feel considerable sympathy for the PLO, if not for its more violent wing. The more acculturated, longer-term residents and citizens, however, find themselves in a terrible dilemma, for they are torn between a desire to see their compatriots achieve a dignified and secure resolution to their disfranchisement in the Middle East and their personal aspirations to become first-class citizens of the Latin American nation many of them now call home. The more deeply they have invested in Central America — in terms of property ownership, capital expenditures, social connections, linguistic and other cultural affiliations — the more they are tempted to draw away from the newer Arab arrivals and their cause.

There is also an interesting reversal of perspective regarding the respective levels of economic development and "modernization" in Honduras and Ephrata. Throughout the first half of this century most Palestinians considered Honduras a backwater in comparison with what they had left behind. Now, however, those born in Honduras — and also some of the newcomers — think of Palestine as being far more "primitive." The new perception is fed by unflattering television views of Bethlehem and East Jerusalem during the intifada and by the somewhat scruffy appearance of visitors and new immigrants as well as by the latters' tales of privations and frustrations at home.

Interestingly, the new mindset has also resulted in a reinterpretation of history. One young man told me that his grandfather had

---

3. Although this incident was said to have received attention in the international press in the early 1980s, I have been unable to locate any such account in the *New York Times*. It is, however, still a vivid and painful memory for Hondurans from all walks of life, including some Palestinians.

"modernized" his wife by bringing her here at the turn of the century via Paris, where he outfitted her in the latest European fashion in preparation for the journey to "America." My friend's tone and laughing manner suggested that he believed Honduras to have been the more "advanced" society, even at that time, and that his grandfather's effort had been aimed at "making a splash" in Honduras. Yet, this account is directly contrary to the way his parents and grandparents remembered it. For their generation, traveling to Paris or other European capitals had been a commonplace life experience even if they themselves had never made the trip. Most Christian Palestinian women were wearing Western dress long before they arrived in Honduras. It seems to have become fashionable to do so about the turn of the century, and the British Mandate furthered the adoption of styles worn in the West. Today in the West Bank, Muslim villagers and the poorer townswomen — as often seen on television — still wear veils, facial and hand tatoos, and long, embroidered gowns, but their Christian counterparts do not. Family photographs a generation old in West Bank Christian homes do occasionally show an ancestor in traditional dress, but questioning often reveals that the clothing was ceremonial, donned for a special occasion, if not for the photograph itself.

The major point here, I believe, involves the same concept introduced in chapter 7 — East versus West. I make this statement mindful of the many historically determined cultural similarities that join Spain (for some eight hundred years a meeting ground, if not melting pot, for European and Arabic thought and style) with both Latin America and the Middle East. Ironically, however, at least one Latin American of Palestinian descent has suggested that pejorative attitudes toward Arabs in Latin America may be laid to the "traditional Latin American and Spanish disdain" for Arabs and Moors (Abugattas 1982:123). Said (1978) has cautioned us not to rely solely upon Western European definitions and configurations of Eastern cultures as though they represented a transcendental truth about "Orientals," and there is some reason to be cautious of the same fallacy in relation to Latin America as that has been defined by adventurers, travelers, and scholars from the United States and elsewhere who call themselves "Latin Americanists."[4] Here we would appear to be faced

---

4. Examples of this abound from throughout the nineteenth century, especially after the independence movements opened up the former Spanish colonies to outside observers. Expec-

with a double dose of such thinking: the alleged Spanish view of the Orient and the Arab view of Latin America. Lest I be chastised by anthropological colleagues, I hasten to add that most of them have resisted such tendencies in their own work and countered them when they discover them in that of others.[5] As Lila Abu-Lughod has pointed out in regard to anthropological studies of the Middle East (1989:273), we tend to construct dichotomies different from those of historians, political scientists, and other academics in explaining what we see or think we see. In relation to the present study I have struggled with the following: Christian versus Muslim; Orthodox versus Catholic; West versus East; Honduran versus Palestinian; native-born versus immigrant; modern versus traditional. All of them break down at one or another point in the analysis, and the categories do not coalesce nor permit compression into merely two.

Having said this, I still maintain that there are distinctions, some subtle but with profound implications for behavior, between Christian and Muslim Palestinians and that, on a continuum between the two, Greek Orthodox Christians are closer to the Muslims than are the Catholics. I further suggest that in Honduras this distinction overrides all the others but tends to coincide with social class on the one hand and acculturation to the Latin American milieu on the other.

### Diverging Life-Styles

In support of my view it will be useful to suggest some points where I see more acculturated Palestinian-Hondurans (regardless of the length of time they have been in America) having diverged from many of the cultural patterns of their ancestors and of present-day residents of Ephrata.

---

tations on the part of the United States and several European countries of forming hegemonic linkages between themselves and the new republics led to descriptions of the "peoples and cultures" of the latter in terms that would make them understandable and, presumably, more accessible. That these descriptions were not necessarily recognizable to the inhabitants of these countries themselves has seldom been discussed. The issue has been treated by Martínez Peláez (1985) for Guatemala, but, ironically, as a Ladino, he has been accused of "creating" a local American Indian culture from his own, rather than their, perspective.

5. Too few anthropologists have studied Arabs in the Americas, except for those in the United States (Abraham and Abraham 1983; Abu-Laban and Zeadey 1975; Aswad 1974) and Canada (Abu-Laban 1980).

*Honduras*

Acculturated Palestinian-Hondurans are thoroughly materialistic and consumer-oriented in their outlook on life. Status is achieved through education, the accumulation of wealth, and conspicuous consumption. Spanish is their primary language, and most of those born in Honduras speak no Arabic or know only a few phrases. They name their children in Honduran style, with two "Christian" names, followed by the patronymic and then the matronymic. The second of the Christian names may or may not be the same as that of the father.

Social class supersedes ethnicity as a determinant of personal interactions outside the family. These new Americans reject arranged marriages, and, although they are still mindful of their families' concerns, increasingly they marry non-Arabs. Formal property transfers at the time of the engagement are no longer customary, although the two sets of parents, depending upon their resources, are expected to give large gifts, including automobiles, houses, and furniture to the couple (assuming, of course, they approve of the union). The young couple's names may be added to the list of stockholders or directors of companies owned by the parents, and the man may be given a more elevated position in the operation of the business.

Although there has been considerable branching out beyond merchandizing and manufacturing, these are still the primary economic activities of Palestinian Hondurans. Professions such as medicine, pharmacy, and engineering, however, have drawn many, and a few have found careers in the armed forces. Yet none in Honduras so far have entered law or the academy. It is difficult to explain the latter, but I suggest it is related to the strength of familial direction in choosing careers and to the low status of university life in Honduras in general. Although scholars are accorded respect in Latin America, they usually rely on family wealth or live in genteel poverty — a luxury for which the immigrant Palestinians have so far not felt themselves ready.[6] The practice of law is also risky in a host society like Honduras, for much of one's success must depend upon effective network-

---

6. Guatemala boasts an important painter named Rodolfo Abularach, descendant of the first Palestinian family to achieve some prominence in the import-export trade of that country.

ing in the larger society. Members of a pariah group would, by definition, have a difficult time in that regard.[7]

Both men and women are fond of dressing and decorating their
homes in the latest fashions, most of which are dictated by what they
see on television and in magazines from the United States, Mexico,
or South America. Extensive socializing within the extended family
is the most prevalent form of entertainment. Weekend and holiday
get-togethers include as many as possible of the local patrilineal kin,
and there is considerable mutual aid among family members. Daily
phone calls between grown sons and daughters and their mothers are
common. In this, Honduran custom is not significantly different from
that in the West Bank.

In their religious behavior Palestinian Hondurans seem neither
more nor less observant than their Old World counterparts, being
careful to attend mass, receive the sacraments as appropriate, and
help maintain the church and its clerics. Their faith seems more a social than a spiritual matter, although there is a fundamental belief in
the truth of Christianity. Some men and women, especially at middle
age, become excessively devout. This may be expressed in public
demonstrations of their piety during the mass;[8] others form prayer
and study groups that meet at private homes, most of which derive
from Catholic fundamentalist thinking, as described in chapter 7.
There is a considerable amount of social prestige connected with sing-
ing in the choir, participating in the ceremony of the mass, and serving on a church committee or as an officer in one of the social clubs
associated with it.

In their turn Palestinian Hondurans are also prejudiced against
persons practicing other religions, although, since they are now living
in a country that is overwhelmingly Christian and Catholic, they do
not feel threatened by the few dissident or non-Christian elements in
their midst. Until recently, even after the establishment of the Israeli

---

7. I was told during the fieldwork in 1988 that there was one man studying for the bar
at that time. This fits in with my other observations concerning the changing status of many
Palestinian Hondurans today. As they commit themselves more and more to Honduras and as
they become more acceptable to other Hondurans, they can be expected to move in many new
directions.

8. In the Orthodox church some worshippers may leave their seats and approach the
priest during prayers and invocations, kneeling before him and covering their heads with the
ceremonial vestment.

state, there has been a comfortable accommodation between Hondurans of Palestinian and Jewish origin. The similarities in their business practices, as well as their common origin in the Middle East, seem to have overcome any rancor that might have been associated with ideological differences. That situation has been reversed now and seems to be directly related to the intifada, especially as that is portrayed in international newscasts.

Muslims are still rare in Honduras, although there seem to be more in recent years than formerly. Such a statement is difficult to document, for written records are nonexistent, but collaborators say that some of the surnames on my list that do not derive from Ephrata "must" be Muslim. In time I came to realize that this was only one possible answer they might have given me in designating the Arab "Other." Some attributed "foreign" (i.e., those with which they were unfamiliar) names to an origin in Ramallah or Nazareth; others cast them even farther from themselves by asserting Syrian, Lebanese, even Egyptian linkages. Whatever they were, they were not from Ephrata, and that made them "different."[9]

For the most part Honduran-born Arabs are secular in their definitions of the state and the origins of the universe and in their explanations of human behavior, although a certain amount of magical thinking still occurs, as is the case in most "modern" nations, even among quite well-educated persons. Women, even teenagers, are permitted considerable freedom of movement, although most parents do try to prevent their daughters from staying out too late and endeavor to instill in them strict moral codes concerning sex and drugs.[10] There is, nevertheless, considerable experimentation with both.

*The West Bank*

In the West Bank there is a continuing reliance upon the immediate and larger family in social intercourse, and marriages are still primarily arranged by parents and grandparents without much, if any, ob-

---

9. A Muslim Palestinian-Israeli from the Galilee area with whom I worked in Maryland failed to recognize as "Palestinian" several of the surnames common, even today, in Bethlehem, Beit Jala, and Beit Sahur.

10. One father, infuriated because his daughter disobeyed him and accompanied a group of young people to an out-of-town party, located the young man with whom she had ridden and beat him savagely, leaving him seriously injured.

jection on the part of the young people. Property transfers are mutually agreed upon by the families and consist at least partially of moveable wealth, such as gold jewelry. Children are given an Arabic "Christian"[11] name, followed by the first name of his or her father, and today by the father's patronymic. The mother's surname is dropped entirely.[12]

Although trade is still an important and prestigious profession for West Bankers, there is a wide variety of "callings" among them. Table 3.3 shows Bethlehem's industrial profile in 1979, suggesting the kinds of skilled and unskilled labor opportunities there at that time. It should be kept in mind that, although many of the workers in these enterprises were immigrant Muslims, most of the owners and managers were Christians.

Large numbers of Bethlehemites who have traveled abroad have come home with higher degrees in disciplines such as political science, sociology, Islamic history, Arabic literature, English, computer science, accounting, medicine, and more. They have found employment as teachers and professors, as well as in private practice. There is considerable intellectual life in Bethlehem, which early in this century spawned several literary clubs and publications (Musallam 1984:18); in the past as well as at present politics lay at the heart of much of their philosophical debate, and most of their literary products have had social protest as a theme.[13]

Like Hondurans, West Bank Palestinians like to live well, but their expectations in that regard are quite different from those of their counterparts in the New World. It is, of course, difficult to measure or evaluate differences in consumption, and it is also the case that the West Bank has seen steady economic decline since 1948, with severe deterioration over the past five years under the intifada. Clothing, automobiles, and household furnishings are modest, even for those who are reasonably well off. Some live in older houses that might once

---

11. Although most surnames are shared across religious communities, given names tend to differ. For example, Muslims frequently name their children after Muhammad or one of his relatives or followers, while Christians avoid these, choosing either biblical or, sometimes, European names. There are, of course exceptions—"Fuad" being popular among both groups, for example.

12. Since cousin marriage is still very common, however, it frequently happens that the mother's surname is the same as that of her husband anyway.

13. Personal communication, Dr. Qustandi Shomali, professor of Arabic Literature, Bethlehem University.

have been termed sumptuous but which are now slightly rundown and in need of repair. These may contain period furnishings of exceptional quality, mostly European, Syrian, or Iranian in origin. Among the newer homes, a few, especially in Beit Sahur, are spacious but furnished with modern items, mostly of lower quality and made either in Israel or the West Bank itself. There may be a mixture of hand-me-downs, heirlooms, and recent acquisitions among the furnishings.

A primary difference is that in the West Bank the homes may house several nuclear families — sons are still expected to bring their wives to live with their parents immediately after marriage. The relationship between women and their daughters-in-law gradually eases into one of comfortable interaction and, eventually, considerable affection. Because the marriages are arranged, the in-marrying women are likely to be known to and perhaps related to their in-laws in some way, and this may also help ease the tensions created by the new living arrangements. As each new family grows, they may build a separate home on an adjoining lot if such may be acquired, or the original plot may be subdivided if it is sufficiently large. In Bethlehem and Beit Jala this is less likely, for both of those towns have nearly reached their limit in use of space, but in Beit Sahur it is common.

These subtle differences in the way different Palestinians perceive and exploit the two social environments seem to me to correspond to the degree of their Westernization and, inevitably, to their aspirations for their own futures. What passes for "civilization" is a relative matter, reflecting what one is used to and the life to which one aspires. Honduras still looks "backward" to many Arab newcomers today, just as the West Bank strikes many Honduran-born Palestinians as quaint and underdeveloped. Probably more objective eyes might have thought them not too different from each other, either at the turn of the century or today. Hamilton's theoretical model would neatly categorize the two views in terms of temporary versus permanent migration strategies (1985), but that would appear to be tautological in that we have no independent criteria by which to judge intentions. I have sometimes contrasted "newcomers" with "oldtimers," but that is not really satisfactory either, since many of the less Westernized have been in Honduras for many years, while some new arrivals fit nicely into the Honduran life-style almost immediately. Many of the latter have invested heavily in the commercial and industrial world of Honduras and often of the United States as well.

It does seem true that those born in Honduras, even when they have spent some time visiting in Ephrata during their lifetimes, are rarely interested in a permanent return. In this sense they are really no longer members of a diaspora as I have defined it in chapter 2. Their preferences are often in stark contrast to those of their parents, who may have migrated to Honduras during their own youth yet still dream of returning "home."

We would appear to have here a classic situation or profile of acculturation, wherein some immigrants, provoked by the desire for financial success and economic assimilation, have chosen to shed some (not all) of their earlier customs and values. Sometimes it is not obvious to them when they reach the point where the old and the new are incompatible. Those born in the new country will have been exposed to foreign ways as a matter of course, and, unless their parents work hard to socialize them as bicultural beings, they may come to disregard or devalue their ancestral culture. Language and religion do seem to be important mechanisms keeping cultural traditions alive. When these are not stressed, as has been the case in Honduras, only the more superficial symbols remain.

It is my view that most native-born Palestinian Hondurans, like their brethren elsewhere in Central America, would prefer to blend in with other Honduran middle-class professionals and bourgeoisie, even when they retain a sense of pride in their origin. Abugattas makes a similar comment in regard to Arabs in Peru, saying that most immigrants have not tried to educate their neighbors in that country regarding Palestine but, instead, have themselves wanted to assimilate (1982:118). In this, Palestinians in both countries would join other "native" Hondurans or Peruvians who identify their ancestors as American Indians, Germans, Spanish, Japanese, Chinese, or what have you.

The conflict between Israel and the West Bank (which in Honduras outweighs that between Jew and Palestinian) has been a magnet for drawing together all those with Arabic surnames. Their sense of Palestinian ethnicity has been enhanced, even when the details of what that might mean are unclear. And therein lies the major problem: The continuing immigration directly from Palestine keeps alive in Honduras an image of the *Oriental* Arab. That figure, like something out of *The Arabian Nights,* is one that many of those born in Honduras would have preferred to forget or, at least, to laughingly push into their past. Their knowledge of Arabic is rudimentary at best; they know little of Middle Eastern ancient or modern history and even less of its culture and literature. Their schooling is in America, by Americans, and it emphasizes the New World.

In contrast, not only do many of the newcomers prefer to speak in Arabic, even in public, but their presentation of self is more direct, more impassioned or emotional when aroused, less superficially polite in Central American fashion,[14] more likely (as was the case for their parents and grandparents) to rely on superstitions to explain the world around them, and more likely to draw boundaries around themselves, shutting out the non-Arab Hondurans. Their fierce rejection of Jews everywhere and their impassioned defense of the Palestinian cause lead many Hondurans of both Palestinian and non-Palestinian origin to refer to them as "fanatics." It would appear that new lines are being drawn that coincide roughly with their level of acculturation.

In all of this the local Orthodox church may be seen as the key symbol of identity for those choosing to retain their Palestinian "peoplehood." As described in chapter 7, its Eastern mien and ritual reflect a basic schism that has existed for centuries between Christian persuasions in the Holy Land. The establishment of the church in San Pedro Sula in 1963 was greeted at first as an overdue and welcome statement of Palestinian presence and pride. It was supported by the leading families, many of whom had no direct knowledge or experience of Orthodoxy, even though their ancestors had adhered to that faith.

The reality of the new religious establishment, however, was apparently not what many Hondurans had expected. Not only was there great difficulty at first in finding a priest who could handle the Spanish language, but the services and rituals left some, now accustomed to Roman Catholicism, feeling that something was missing. Some told me that, even though they knew both persuasions were basically Christian, they did not feel as though they had been to church after an Orthodox mass. Some objected to the custom of kneeling in the aisles during the processional as the priest and his assistants carry reli-

---

14. Ironically, in the Middle East Muslims are often thought to be more polite than Christians or Jews — perhaps because they are less direct and open in saying exactly what they think, especially when the latter is unflattering to the listener. The corollary to this is that, when angry, they are perhaps even more capable of hyperbole and insult.

gious objects to their proper place on the altar. Others complained that they felt it unsanitary for everyone to kiss the cross in succession at the end of the service.

A major difference between the Orthodox and Catholic churches, apparent to all but generally not well understood by most Hondurans, is in their methods for determining the date of Easter, which throughout Christendom is the basis for determining other "movable feasts." The replacement of the civil and ecclesiastical Julian calendar by the Gregorian occurred at different times in different countries and by different sects, starting in Rome under Pope Gregory XIII in 1582. It was not adopted by Russians until the advent of the Soviet government in 1917. The Greek Orthodox church, even after adopting the Gregorian calendar, still computes the date of Easter according to lunar movements as measured in Jerusalem and in accordance with Jewish calculations of the date of Passover. Thus, Orthodox Easter and Christmas celebrations generally fall at a slightly different time — no more than a week apart, however — than in the Catholic church. In the Holy Land, where multiple religious calendars are legion, this poses no dilemma, but in Honduras it presents an awkwardness that is at best inconvenient and at worst an apparent blasphemy. Still, it definitely serves to set the Orthodox apart from other Christians. Some Orthodox Palestinian Hondurans end by celebrating both sets of holidays; others party on the beach during the Catholic holy week, returning to spend much of the second week attending the more dramatic nightly events of the Eastern church.

There is evidence, discussed in chapter 7, that the Greek Orthodox church has long been seen as a symbol of the Palestinian nationalist cause in the Middle East. That perception may well have contributed to the tide that eventually swept it into existence in San Pedro Sula. The date of its founding was only a few years before the establishment of the PLO with the help of then-president Nasser of Egypt. As the violent conflict in their homeland escalated, however, and particularly after the PLO began to be portrayed in the Western press as a terrorist organization, many of the "old guard" Hondurans began to pull away from association with both of these institutions. In the case of the church its very different worship service was the reason given, which was convenient because one was not required to reject publicly the Palestinian label. The PLO, on the other hand, as it increasingly came to view itself as a nation with territorial ambitions, made more salient the question — for some a real dilemma — of defining its nationality, as opposed to mere ethnicity.

## Nationhood and Nationalism

Nationhood has not come easily to either Honduras or the West Bank, the former as a result of its having been a relatively poor sector of the Central American region since colonial times. Despite the presence of silver and gold, Honduras was never the seat of colonial or creole elite power and influence; it was always secondary to Guatemala and El Salvador. After the Central American confederation — led by a native Honduran named Francisco Morazán — was dissolved the country continued to sink into even greater poverty and oblivion until the "green gold" of bananas was discovered just before the turn of the twentieth century. Chapter 4 has described its growth since then, especially on the north coast. Thus although the country has a clear sense of being "different" from the other Central American countries, and even fought the so-called "Soccer War" with El Salvador in 1972 (Durham 1979), Hondurans of several ancestries interviewed for this study had difficulty defining the differences between themselves and other Central Americans except in stereotypical terms that are commonly the basis of joking behavior when they find themselves in each others' company.

In San Pedro Sula, and in many others of the coastal cities and towns, Arab culture (or, rather, a Latin American adaptation of some of its elements, put together in a new form) is actually more salient and might eventually have become acceptable as one of several ancestral roots for modern Hondurans had it not been for the development of the present state of affairs in the Middle East and consequent problems in Honduras. The country is bereft of symbols by which its citizens may define themselves as a people and about which they can rally, a problem faced by all the Central American republics and described in some detail for Guatemala by Moore (1989).

In recent years there has been an effort to establish a claim to the Mayan heritage, particularly as a result of the excavations and reconstructions at Copán. But even that city was on the fringes of Mayan civilization, and Mayan sites in Honduras are fewer, less spectacular (with the exception of the magnificent Copán), and relatively recent in comparison with those in Mexico and Guatemala. Borrowings of artistic motifs, music, and dance from other American Indian groups — such as the Rama, the Miskito, and even the hybrid Garifuna — have been used as well. But here again there is no real sense of attachment to these symbols by most Hondurans.

As Honduras continues to search for and struggle toward nationhood, it needs something that can unite its different population segments, or identity groups. As Domínguez has shown for Israel (1989), there is a tendency to search for folkloric symbols among the country's minority ethnic groups, and, although no one group can "stand in" for the whole, something can be made of the mix. When any one group is perceived with disdain or fear, however, its culture is not likely to appeal to the others or to be adopted as part of a collective representation. This element seems to be present in Israel, in relation to both minority Jewish groups and Arabs, as well as in Honduras. The extreme cultural diversity in both states makes it difficult for them to define and celebrate their nationhood.

But the West Bank is not Israel — or at least not yet, despite having been occupied by that state for more than twenty years. Increasingly, there are Jewish (Israeli and immigrant) settlers established in official colonies throughout its territory, and, even if some agreement is finally reached between Israeli and Palestinian leaders to exchange "land for peace," there will be continuing problems due to the differing values and goals among this mixed population. The Israelis will not want to give up their land and homes, much less their Israeli citizenship. Some Palestinians with whom I discussed this matter thought it could be worked out by allowing Israelis already in the territories certain privileges as resident foreigners, with appropriate taxation of them in this regard. Others insisted all Jews would have to return to Israel proper, exchanging their properties with Arabs, who would all move to the West Bank. Such a solution does not seem likely to appeal greatly to either Arabs or Jews.

In addition to these "human" problems the West Bank has other deficiencies making it relatively unattractive as an independent state. It has few natural resources; its land is in many places poor for agriculture; it has no seaport (although with Gaza, such could be created), no navigable rivers, no railroads, no airport, and generally poor highways. Its infrastructure, such as schools, hospitals, government buildings, and the like, has not been well maintained during the occupation. It has no heavy industry, and a populace largely unskilled and poor. Many feel that in the event of independence most Arabs would continue working in the lower echelons of Israeli society, as they do now, but probably with even fewer rights and protections.

The other side of this picture is Israel's continuing need for more space to house its own population, expanding both through natural increase and through immigration. Palestinian birthrates are higher than those of Jews within Israel, but oriental and Orthodox Jews are not far behind the Arabs. There must be a place for them in succeeding generations. There is also the matter of water supply and the desire to have a buffer zone between Israel proper and Jordan.

This is not the place to go into the details of these needs, but it is clear that establishment of an independent Palestinian state in the West Bank is far from being a simple matter for either Arabs or Israelis. Even if it were feasible in terms of ethnic interaction, politics, capital, and technical assistance, the question is whether it would be sustainable over time. Israel will never permit such a close neighbor to have an army or other defense mechanisms, but perhaps even more serious is the question of productivity in a global market. At the present time there is simply no marketable product or resource in the West Bank or Gaza which could sustain an independent government and a free people with a decent standard of living.

A return to tourism is a distinct possibility—this is currently of great economic significance to Israel. But without Jerusalem (and perhaps Bethlehem, which may well end up being annexed as a suburb of Jerusalem), much of the spiritual return to pilgrims as well as the touristic glamour would be missing. New facilities, perhaps even the "discovery" of new sites holy to all three major religions, would be in order. Even Jordan has more sites of potential interest to tourists than has the West Bank.

Any discussion of just where an independent Palestinian state might be located must consider Jordan. As noted above, a majority of that country's present population considers itself Palestinian. Unfortunately, there has also developed a strong sense of nationality among those calling themselves Jordanians, even though the country has only existed as a distinct entity since 1927, when "Transjordan" became an independent constitutional entity, although still under British tutelage. In 1946 Abdullah (grandfather of the present king, Hussein), was crowned as first monarch of the "Hashemite Kingdom of Jordan." In 1948–49 thousands of Palestinians were uprooted and deported from their homes inside the new Israeli state, and others fled as a result of threats against them. Many fled across the river to Jordan, and in 1952 that country absorbed the entire West Bank and Gaza, granting Jordanian citizenship to all Palestinians in those territories. Even after 1967, when Israel took the area back by military conquest, Jordan recognized West Bankers as its citizens. This policy was revoked in 1988 when King Hussein formally relinquished Jordanian claims to the territory, ostensibly to clear the way for the PLO to gain recognition as the only authoritative bargaining entity on behalf of Palestinians everywhere.

Thus, there have been only two generations of Jordanian existence, and Palestinians have been an integral part of that nation for one of them. It is virtually impossible to distinguish Jordanians and Palestinians by physical characteristics, speech, dress, diet, or other custom.[15] Young people born east of the Jordan have only mixed impressions, from the media on the one hand and from their parents on the other, of what life is like in Israel and in the West Bank, and most have little desire to move there.

On the other hand, despite the outward similarities in what usually pass for ethnic symbols, Jordanians and Palestinians often hate and mistrust each other. This animosity ranges all the way from Palestinian university students who cite discriminatory practices in everything from acceptance into prestigious majors to grading, to men and women in the marketplace who hurl ethnic epithets at each other in the course of daily commerce. The continuing presence of large groups of poor Palestinians concentrated in "camps" is offensive to their primarily Jordanian neighbors, even when their standards of living do not differ significantly.

There is no doubt that the abortive 1970 "Black September" coup attempt against King Hussein by local Palestinians supported by the PLO exacerbated the tensions and left scars on both sides. These persist despite the 1984 rapprochement between King Hussein and the PLO leadership that, according to Day (1986:62), made it

---

15. When I first arrived in Jordan the United States ambassador was fond of telling people that my "mission" there as a Fulbright scholar was to discover and relate to the world just what the differences were. At gatherings he made a point, at least in my presence, of asking people whether they were "East Bankers" or "West Bankers." Although obviously embarrassed by the question, there seemed little hesitancy on the part of either Palestinians or Jordanians to confess their allegiance.

"less difficult to be both a Palestinian and a Jordanian." Many Jordanians told me of being insulted by their Palestinian neighbors during the hostilities, who boasted that "soon" the Jordanians would be made to flee and give up their homes. When Hussein's forces prevailed many of the Palestinians suffered that fate instead, much to the glee of the Jordanians watching from down the road.

The monarchy does not sit well with many Palestinians, even those who have prospered and risen to relatively affluent positions within Jordan. The authority of the king is sanctioned, according to government officials with whom I spoke, by his having descended directly from Muhammad.[16] Quite apart from the fact that many Muslims disapprove of his regime, members of other religions — in this case Christians — find descent from a religious leader ludicrous as a basis for governmental power. It is more realistic to point out that his authority was established by Britain and is upheld by one of the strongest military establishments in the Middle East and by an effective secret police.

Palestinian-Hondurans, now accustomed to a more secular state (albeit one in which Christianity is virtually the only religion) and one in which democracy is an articulated ideal (even though many would argue that the vote is manipulated and the people exploited), are even less enthusiastic about monarchies.[17] It is extremely doubtful that many of them would return to Jordan, despite the fact that many of their compatriots have done very well there. A constitutional monarchy in which an elected official such as a prime minister held the reins of power, or a republic might suit them better, but only if they could be assured of true religious freedom.

## Summary and Conclusions

In summary Palestinian Hondurans in general, and some of them in particular, have been exceedingly successful in the New World, and,

---

16. King Hussein, like other Hashemites, traces his ancestry to Fatima, Muhammad's daughter, and her husband, 'Ali, the fourth caliph. Genetically, he is, then, a direct descendant of the Prophet. In a patrilineal system of reckoning, however, Muhammad had no descendants, for he had no sons.

17. There are some Palestinian-Hondurans, especially women, who idolize the Jordanian royal family, following its successes and travails much as occurs in Britain. This in no way contradicts my general observation that they would prefer to live under a more democratic regime.

although they are torn with anguish over the plight of their brethren in the Middle East, most of them today have no intention of returning there to live. Those who do entertain such hopes tend to be found among the more recent immigrants, but the more successful they are on a day-to-day basis, the less likely they will be to return.

As in the Jewish diaspora, religion plays a significant part in their self-identification and in their decisions about where to live. Finding themselves in a predominantly Christian polity for the first time in their lives, the new emigrants have relaxed, and many of the Orthodox have thrown in their lot with the local Roman Catholics. This has furthered their acculturation to Latin American culture, made them more acceptable to Honduran society, and drawn them away from the Eastern rite.

Still, their ambivalence about citizenship, their reluctance to cut off ties to their home community, and, most especially, the pressures that have been put upon them by the latter to support them over the past forty years have maintained and widened the gulf between themselves and members of the host society. Once pariah entrepreneurs, they are now among the most wealthy and powerful industrialists in the country. In short, they are on the verge of being accepted along class lines, rather than being rejected on the basis of ethnicity. It is not likely that they will be willing to give up such a status, and it is my view that once the Palestinian-Israeli dispute is settled—regardless of the details of that settlement—Palestinian-Hondurans will for the most part give up that cause and devote themselves to Honduras.

It may be, as has often been stated, that Palestinian nationalism has itself been a product of Zionism. It is certainly the case that both arose at about the same time, toward the end of the nineteenth century. In the one case we have witnessed a people in search of a country, which, once achieved, now finds itself in search of its "peoplehood" (Domínguez 1989). In the other case we have a people who have never had a country of their own but whose peoplehood has been reinforced by the denial to them of even the lands upon which they were born and raised. Palestinians—whether they once designated themselves Bethlehemites, Syrians, Galileans, or other—are today united as a people or a nation as never before. They are likely, in my opinion, to find power in that unity at the same time that they preserve the right to maintain a transnationalism when it comes to citizenship.

My hope is that other Hondurans will come to recognize that transnationalism does not indicate lack of patriotism for either country and may contribute strength to both.

# Appendix: Arab Names in Central America, Mexico, and the Caribbean

| Name | Origin | Locations | Current | Date |
|------|--------|-----------|---------|------|
| Abbassy | Acre | H | H | 1948–67 |
| Abboud | Syria | H G | H G | 1918–48 |
| Abdalah | ? | H G N | H G | 1948–67 |
| Abdelnur | BL | H | H | 1918–48 |
| Abdo | BL | H G N | all | 1918–48 |
| Abedrabo | BJ | H | H | 1948–67 |
| Abou Jamous | BJ | G | G | after 1950 |
| Abou-nehra | ? | H | H | after 1950 |
| Abouchaibe | BJ | H | none | after 1950 |
| Aboukalil | BL | S | | after 1950 |
| Aboumohor | BJ | H | H | 1948–67 |
| Abraham | BS | H G | H | |
| Abucharar | BL | S | | after 1950 |
| Abudeye | BJ | H | H | 1918–48 |
| Abudoj | BL | H | | after 1950 |
| Abufele | BL | H | H | 1918–48 |
| Abugaber | BL | H G M | G | 1918–48 |
| Abugarade | BL | S M | | after 1950 |
| Abugattas | BJ | H | H | after 1950 |
| Abugosh | BJ | | none | after 1950 |
| Abuid | BJ | H | H | |
| Abularach | BL | H G M | G S | 1900–1917 |

B = Belize
DR = Dominican Republic
G = Guatemala
H = Honduras
M = Mexico
N = Nicaragua
S = El Salvador

Dates were assigned as follows: If Jacir or Musallem noted them in 1955, "1950" was noted. If Jacir or Musallem did not note them, "after 1950" was noted. Other dates were assigned according to entries in baptismal, marriage, death, or telephone records seen during the research.

| Name | Origin | Locations | Current | Date |
|------|--------|-----------|---------|------|
| Abumojor | BJ | H | H | after 1950 |
| Abureyes | ? | H | H | after 1950 |
| Aburuman | BJ | H | H | |
| Abuyiries | BJ | H | H | after 1950 |
| Adib | Ramallah | G | G | after 1950 |
| Affaneh | BL | S | | 1950 |
| Affif | ? | H | H | 1950 |
| Ahmad | Jerusalem | H B | H B | 1918–48 |
| Akel | Ramalleh | N | none | 1950 |
| Al Hayek | Syria | H | H | after 1950 |
| Alam | BJ | G | G | after 1950 |
| Alburez | ? | G | G | |
| Ali | BL | H | | 1950 |
| Aljobhan | ? | H | H | after 1950 |
| Amer | ? | H | H | after 1950 |
| Andonie | BL | H Haiti | H | 1900–1917 |
| Andraus | ? | G | G | after 1950 |
| Anton | ? | G | G | after 1950 |
| Asfura | BL | H G S | H | 1918–48 |
| Assaf | BL | H G | H | 1900–1917 |
| Atallah | ? | H S | H | 1950 |
| Atti | BL | H | H | 1900–1917 |
| Atuan | BL | H | H | after 1950 |
| Awad | BL BJ BS | H | H | 1950 |
| Ayoub | Lebanese | G B | B | after 1950 |
| Azar | Lebanese | H G | H G | 1967–87 |
| Azize | BL | H | H | 1948–67 |
| Azzad | ? | H | H | after 1950 |
| Babun | BL | H G S Haiti | same | 1948–67 |
| Bader | BJ | H | H | 1900–1917 |
| Bahaiah | BL | S | | 1950 |
| Bamar | ? | H | H | 1918–48 |
| Banayotti | BL (Greek) | H | H | 1918–48 |
| Bandak | BL | H S M N Haiti H G | same | 1918–48 |
| Bandy | BJ | H N | H | 1918–48 |
| Baracat | Jordan | H | H | after 1950 |
| Barake | BL | S | | 1950 |
| Barduri | BJ | H | | 1918–48 |
| Barhum | BS | H | H | 1918–48 |
| Barjun | BL | H | H | 1950 |
| Bassila | BL | G | G | after 1950 |
| Batarse | BL | H S G M | H G | 1900–1917 |
| Bazir | ? | G | G | after 1950 |
| Bedran | ? | H | H | after 1950 |

| Name | Origin | Locations | Current | Date |
|------|--------|-----------|---------|------|
| Bichara | BJ | H S | H | 1950 |
| Bigit | BL | S | | 1950 |
| Boadla | ? | H | H | 1918–48 |
| Botto | BL | H | H | 1900–1917 |
| Boukeleh | ? | S | | 1950 |
| Burbura | BL | H | H | 1967–87 |
| Busmail | ? | H | H | 1950 |
| Cader | ? | S | | 1950 |
| Camal | BL | H | | 1950 |
| Canahuati | BL | H S | H S | 1900–1917 |
| Carr | Lebanese | B | B | |
| Carraah | BL | S | | 1950 |
| Cassis | BL BJ BS | H S M | H | 1900–1917 |
| Chahin | BL | H S | H | 1900–1917 |
| Chamieh | BL | H | | 1948–67 |
| Charara | BL | S M | | 1950 |
| Charur | BL | G | | 1950 |
| Chehadeh | BJ | H | H | 1918–48 |
| Cokali | ? | H | | 1900–1917 |
| Comandari | BL | H S | H | 1948–67 |
| Cronfel | BL | H | H | 1948–67 |
| Cury | BL BJ | H | H | 1900–1917 |
| Dabbah | BJ | G | G | after 1950 |
| Dabdoub | BL | H S M G | H G | 1900–1917 |
| Dacak | Lebanese | B | B | |
| Dacaret | BL | H G Haiti | H G | 1918–48 |
| Dada | BL | S | G | 1948–67 |
| Dahboura | BL | S | | 1950 |
| Dahuabe | BL | S | | 1950 |
| David | BL | H G | H | 1918–48 |
| Dawa | BJ | H | | 1918–48 |
| Dewane | ? | H | | 1918–48 |
| Diab | Lebanese | B | B | |
| Dieck | BL | H M G | H G | 1918–48 |
| Dip | Ramallah | H M N | H | 1900–1917 |
| Dogadher | ? | H | H | after 1950 |
| Duaje | Lebanon | H | H | 1948–67 |
| Eid | ? | H B | H B | 1948–60 |
| El Hayek | Syria | H | H | 1960–80 |
| El-Sayed | Lebanese | B | B | |
| Elias | Lebanese | H G S N | H G | 1918–48 |
| Ennabe | Ramallah | H | H | 1900–1917 |
| Esmahan | ? | S | | 1950 |
| Espat | Lebanese | B | B | |

| Name | Origin | Locations | Current | Date |
|------|--------|-----------|---------|------|
| Facusse | BL | H | H | 1900–1917 |
| Fadul | ? | G | G | after 1950 |
| Fanous | Leb? Egypt? | H | H | after 1950 |
| Farach | BS | G | G | 1918–48 |
| Faraj | BS BJ | H | H | 1918–48 |
| Fattaleh | Jerusalem | H | H | 1967 |
| Fawzi | ? | G | G | after 1950 |
| Fayad | ? | H | H | after 1950 |
| Flefil | BL | H | H | before 1900 |
| Frech | BL | H N M | H | 1918–48 |
| Fuadi | ? | H | H | after 1950 |
| Gabrieh | BL | H G | H | 1900–1917 |
| Gadallah | BL | DR S G | G S | 1918–48 |
| Ganem | BS | H | H | 1948–60 |
| Gattas | BL | H G S M | H | 1900–1917 |
| Gawy | ? | H | H | after 1950 |
| Gazanabbi | ? | B | B | |
| Gazzawi | BL | Haiti G | G | 1950 |
| Giacoman | BL | H G S N | H G | 1900–1917 |
| Giafar | ? | S | | 1950 |
| Gidi | BL | M | | 1950 |
| Giha | BL | H | | 1918–48 |
| Gindi | BS | B | B | |
| Goljami | ? | H | | 1900–1917 |
| Habet | Lebanese | B | B | |
| Haddad | Lebanese | B G | B | after 1950 |
| Hakin | BL | G | G | after 1950 |
| Hamame | ? | G | G | after 1950 |
| Hamdan | ? | S N | | 1950 |
| Hamdy | BL | G | G | after 1950 |
| Hamis | BJ | H | H | 1918–48 |
| Hanania | BL | H S | H | 1948–60 |
| Handal | BL | H G Haiti M G S | H G S | 1900–1917 |
| Harari | Lebanese | G | G | |
| Hasbun | BL | H G S Haiti M | all | 1900–1917 |
| Hassan | BL | B | B | |
| Hassim | BL | H | H | after 1950 |
| Hawit | Jerus or Ram | H | H | 1918–48 |
| Hawzs | Lebanese | B | B | |
| Hegar | Lebanese | B | B | |
| Helife | ? | G | G | after 1950 |
| Hiaczi | ? | H | H | after 1950 |
| Hid | BL | S | | 1950 |
| Hilsaca | BL | H | H | after 1950 |

| Name | Origin | Locations | Current | Date |
|------|--------|-----------|---------|------|
| Hoch | BL | H | H | 1918–48 |
| Hode | BJ | H | H | 1918–48 |
| Hreizi | BL | H S | H | 1948–60 |
| Husman | Lebanese | B | B | |
| Ibrahim | BJ | H | H | after 1950 |
| Ictech | BL | H | H | 1948–60 |
| Isabrin | BJ BS | H | H | after 1950 |
| Ismael | ? | H | | 1950 |
| Jaar | BL | H Haiti DR M | H | 1900–1917 |
| Jacaman | BL | H | H | 1918–48 |
| Jalal | BS | H | H | after 1950 |
| Jamal | BL | H | H | after 1950 |
| Jarufe | BJ | H | H | 1918–48 |
| Jasbufum | ? | H | | 1918–48 |
| Jassir | BL | G S | | 1950 |
| Jibrin | ? | H | H | 1918–48 |
| Jiha | BL | Haiti | | 1950 |
| Jobez | BL | H G S | | 1950 |
| Jorge | Lebanese | H DR | H DR | 1900–1917 |
| Kafati | BJ | H S | H | 1948–60 |
| Kafie | ? | H | H | 1918–48 |
| Kaled | ? | H | H | |
| Kamandari | BL | H S | H | 1948–60 |
| Kamar | BL Jerus | H | H | 1918–48 |
| Kattan | BL BJ | H | H G | 1900–1917 |
| Kawas | BL | H Haiti M | H | 1900–1917 |
| Kebani | ? | G | G | |
| Khalil | BL | H | | 1950 |
| Khoury | BJ | H S | H | 1900–1917 |
| Konkar | BJ | H | H | |
| Ladat | BL | H | H | 1918–48 |
| Lajud | ? | G | G | |
| Lama | BL | H G Haiti | H G | 1918–48 |
| Larach | BJ | H | H | 1900–1917 |
| Magads | ? | H | | 1918–48 |
| Mahchi | BL Jeru | H | H | 1918–48 |
| Mahmud | ? | H N | | 1950 |
| Mahomar | BL | H S | H | 1900–1917 |
| Maloff | Lebanese | H G | H G | 1918–48 |
| Manzur | BL BJ | H G | G | 1918–48 |
| Marcos | BL | H M N | H | 1900–1917 |
| Maria | BL | S G | G | 1950 |
| Marzouka | BL | H Haiti | H | 1948–60 |
| Massou | BL BJ | H | H | 1967 |

| Name | Origin | Locations | Current | Date |
|------|--------|-----------|---------|------|
| Michalen | BL | H DR | DR | 1950 |
| Michel | BL | H S M N | H | 1918–48 |
| Mikel | BL | H | H | 1950 |
| Miladeh | BL | H | H | after 1950 |
| Miselem | BL | H M | H | 1918–48 |
| Misleh | BJ BS | H | H | 1967–87 |
| Mitri | BL BJ | H DR | H | 1918–48 |
| Muadi | BL | G | G | after 1950 |
| Mukaquer | BJ | H | H | 1948–60 |
| Murra | BL | H M Haiti | H | 1948–60 |
| Musa | ? | B G | B G | |
| Musalam | BL | H G | G H | |
| Mussan | ? | G | G | after 1950 |
| Nafky | ? | H | H | after 1950 |
| Nahhas | ? | G | G | after 1950 |
| Nahomed | ? | H | H | 1960–67 |
| Nahum | ? | H | H | 1967 |
| Nassad | ? | H | H | 1960–67 |
| Nasser | BL | H S G | H | 1900–1917 |
| Nastas | BL | H Haiti N S | H | 1918–48 |
| Nazrala | BJ | H | H | 1948–60 |
| Nicoli | BL | H | H | 1900–1917 |
| Nimer | Ramallah | H G | H G | after 1950 |
| Numman | Ramallah | H | H | 1918–48 |
| Nustass | BL | H S | | 1950 |
| Odeh | BL | H | H | 1918–48 |
| Padra | BS | Haiti | | 1950 |
| Paranky | BL (Greek) | H | H | 1900–1917 |
| Rabat | ? | H | H | after 1950 |
| Rafeq | ? | H | H | after 1950 |
| Richmawy | BS | H | H | 1918–48 |
| Rizk | BJ | M | | 1950 |
| Rock | BL | H | H | 1967 |
| Roman | BJ | H | H | 1918–48 |
| Saad | BL | H | H | 1950 |
| Saade | BL | H G S M | H | 1918–48 |
| Saba | BJ | Haiti | | 1950 |
| Sabat | BL | H Haiti | H | 1918–48 |
| Saca | BL | H G S | H | 1948–60 |
| Sacaan | BL | H | H | 1948–60 |
| Safie | BL | H S G | H | 1948–60 |
| Sahury | BL | H | H | 1918–48 |
| Said | ? | H | H | after 1950 |
| Sajia | Lebanese | B | B | |

| *Name* | *Origin* | *Locations* | *Current* | *Date* |
|---|---|---|---|---|
| Sakalha | ? | G | G | after 1950 |
| Sakhel | BJ | H | H | after 1950 |
| Salame | BL BJ BS | H S | H | 1918–48 |
| Saleh | BJ | S G | | 1950 |
| Salem | BL | H | H | 1918–48 |
| Salman | BL BJ | H DR M | H | 1900–1917 |
| Salomon | BL | H | H | |
| Salty | BL | H N | H | 1948–60 |
| Samara | BL | H S | H | 1948–60 |
| Samury | BL | G | G | after 1950 |
| Sansur | BL BJ | H M | H | 1948–60 |
| Saybe | BL | H | H | 1900–1917 |
| Segebre | BJ | H | H | 1967–87 |
| Sekali | ? | H | | before 1900 |
| Selim | ? | H | | 1918–48 |
| Shahin | BL BJ | S | | 1950 |
| Shaleh | BJ | H | | 1967 |
| Shamah | BL | H B | B | 1960 |
| Shaya | BJ | H | | before 1900 |
| Shekae | Jerusalem | H | | 1900–1917 |
| Shoman | ? | G B | G B | after 1950 |
| Sicre | ? | G | G | after 1950 |
| Sikaffy | BL | H | H | 1900–1917 |
| Silhy | ? | S | | 1950 |
| Siman | BJ | H S | H | 1948–60 |
| Simeri | BL | H | | 1918–48 |
| Simon | ? | H S | H | 1950 |
| Sirene | BJ | H | H | after 1950 |
| Sirgi | ? | H | | 1950 |
| Siwady | BL | H S | H | 1900–1917 |
| Skai | ? | H | | 1900–1917 |
| Soliman | BL | H | H | 1900–1917 |
| Sowadi | BL | S | H | 1950 |
| Stefan | BL | H | H | 1950 |
| Surur | ? | G | G | after 1950 |
| Tabush | BL | G | G | after 1950 |
| Talamas | BL | Haiti M | | 1950 |
| Talgie | BL | M | | 1950 |
| Talhami | BL | H | H | 1918–48 |
| Tanas | ? | S | | 1950 |
| Tanios | ? | H | H | after 1950 |
| Tarazi | ? | S | | 1950 |
| Tome | BJ | H | H | 1918–48 |
| Touche | ? | H M | | 1950 |

| Name | Origin | Locations | Current | Date |
|---|---|---|---|---|
| Tueme | BL | M | | 1950 |
| Turjuman | ? | G | G | after 1950 |
| Yacaman | BL | H G | H G S | 1900–1917 |
| Yacoub | BJ BS | H | H | after 1950 |
| Yaghmur | ? | H | H | after 1950 |
| Yamani | ? | H | H | after 1950 |
| Yarur | ? | S | | 1950 |
| Yazbek | ? | H | H | after 1950 |
| Yeres | BJ | H | | 1918–48 |
| Yibrin | ? | H | H | after 1950 |
| Yones | BL | H | H | 1900–1917 |
| Youssef | ? | G | G | after 1950 |
| Yuja | BL | H Haiti | H | 1918–48 |
| Zabaneh | ? | S | | 1950 |
| Zabath | BL | H | H | after 1950 |
| Zablah | BL | H S M | H | 1918–48 |
| Zacarias | BS | H G M | H G | 1948–60 |
| Zaghi | ? | G | G | after 1950 |
| Zahran | ? | N | | 1950 |
| Zaidan | BJ | S DR | | 1948–60 |
| Zakieh | ? | H | H | after 1950 |
| Zarky | ? | H | H | after 1950 |
| Zaror | BJ | H G | H | 1948–60 |
| Zarruck | BL | H N | H | 1918–48 |
| Zarzar | BL | H M S | H | 1948–60 |
| Zimeri | ? | G Haiti | G | 1950 |
| Zoghbi | BL | H | H | after 1950 |
| Zummar | BS | H | H | 1918–48 |
| Zurehe | H | H | | 1918–48 |

# References

## Abbreviations Used

INA   Israeli National Archives (Jerusalem)
PRO   Public Record Office (Kew, England)

## Published Works

Aamiri, M. A.
1978   *Jerusalem: Arab origin and heritage.* Bath: Longman.
Abir, M.
1970   *Local leadership and its reaction to early reforms in Palestine, 1826–1834.* Jerusalem: Hebrew University.
Abraham, Sameer Y., and Nabeel Abraham, eds.
1983   *Arabs in the New World: Studies on Arab-American communities.* Detroit: Wayne State University, Center for Urban Studies.
Abugattas, Juan
1982   The perception of the Palestinian question in Latin America. *Journal of Palestine Studies* 11 (3): 117–28.
Abu-Laban, Baha
1980   *An olive branch on the family tree: The Arabs in Canada.* Toronto: McClelland and Stewart
Abu-Laban, Baha and Faith T. Zeadey, eds.
1975   *Arabs in America: Myths and realities.* Wilmette (Illinois): Medina University Press.
Abu-Lughod, Janet
1971   The demographic transformation of Palestine. In *The transformation of Palestine,* ed. Ibrahim Abu-Lughod, 139–65. Evanston: Northwestern University Press.
Abu-Lughod, Lila
1989   Zones of theory in the anthropology of the Arab world. *Annual Review of Anthropology* 18:267–306.
Adams, William Y.
1981   Dispersed minorities of the Middle East: A comparison and a lesson. In *Persistent peoples,* ed. George Pierre Castile and Gilbert Kushner, 3–25. Tucson: University of Arizona Press.

Alexander, Yonah
1973    *The role of communications in the Middle East conflict: Ideological and religious aspects.* New York: Praeger.
Allison, Norman Ernest, Jr.
1977    *A case of honor: Arab Christians in a Jordanian town.* Ph.D. diss. University of Georgia, Athens.
Amado, Jorge
1962    *Gabriela, Cloves and Cinnamon.* New York: Knopf.
American Christian Palestine Committee
1948    *The people speak on Palestine: American public opinion on the U.S. and the U.N.* New York: American Christian Palestine Committee.
Ammar, Nellie
1970    They came from the Middle East. *Jamaica Journal* 4 (1): 2-6.
Anglo-American Committee of Inquiry
1946    *A survey of Palestine.* Jerusalem: Government Printer.
*Anthropology Newsletter*
        Washington, D.C.: American Anthropological Association.
Armstrong, John A.
1976    Mobilized and proletarian diasporas. *American Political Science Review* 70:393-408.
Aruri, Naseer H., and Samih Farsoun
1980    Palestinian communities and Arab host countries. In *The sociology of the Palestinians,* ed. Khalil Nakhleh and Elia Zureik, 112-46. New York: St. Martin's.
Ashkenasi, Abraham
1981    *The structure of ethnic conflict and Palestinian political fragmentation.* Berlin: Der Freien Universitat.
Aswad, Barbara
1974    *Arabic speaking communities in American cities.* Staten Island, N.Y.: Center for Migration Studies.
Ata, Ibrahim Wade
1986    *The West Bank Palestinian family.* New York: Routledge and Kegan Paul.
Atiya, Aziz S.
1962    *The Crusade: Historiography and bibliography.* Bloomington and London: University of Indiana Press.
Awartani, Hisham
1979    *A survey of industries in the West Bank and the Gaza Strip.* Nablus: Birzeit University Publications.
Bach, R. L., and L. A. Schraml
1982    Migration, crisis and theoretical conflict. *International Migration Review* 16:320-41.
Bahbah, Bishara
1986    *Israel and Latin America: The military connection.* New York: St. Martin's.
Bailey, Clinton
1966    *The participation of the Palestinians in the politics of Jordan.* New York: Columbia University.

Bandak, Tasso, and Norma Bandak
1988 Jamileh Bandak, 1897–1980: Palestinian indomitability and perseverance. *Bethlehem Newsletter* 1 (8): 13.

Banoura, Thouma
1981 *History of Belen, Beit Jalla, Beit Sahour, Efrate* (in Arabic). Jerusalem.

Baster, James
1954 Economic aspects of the settlement of the Palestine refugees. *Middle East Journal* 8 (1): 54–68.

Belisle, Jean-Francois
1988 Los inmigrantes y la economia ecuatoriana en la primera mitad del siglo XX. Paper delivered at International Congress of Americanists, Amsterdam.

Ben-Arie, Y.
1970 The population of the large towns in Palestine during the first eighty years of the nineteenth century according to Western sources. International Seminar on the History of Palestine and its Jewish Settlement during the Ottoman Period. Jerusalem: Hebrew University.

Ben-Porath, Yoram
1980 The F-connection: Families, friends, and firms and the organization of exchange. *Population and Development Review* 6:1–30.

Benvenisti, Meron
1972 *The Crusaders in the Holy Land.* New York: Macmillan.
1986 *Demographic, economic, legal, social and political developments in the West Bank.* Boulder: Westview.

Benzinger, J.
1903 Researches in Palestine. In *Explorations in Bible lands during the nineteenth century,* ed. Herman V. Hilprecht, 582–84. Philadelphia: A. J. Holman.

Bertelson, Judy S., ed.
1977 *Nonstate nations in international politics: Comparative systems analysis.* New York: Praeger.

Betts, Robert Brenton
1978 *Christians in the Arab East: A political study.* Athens: Lycabettus.

Blitzer, Wolf
1985 *Between Washington and Jerusalem: A reporter's notebook.* New York: Oxford University Press.

Blondeel Van Cuelebrouk, M.
1846 *Colonie de Santo-Tomas.* Brussels: Le Ministre des Affaires Etrangeres.

Blumberg, Arnold
1980 *A view from Jerusalem, 1849–1858: The consular diary of James and Elizabeth Anne Finn.* Rutherford: Fairleigh Dickinson University Press.

Bock, Philip K., ed.
1969 *Peasants in the modern world.* Albuquerque: University of New Mexico Press.

Bonacich, E.
1973 A theory of middleman minorities. *American Sociological Review* 38:583–94.

Bowman, Glenn
1988    Pilgrimage conference. *Anthropology Today* 4 (6): 20–23.
Braude, Benjamin, and Bernard Lewis, eds.
1982    *Christians and Jews in the Ottoman Empire: The functioning of a plural society,* vols.
        1 and 2. New York: Holmes and Meier.
Bray, Donald W.
1962    The political emergence of Arab-Chileans. *Journal of Interamerican Studies*
        4:557–62.
Brettell, Caroline
1979    Emigrar para voltar: A Portuguese ideology of return migration. *Papers in
        Anthropology* 20:1–20.
1986    *Men who migrate, women who wait: Population and history in a Portuguese parish.*
        Princeton: Princeton University Press.
Brouwer, L., and M. Priester
1983    Living in between: Turkish women in their homeland and in the Nether-
        lands. In *One way ticket: Migration and female labour,* ed. A. Phizacklea,
        113–29. London: Routledge and Kegan Paul.
Bryce-Laporte, Roy Simon
1980    *Sourcebook on the new immigration: Implications for the United States and the interna-
        tional community.* New Brunswick, N.J.: Transaction Books.
Buckingham, James Silk
1822    *Travels in Palestine.* London: Longman.
1825    *Travels among the Arab tribes inhabiting the countries east of Syria and Palestine.*
        London: Longman.
Burckhardt, John Lewis
1822    *Travels in Syria and the Holy Land.* London: J. Murray.
Burns, Allen F.
1989    Internal and external identity among Kanjobal Mayan refugees in Florida.
        In *Conflict, migration, and the expression of ethnicity,* ed. Nancie L. González
        and Carolyn S. McCommon, 46–59. Boulder: Westview.
Burton, Isabel
1875    *The inner life of Syria, Palestine and the Holy Land.* London: H. S. King.
Caldarola, Carlo
1975    Fundamentalist Christianity: Israel and the second coming. In *Arabs in
        America,* ed. Baha Abu-Laban and Faith T. Zeadey, 171–83. Wilmette:
        Medina University Press.
Carmack, Robert M., ed.
1988    *Harvest of violence.* Norman: University of Oklahoma Press.
Cash, William Wilson
1937    *Christendom and Islam: Their contacts and cultures down the centuries.* New York:
        Harper & Brothers.
Census of Palestine
1922    Jerusalem. Printed at the Greek Convent Press.
Census of Palestine, 1931
1933    Alexandria: Printed for the Gov't. of Palestine by Whitehead Morris.

Center for Migration Studies
1986    Temporary workers and migration. *International Migration Review* 20 (4). New York: Center for Migration Studies.
Cernea, Michael M.
1989    Anthropology, policy and involuntary resettlement. *Newsletter of the British Association for Social Anthropology in Policy and Practice* 4:3-6.
Cheek, Charles, and Nancie L. González
1986    Black Carib settlement patterns in early eighteenth century Honduras: The search for a livelihood. In *Ethnohistory: A researcher's guide,* ed. Dennis Weidman, 403-30. Williamsburg, Va.: College of William and Mary.
Chiha, Michel
1969    *Palestine.* Beirut: Trident.
Choldin, Harvey M.
1973    Kinship networks in the migration process. *International Migration Review* 7:163-76.
Chomsky, Noam
1983    *The fateful triangle: United States, Israel and the Palestinians.* Boston: South End Press.
Chuaqui, Benedicto
1952    Arabs in Chile. *Americas* 4 (12): 17-29.
Clarke, Duncan L.
1989    *American defense and foreign policy institutions: Toward a sound foundation.* New York: Harper and Row.
Clarke, E. C.
1974    The Ottoman industrial revolution. *International Journal of Middle Eastern Studies* 5:65-76.
Clermont-Ganneau, Charles Simon
1875    *The Arabs in Palestine,* 199-214. London: Palestine Exploration Society.
Coate, Winifred
1953    The condition of Arab refugees in Jordan. *International Affairs* 29:449-56.
Cohen, Abner
1965    *Arab border villages in Israel.* Manchester: Manchester University Press.
1970    The politics of marriage in changing Middle Eastern stratification systems. In *Essays in comparative social stratification,* ed. Leonard Plotnicov and Arthur Tuden, 195-209. Pittsburgh: University of Pittsburgh Press.
1971    Cultural strategies in the organization of trading diasporas. In *The development of indigenous trade and markets in West Africa,* ed. Claude Meillassoux, 266-81. London: International African Institute.
Colson, Elizabeth
1971    *The social consequences of resettlement.* Manchester: Manchester University Press.
Conder, Claude R.
1879    *Tent work in Palestine,* 2 vols. London: Richard Bentley and Son.
Conder, Claude R. and H. H. Kitchener
1883    *The survey of Western Palestine,* Vol. 3: *Memoirs,* London: The Committee of the Palestine Exploration Fund.

Coon, Carleton S.
1965    *Caravan: The story of the Middle East.* New York: H. Holt.
Coughlin, Richard J.
1960    *Double identity: The Chinese in Thailand.* Hong Kong: Hong Kong University Press.
Crowley, William K.
1974    The Levantine Arabs: Diaspora in the New World. *Proceedings of the Association of American Geographers* 6:137–42.
n.d.a    *The Arabs of Central America.* Unpub. MS.
n.d.b    *Palestinian immigration to Honduras.* Unpub. MS.
Danzinger, Nera
1984    The contagion effect, an additional aspect in the dynamics of emigration: The case of Israel. *International Migration Review* 22 (1): 33–44.
Davies, W. D.
1974    *The gospel and the land: Early Christianity and Jewish territorial doctrine.* Berkeley and Los Angeles: University of California Press.
1982    *The territorial dimensions of Judaism.* Los Angeles: University of California Press.
Dawson, R.
1971    Closing impressions of San Pedro Sula. Unclassified, unpub. State Department doc. Tegucigalpa: American Embassy.
Day, Arthur R.
1986    *East Bank / West Bank: Jordan and the prospects for peace.* New York: Council on Foreign Relations.
Domínguez, Virginia
1989    *People as subject, people as object: Selfhood and peoplehood in modern Israel.* Madison: University of Wisconsin Press.
Durham, William
1979    *Scarcity and survival in Central America: Ecological origins of the Soccer War.* Stanford: Stanford University Press.
Dumett, Raymond E.
1983    African merchants of the Gold Coast, 1860–1905: Dynamics of indigenous entrepreneurship. *Comparative Studies in Society and History* 25 (4): 661–93.
Earle, Duncan M.
1988    Mayas aiding Mayas: Guatemalan refugees in Chiapas, Mexico. In *Harvest of violence,* ed. Robert M. Carmack, 256–73. Norman: University of Oklahoma Press.
Edwards, Mike
1983    Honduras: Eye of the storm. *National Geographic* 164 (5): 608–37.
Eickelman, Dale F.
1981    *The Middle East: An anthropological approach.* Englewood Cliffs, N.J.: Prentice-Hall.
Falla, Ricardo
1988    Struggle for survival in the mountains: Hunger and other privations inflicted on internal refugees from the Central Highlands. In Carmack, *Harvest of violence,* 235–55.

Feinberg, Richard, and Cynthia Carlisle
1989    *Immigration from Central America: Some thoughts on its causes and cures.* Washington, D.C.: Commission for the Study of International Migration and Cooperative Economic Development.

Feintuch, Yossi
1987    *United States policy on Jerusalem.* Westport, Conn.: Greenwood Press.

Findley, Paul
1985    *They dare to speak out: People and institutions confront Israel's lobby.* Westport, Conn.: Lawrence Hill.

Finn, Elizabeth Anne
1879    The Fellaheen of Palestine. *Palestine Exploration Fund Quarterly Statement* 11:33–48, 72–87.

1882    *A home in the Holy Land.* New York: T. Y. Crowell.

1923    *Palestine peasantry: Notes on their clans, warfare, religion and laws.* London: Marshall Brothers.

Finn, J.
1868    *Byways in Palestine.* London. n.p.

Fitzhugh, William W.
1985    Early contacts north of Newfoundland before A.D. 1600: A review. In *Cultures in contact,* ed. William W. Fitzhugh, 23–43. Washington, D.C.: Smithsonian Institution.

Fong, Ng Bickleen
1959    *The Chinese in New Zealand.* Hong Kong: Hong Kong University Press.

Foster, Brian L.
1974    Ethnicity and commerce. *American Ethnologist* 1:437–48.

Foster, George M., and Robert V. Kemper, ed.
1974    *Anthropologists in cities.* Boston: Little, Brown.

Friedl, Ernestine
1976    Kinship, class and selective migration. In *Mediterranean family structures,* ed. J. G. Peristiany, 363–87. Cambridge: Cambridge University Press.

Gallagher, Dennis, ed.
1986    *Refugees: Issues and directions.* New York: Center for Migration Studies.

Gardner, Betty, and Eleanor Olson
1986    *New England centennial: 1886–1986.* Bismarck, N.D.: Richtman's.

Garfinkle, Adan M.
1984    Chapter 1: Genesis. In *The Arab-Israeli conflict: Perspectives,* ed. Alzin Z. Rubinstein, 1–39. New York: Praeger.

Geiser, Peter
1981    *Cairo's Nubian families.* Cairo: American University.

Georges, Eugenia
1990    *The making of a transnational community.* New York: Columbia University Press.

Geramb Marie, Joseph de
1840    *A pilgrimage to Palestine, Egypt and Syria.* London: H. Colburn.

Gerber, Haim
1982    Modernization in nineteenth century Palestine: The role of foreign trade. *Middle Eastern Studies* 18 (3): 250–64.
Gersony, Robert
1989    Why Somalis flee: Conflict in northern Somalia. *Cultural Survival Quarterly* 13 (4): 45–58.
Ghosh, Amitav
1989    *The shadow lines*. New York: Viking.
Glick, Clarence E.
1980    *Sojourners and settlers: Chinese migrants in Hawaii.* Honolulu: Hawaii History Center and the University Press of Hawaii.
Glick, Thomas F.
1979    *Islamic and Christian Spain in the early Middle Ages: Comparative perspectives on social and cultural formation.* Princeton: Princeton University Press.
Glick, Thomas F., and O. Pi-Sunyer
1969    Acculturation as an explanatory concept in Spanish history. *Comparative Studies in Society and History* 11 (3): 136–55.
Glick-Schiller, N., L. Basch, and C. Blanc-Szanton
1991    Transnationalism: A new analytic framework for understanding migration. In *Towards a transnational perspective on migration: Race, class, ethnicity, and nationalism reconsidered,* ed. N. Glick-Schiller, L. Basch, and C. Blanc-Szanton, New York: New York Academy of Sciences.
Gmelch, George
1980    Return migration. *Annual Review of Anthropology* 9:135–59.
Gmelch, Susan Bohn
1986    Groups that don't want in: Gypsies and other artisan, trader, and entertainer minorities. *Annual Review of Anthropology* 15:307–30.
Goitein, S. D.
1978    *A Mediterranean society: The Jewish communities of the Arab world as portrayed in the documents of the Cairo Geniza,* vol. 3: *The family.* Berkeley: University of California Press.
Goldberg, Harvey E., ed.
1977    Ethnic groups in Israeli society. *Ethnic Groups* 1 (3): 163–262.
González, Nancie L.
1961    Family organization in five types of migratory wage labor. *American Anthropologist* 63:1264–68.
1969    *Black Carib household structure: A study of migration and modernization.* Seattle: University of Washington Press.
1988    *Sojourners of the Caribbean: Ethnogenesis and ethnohistory of the Garifuna.* Urbana: University of Illinois Press.
1989    The Christian Palestinians of Honduras: An uneasy accommodation. In *Conflict, migration, and the expression of ethnicity,* ed. Nancie L. González and Carolyn S. McCommon, 75–90. Boulder: Westview.
González, Nancie L. and Carolyn S. McCommon, ed.
1989    *Conflict, migration, and the expression of ethnicity.* Boulder: Westview.

Granovetter, Mark
1985     Economic action and social structure: The problem of embeddedness. *American Journal of Sociology* 91 (3): 481–510.
1990     *Economy and society.* Unpub. MS.
Granqvist, Hilma N.
1931     *Marriage conditions in a Palestinian village.* Helsingfors (Finland): Societas Scientiarum Fennica.
1935     *Marriage conditions in a Palestinian village,* vol. 2. Helsingfors (Finland): Societas Scientiarum Fennica.
1947     *Birth and childhood among the Arabs: Studies in a Muhammadan village in Palestine.* Helsingfors (Finland): Soderstrom.
1950     *Child problems among the Arabs: Studies in a Muhammadan village in Palestine.* Helsingfors (Finland): Soderstrom.
1965     *Muslim death and burial: Arab customs and traditions: Studies in a village in Jordan.* Helsingfors (Finland): Societas Scientiarum Fennica.
Green, Stephen
1988     *Living by the sword: America and Israel in the Middle East.* Brattleboro: Amana Press.
Gregory, Peter
1989     *The determinants of international migration and policy options for influencing the size of population flows.* Working Paper no. 2. Washington, D.C.: Commission for the Study of International Migration and Cooperative Economic Development.
Griffith, William Joyce
1965     *Empires in the wilderness: Foreign colonization and development in Guatemala, 1834–1844.* Chapel Hill: University of North Carolina Press.
1972     Attitudes toward foreign colonization: The evolution of nineteenth-century Guatemalan immigration policy. In *Applied enlightenment: Nineteenth-century liberalism,* ed. William Joyce Griffith, pt. 4. New Orleans: Tulane University Press.
Guatemala
1909     *Ley de inmigración.* Guatemala: National Legislative Assembly.
Hadawi, Sami
1967     *Bitter harvest: Palestine between 1914–1967.* New York: New World Press.
Hagopian, Elain C.
1969     *The Arab-Americans: Studies in assimilation.* Wilmette, Ill.: Medina University Press.
Haiek, Joseph R., ed.
n.d.     *The American Arabic-speaking community almanac.* Los Angeles. n.p.
Haller, Charles Lewis von (Karl Ludwig)
1872     *Orientalische ausfluge.* Stuttgart: Schaffhausen.
Hamilton, Gary G.
1978     Pariah capitalism: A paradox of power and dependence. *Ethnic Groups* 2:1–15.
1985     Temporary migration and the institutionalization of strategy. *International Journal of Intercultural Relations* 9:405–25.

Hansen, Arthur, and Anthony Oliver-Smith, eds.
1982    *Involuntary migration and resettlement.* Boulder: Westview.

Harbison, Frederick, and Charles A. Myers
1959    *Management in the industrial world: An international analysis.* New York: McGraw-Hill.

Harris, Lis
1985    *Holy days: The world of a Hasidic family.* New York: Collier (Macmillan).

Hassan, Bin Talal
1981    *Palestinian self-determination: A study of the West Bank and Gaza Strip.* New York: Quartet Books.

Hendricks, Glenn
1974    *The Dominican diaspora.* New York: Teachers College Press.

Hernández Alvarez, José
1967    *Return migration to Puerto Rico.* Westport, Conn.: Greenwood Press.

Herring, Hubert
1964    *A history of Latin America.* 2d rev. ed. New York: Knopf.

Hinshaw, Robert
1975    *Panajachel: A Guatemala town in thirty-year perspective.* Pittsburgh: University of Pittsburgh Press.

Hitti, Philip K.
1965    *Arabs: A short history.* London: Macmillan.

Holzberg, Carol S.
1987    *Minorities and power in a black society: The Jewish community of Jamaica.* Lanham, Md.: North-South Publishers.

Houghton, R. B.
1969–70 Central Americans from the Arab world. U.S. Department of State Case Study, 11th sess., Senior Seminar in Foreign Policy. Washington, D.C. Unpub. MS.

Hourani, Albert H.
1947    *Minorities in the Arab world.* London: Oxford University Press.
1968    Ottoman reform and the politics of notables. In *The beginnings of modernization in the Middle East,* ed. William R. Polk and Richard C. Chambers, 41–68. Chicago: University of Chicago Press.
1991    *A history of the Arab peoples.* Cambridge: Harvard University Press.

Howell, Nancy
1990    *Surviving fieldwork: A report of the advisory panel on health and safety in fieldwork.* Washington, D.C.: American Anthropological Association.

Ingrams, Doreen
1972    *Palestine papers, 1917–1922.* London: John Murray.

Israeli National Archives (INA) Jerusalem

Issawi, Charles Philip
1955    The entrepreneur class. In *Social forces in the Middle East,* ed. Sydney N. Fisher, 116–36. Ithaca: Cornell University Press.
1982    *An economic history of the Middle East and North Africa.* New York: Columbia University Press.

1987    *The Fertile Crescent, 1800–1914.* New York: Oxford University Press.

Issawi, Charles Philip, ed.

1966    *The economic history of the Middle East, 1800–1914.* Chicago: University of Chicago Press.

Jacir, Nasri Salomon

1955–57    *Boletín de la Sociedad Caritativa de Belén.* Jerusalem: Commercial Press.

Jackson, William F. B.

1873    *Cities of the Bible.* Philadelphia: A. J. Holmes.

Jamail, Milton, and Margo Gutiérrez

1986    *It's no secret: Israel's military involvement in Central America.* Belmont, Mass.: Association of Arab-American University Graduates.

Jansen, Michael E.

1970    *The United States and the Palestinian people.* Beirut: Institute for Palestine Studies.

Jiryis, Sabri

1988    Forty years since the seizure of Palestine. *Journal of Palestine Studies* 18 (1): 83–95.

Joseph, Suad

1978    Muslim-Christian conflicts: A theoretical perspective. In *Muslim-Christian conflicts: Economic, political and social origins,* ed. Suad Joseph and B. L. K. Pillsbury, 1–60. Boulder: Westview.

Kanafani, G.

1978    *The 1936–39 revolt in Palestine.* Washington, D.C.: Committee for Democratic Palestine.

Karpat, Kemal H.

1968    The land regime, social structure, and modernization in the Ottoman Empire. In *The beginnings of modernization in the Middle East: The nineteenth century,* ed. William R. Polk and Richard C. Chambers, 69–90. Chicago: University of Chicago Press.

1974    Ottoman immigration policies and settlement in Palestine. In *Settler regimes in Africa and the Arab world,* ed. Ibrahim Abu-Lughod and Baha Abu-Laban, 57–72. Wilmette, Ill.: Medina University Press.

1985    The Ottoman emigration to America, 1860–1914. *International Journal of Middle Eastern Studies* 17:175–209.

Katibah, Habib I.

1946    *Arab-speaking Americans.* New York: Institute of Arab American Affairs.

Kayyali, Abdul al-Wahhab

1978    *Palestine: A modern history.* London: Croom Helm.

Kearney, Michael

1986    From the invisible hand to visible feet: Anthropological studies of migration and development. *Annual Review of Anthropology* 15:331–61.

Kedourie, Elie

1970    Religion and politics. In *The Chatham House version and other Middle Eastern studies,* ed. Elie Kedourie, 317–50. London: Weidenfeld and Nicolson.

Kemper, Robert V.
1877    *Migration and adaptation: Tzintzuntzan peasants in Mexico City.* Beverly Hills
        and London: Sage.
Kerns, Virginia
1983    *Women and the ancestors.* Urbana: University of Illinois Press.
1984    Past and present evidence of interethnic mating. In *Current develop-
        ments in anthropological genetics,* vol. 3: *Black Caribs: A case study in biocultural
        adaptation,* ed. Michael H. Crawford, 95–114. New York: Plenum
        Press.
Khadduri, Majid
1955    *War and peace in the law of Islam.* Baltimore: Johns Hopkins Press.
Khalaf, Samir, and Emilie Shwayri
1966    Family firms and industrial development: The Lebanese case. *Economic De-
        velopment and Cultural Change* 15 (1): 59–69.
Khalidi, Walid
1988    Plan Dalet: master plan for the conquest of Palestine. *Journal of Palestine
        Studies* 18 (1): 4–70.
Kimche, David
1972    The opening of the Red Sea to European ships in the late eighteenth cen-
        tury. *Middle Eastern Studies* 8:63–71.
Kincaid, Jamaica
1988    *A small place.* New York: New American Library.
King-Crane Commission
1922    King-Crane report on the Near East: A suppressed official document of the
        U.S. government. *Editor and Publisher* 60 (27): 2, pp. 1–xxvii.
Kirk, George
1964    *A short history of the Middle East from the rise of Islam to modern times,* New York:
        Praeger.
Kiste, Robert C.
1974    *The Bikinians: A study in forced migration.* Menlo Park: Cummings.
Knowlton, Clark S.
1955    *Spatial and social mobility of the Syrians and Lebanese in the city of Sao Paulo, Brazil.*
        Ph.D. diss. Vanderbilt University.
Kocka, Jurgen
1971    Family and bureaucracy in German industrial management. *Business His-
        tory Review* 45:133–56.
Kubat, D., ed.
1983    *The politics of return: International return migration in Europe.* New York: Center
        for Migration Studies.
Laham, Lutfi
1987    Letter to our sisters and brothers, friends and pilgrims. Jerusalem: Greek
        Catholic Patriarchate. Mimeo.
Le Strange, Guy
1892 [1886] *Mukaddasi's description of Syria and Palestine.* London: Palestine Pilgrim's
        Text Society.

Lesch, Ann Mosely
1979a   Israeli deportation of Palestinians from the West Bank and the Gaza Strip,
        1967–1978, pt. 1. *Journal of Palestine Studies* 8 (2): 101–31.
1979b   Israeli deportation of Palestinians from the West Bank and the Gaza Strip,
        1967–1978, pt 2. *Journal of Palestine Studies* 8 (3): 81–112.
1979c   *Arab politics in Palestine, 1917–1939.* Ithaca: Cornell University Press.
Lessinger, Johanna
1991    Investing or going home? A transnational strategy among Indian im-
        migrants to the United States. Forthcoming in *Towards a transnational per-
        spective on migration: Race, class, ethnicity, and nationalism reconsidered,* ed. N.
        Glick-Schiller, L. Basch, and L. Blanc-Szanton, New York: New York
        Academy of Sciences.
Levin, Barry, ed.
1985    *Caribbean exodus.* New York: Praeger.
Levine, Robert, and Donald Campbell
1972    *Ethnocentrism: Theories of conflict, ethnic attitudes, and group behavior.* New York:
        Wiley and Sons.
Lewis, Oscar
1959    *Five famililes.* New York: Basic Books.
Lind, Andrew
1958    Adjustment patterns among Jamaican Chinese. *Social and Economic Studies*
        7:144–64.
Lindbeck, George
1979    Christians between Arabs and Jews. *Worldview* 22:25–26, 35–39.
Liptak, Dolores Ann
1987    *European Immigrants and the Catholic Church in Connecticut, 1870–1920.* New
        York: Center for Migration Studies.
Lowenthal, David
1972    *West Indian societies.* New York: Oxford University Press.
Luque, Gonzalo R.
1979    *Memorias de un Sampedrano.* San Pedro Sula: n.p.
Macalister, R. A. Stewart
1909    Rauwolff's travels in Palestine, 1573. *Palestine Exploration Fund Quarterly
        Statement,* July, 210–18.
Maloof, Louis J.
1958    *A sociological study of Arabic-speaking people in Mexico.* Ph.D. diss. Gainesville:
        University of Florida.
Mandel, Ruth
1989    Ethnicity and identity among guestworkers in West Berlin. In González
        and McCommon, *Conflict, migration, and the expression of ethnicity,* 60–74.
Ma'oz, Moshe
1968    *Ottoman reform in Syria and Palestine, 1840–1861: The impact of the Tanzimat on
        politics and society.* Oxford: Clarendon.
1982    Communal conflicts in Ottoman Syria during the reform era: The role of
        political and economic factors. In *Christians and Jews in the Ottoman Empire:*

*The functioning of a plural society,* vol. 2, ed. Benjamin Braude and Bernard Lewis, 91–105. New York: Holmes and Meier.

Ma'oz, Moshe, ed.

1975    *Studies on Palestine during the Ottoman period.* Jerusalem: Magnes.

Maqsud, Clovis

1968    Who is an Arab? Arab nationalism and the problem of minorities. In *Political and social thought in the contemporary Middle East,* ed. Kemal H. Karpat, 59–63. New York: Praeger.

Marshall, Paule

1984    *Praisesong for the widow.* New York: Dutton.

Martínez Peláez, Severo

1985    *La patria del criollo: Ensayo de interpretación de la realidad colonial guatemalteca.* Costa Rica: EDUCA.

Mathias, Charles McC.

1980    Ethnic groups and foreign policy. *Foreign Affairs* 59 (5): 975–98.

Maundrell, Henry

1963    *Journey from Aleppo to Jerusalem in 1697.* Beirut: Khayats.

McCarthy, Justin

1990    *The population of Palestine: Population statistics of the late Ottoman period and the Mandate.* New York and Oxford: Columbia University Press.

McCommon, Carolyn S.

1989    Refugees in Belize: A cauldron of ethnic tensions. In González and McCommon, *Conflict, migration, and the expression of ethnicity,* 91–102.

McGarvey, J. W.

1881    *Lands of the Bible.* Philadelphia: Lippincott.

McTague, John J., Jr.

1978    The British military administration in Palestine, 1917–1920. *Journal of Palestine Studies* 7 (3): 55–76.

Mendenhall, George

1985    *The syllabic inscriptions from Byblos.* Beirut: American University Press.

Migdal, Joel S., ed.

1980    *Palestinian society and politics.* Princeton: Princeton University Press.

Mishal, Shaul

1978    *West Bank / East Bank: The Palestinians in Jordan, 1949–1967.* New Haven: Yale University Press.

Mogannam, Matiel E. T.

1937    *The Arab woman and the Palestine problem.* London: Herbert Joseph.

Monterrosa Sicilia, R.

1967    *La inmigración Palestina a El Salvador, el desarrollo económico y 'los 14 grandes.'* San Salvador: Unpub. MS.

Moore, Alexander

1989    Symbolic imperatives for a democratic peace in Guatemala. In González and McCommon, *Conflict, migration, and the expression of ethnicity,* 28–45.

Murga Frassinetti, A.

1978    *Enclave y sociedad en Honduras.* Tegucigalpa: Universidad Nacional Autónoma.

Murray, C.
1981    *Families divided: The impact of migrant labor in Lesotho.* Cambridge: Cambridge University Press.

Musallam, Adnan A.
1981    *Bethlehem's intellectual and press history, 1919–1948, with a study of Arab press and society in Palestine in the Ottoman and British eras.* Ann Arbor: University of Michigan.

Musallam, Ayyub
1964    Our emigration to the Americas (in Arabic). *Al-Manar* (Jerusalem) 1266 (23 July).

Muslih, Muhammad Y.
1988    *The origins of Palestinian nationalism.* New York: Columbia University Press.
1990    Towards coexistence: An analysis of the resolutions of the Palestine National Council. *Journal of Palestine Studies* 19 (4): 3–29.

Naff, Alixa
1983    Arabs in America: A historical overview. In *Arabs in the New World,* ed. Sameer Y. Abraham and Nabeel Abraham, 9–29. Detroit: Wayne State University Press.

Nakhleh, Khalil
1975    Cultural determinants of Palestinian collective identity: The case of the Arabs in Israel. *New Outlook* 18 (7): 31–40.
1977    Anthropological and sociological studies on the Arabs in Israel: A critique. *Journal of Palestine Studies* 6 (4): 41–70.

Nakhleh, Khalil, and Elia Zureik, eds.
1980    *The sociology of the Palestinians.* New York: St. Martin's.

Neff, Donald
1988a   U.S. policy and the Palestinian refugees. *Journal of Palestine Studies* 18 (1): 96–111.
1988b   *Warriors against Israel: America comes to the rescue.* Brattleboro: Amana Press.

Nimer de Bendeck, Betty
1979    *El arte culinario de oriente.* San Pedro Sula: Honduras Industrial, S.A.

Ong, Aihwa
1991    Trans-Pacific entrepreneurs: Hong Kong enrepreneurs and cultural citizenship in a Pacific rim state. Forthcoming in Glick-Schiller, Basch, and Blanc-Szanton, *Towards a transnational perspective on migration.*

Owen, Roger, ed.
1982    *Studies in the economic and social history of Palestine in the nineteenth and twentieth centuries.* Oxford: St. Antony's College.

Páez Oropeza, Carmen
1984    *Los libaneses en México: Asimilación de un grupo étnico.* México: Instituto Nacional de Antropología e Historia.

Palestine
1944–45 *Statistical abstract of Palestine.* Jerusalem: Government Printer.

Palmer, P.
1895    Das jetzige Bethlehem. *Zeitschrift des deutschen Palaestina-Vereins* (Wiesbaden) 17:89–97.

Palumbo, Michael
1987    *The Palestinian catastrophe: The 1948 expulsion of a people from their homeland.* London: Faber and Faber.

Pamuk, Sevket
1987    *The Ottoman Empire and European capitalism, 1820–1913: Trade, investment, and production.* Cambridge: Cambridge University Press.

Papers of the British Mandate
1917–
1948    Certification of marriage of Palestinian citizens in foreign countries. Jerusalem: Israeli National Archives.

1929    Celebration of religious marriages abroad. Jerusalem: Israeli National Archives.

Parfitt, Tudor
1987    *The Jews in Palestine, 1800–1882.* Woodbridge, Suffolk: Boydell.

Patai, Raphael
1969    *Golden river to golden road.* Philadelphia: University of Pennsylvania Press.

Peres, Yochanan
1970    Modernization and nationalism in the identity of the Israeli Arab. *Middle East Journal* 24 (4): 479–92.

Peretz, Don, Richard J. Ward, and Evan M. Wilson
1977    *The Palestinian state: A rational approach.* Port Washington, N.Y.: Kennikat.

Persson, Sune O.
1979    *Mediation and assassination: Count Bernadotte's mission to Palestine 1938.* London: Ithaca.

Philpott, S. B.
1971    The implications of migration for sending societies: Some theoretical considerations. In *Migration and anthropology,* ed. R. F. Spencer, 9–20. Seattle: University of Washington Press.

Plascov, Avi
1981    *The Palestinian refugees in Jordan, 1948–1957.* London: Frank Cass.

1982    The Palestinians of Jordan's border. In *Studies in the economic and social history of Palestine,* ed. Roger Owen, 203–41. Oxford: St. Antony's College.

Platt, Desmond Christopher M.
1972    *Latin America and British trade, 1806–1914.* London: Adam and Charles Black.

Plattner, Stuart M.
1975a   The economics of peddling. In *Formal methods in economic anthropology,* ed. S. M. Plattner, 55–76. Washington, D.C.: American Anthropological Association.

1975b   Pedlar: A computer game in economic anthropology. In Plattner *Formal methods in economic anthropology,* 197–215.

1976    Periodic trade in developing areas without markets. In *Regional analysis,* vol. 1: *Economic systems,* ed. Carol A. Smith, 68–89. New York: Academic Press.

Poitevin, René
1977    *El proceso de industrialización en Guatemala.* Costa Rica: EDUCA.

Polk, William R., and Richard C. Chambers, eds.
1968 *The beginnings of modernization in the Middle East.* Chicago: University of Chicago Press.

Posas, Mario, and Rafael del Cid
1981 *La construcción del sector público y del estado nacional de Honduras, 1876-1979.* Ciudad Universitaria Rodrigo Facio (Costa Rica): EDUCA.

Posnansky, Merrick
1983 Towards an archaeology of the Black diaspora. *Proceedings of the International Congress for the Study of Pre-Columbian Cultures in the Lesser Antilles* 9:443-50.

Prescott, Hilda F. M.
1950 *Friar Felix at large: A fifteenth-century pilgrimage to the Holy Land.* New Haven: Yale University Press.
1954 *Jerusalem journey: pilgrimages to the Holy Land in the fifteenth century.* London: Eyre and Spottiswoode.

Rand, Christopher
1963 *Christmas in Bethlehem.* New York: Oxford University Press.

Rekhess, Elie
1979 Attitudes towards Islam: Findings of a field study among the professional elite in the West Bank. In *The contemporary Middle Eastern scene,* ed. Gustav Stein and Udo Steinbach, 133-38. Opladen (W. Germany): Leske und Budrich.

República de Honduras
1906 *Ley de inmigración.* Tegucigalpa: Tipografía Nacional.
1929 *Ley de inmigración.* Tegucigalpa: Tipografía Nacional.
1934 *Ley de inmigración.* Tegucigalpa: Tipografía Nacional.

Rhoades, R.
1979 Toward an anthropology of return migration. *Papers in Anthropology* 20:1-111.

Rivera y Morillo, Humberto
1986 Early years in San Pedro Sula. San Pedro Sula, Honduras. Unpub. MS.

Robinson E.
1874 Biblical researches in Palestine. In *Journal of travels in the year 1838,* ed. E. Robinson and E. Smith, 2 vols.; and Later Biblical researches in Palestine and in the adjacent regions. *A journal of travels in the year 1852,* ed. E. Robinson and E. Smith, vol. 3. Boston: Crocker and Brewster.

Robinson, George
1837 *Travels in Palestine and Syria,* vol. 1: *Palestine.* London: Henry Colburn.

Rogers, M. E.
1862 *Domestic life in Palestine.* London: Bell and Daldy.

Rosa, Marco Antonio
1978 [1967] *La Tegucigalpa de mis recuerdos.* Tegucigalpa: Centro Técnico Tipo-Litográfico Nacional (CETTNA).

Rosenfeld, Henry
1973 Hamula. *Journal of Peasant Studies* 1:243-44.

1978    The class situation of the Arab national minority in Israel. *Comparative Studies in Society and History* 20:374–407.

Rouse, Irving

1986    *Migrations in prehistory.* New Haven: Yale University Press.

Rubenberg, Cheryl A.

1986a    The United States, Israel, and Guatemala: Interests and conflicts. Paper presented at the Meetings of the Latin American Studies Association, Boston.

1986b    Israeli foreign policy in Central America. *Third World Quarterly* 8:896–915.

1986c    *Israel and the American national interest: A critical examination.* Urbana: University of Illinois Press.

1989    Lebanon's protracted conflict: causes and consequences. In González and McCommon, *Conflict, migration, and the expression of ethnicity,* 103–37.

Rubinstein, Hymie

1983    Remittances and rural underdevelopment in the English-speaking Caribbean. *Human Organization* 42 (4): 295–306.

Rubio, J. Francisco

1982    *Diccionario de voces usadas en Guatemala.* Guatemala: Editorial Piedra Santa.

Runciman, Steven

1968    *The historic role of the Christian Arabs of Palestine.* London: Longman.

Rustow, Dankwart A.

1979    Western nationalism and the Ottoman Empire. In *The mutual effects of the Islamic and Judeo-Christian worlds: The East European pattern,* ed. Abraham Ascher, T. Halasi-Kun, and B. K. Kiraly, 65–76. Brooklyn: Brooklyn College Press.

Sabella, Bernard

1987    *The Christian community in Jerusalem and the West Bank employment prospects in the next five to ten years.* Unpub. MS.

Sahliyeh, Emile F.

1988    The West Bank Palestinians and the politics of marginalization. In *The Arab-Israeli conflict: Two decades of change,* ed. Yehuda Lukacs and Abdalla M. Battah, 83–92. Boulder and London: Westview.

Said, Edward W.

1979    *Orientalism.* New York: Vintage Books.

Salam y Massarueh, Abdul

1986    The Palestinians: Exiles in the diaspora. *Middle East Insight* 4 (6): 27.

Sapper, Karl T.

1928    *Mexico, land, volk und wirtschaft.* Wien: L. W. Seidel.

Sayegh, Rosemary

1979    *The Palestinians: From peasants to revolutionaries.* London: Zed.

Sayegh, Yusif

1962    *Entrepreneurs of Lebanon.* Cambridge: Harvard University Press.

Schick, Robert

1987    *The fate of the Christians in Palestine during the Byzantine-Umayyad transition,* A.D. *600–750,* 3 vols. Ph.D. diss. Chicago: University of Chicago.

Schmelz, U. O.
1981    Notes on the demography of Jews, Muslims and Christians in Jerusalem. *Middle East Review* 13:62–69.
Scholch, Alexander
1982    European penetration and the economic development of Palestine, 1856–1882. In *Studies in the economic and social history of Palestine in the nineteenth century*, ed. Roger Owen, 10–87. Oxford: St. Antony's College.
Schumacher, G.
1890    Das jetzige Nazareth. *Zeitschrift des deutschen Palaestina-Vereins* (Wiesbaden) 13:235–45.
Scudder, Thayer
1973    The human ecology of big projects: River basin development and resettlement. In *Annual Review of Anthropology*, ed. B. Siegel, 45–55. Palo Alto, Calif.: Annual Reviews.
Seeger, Anthony
1981    *Nature and society in central Brazil.* Cambridge: Harvard University Press.
Sengstock, Mary C.
1977    Social change in the country of origin as a factor in immigrant conceptions of nationality. *Ethnicity* 4:54–70.
Shammas, Anton
1991    Amerka, Amerka: A Palestinian abroad in the land of the free. *Harpers* 282 (1689): 55–61.
Shankman, Paul
1976    *Migration and underdevelopment: The case of Western Samoa.* Boulder: Westview.
Sharif, Regina
1977    Latin America and the Arab-Israeli conflict. *Journal of Palestine Studies* 7:98–122.
Shinar, Dov
1987    *Palestinian voices: Communication and nation building in the West Bank.* Boulder: Lynne Reinner.
Shipler, David
1986    *Arab and Jew: Wounded spirits in a promised land.* New York: Times Books.
Shirey, Ruth I.
1971    The immigrant entrepreneur and industrial development in Tegucigalpa and San Pedro Sula, Honduras. Paper presented at the Meetings of the Pennsylvania Academy of Science, Philadelphia.
Skinner, Kenneth A., and Glenn L. Hendricks
1979    The shaping of ethnic self-identity among Indochinese refugees. *Journal of Ethnic Studies* 7 (3): 25–41.
Smith, Pamela Ann
1984    *Palestine and the Palestinians, 1876–1983.* New York: St. Martin's.
Smooha, Sammy, ed.
1984    *Social research on Arabs in Israel, 1977–1982: A bibliography.* Haifa: University of Haifa.

Sorsby, William S.
1972　Spanish colonization of the Mosquito Coast, 1787–1800. *Revista de la historia de America* 73–74:145–53.

Sorury, Kathryn Marlett
1985　*Palestine: The Palestinian and anti-Zionist viewpoints.* Monticello: Vance Bibliographies.

Spayd, Liz, and D'Vera Cohn
1991　Montgomery takes on rainbow cast. *Washington Post,* 24 February, A-1, A-19.

Spencer, R. F., ed.
1971　Migration and anthropology. *Proceedings of the American Ethnological Society.* Seattle: University of Washington Press.

Spicer, Edward H.
1971　Persistent cultural systems. *Science* 174: 795–800.

Spyridon, S. N., ed.
1938　*Annals of Palestine, 1821–1841. Manuscript of Monk Neophytus of Cyprus.* Jerusalem: n.p.

Stillman, Yedida Kalfon
1979　*Palestinian costume and jewelry.* Albuquerque: University of New Mexico Press.

Stinner, William F., Klaus de Albuquerque, and Roy S. Bryce-Laporte, eds.
1982　*Return migration and remittances: Developing a Caribbean perspective.* Washington, D.C.: Research Institute on Immigration and Ethnic Studies, Smithsonian Institution.

Stockton, E. D.
1967　*The stone age of Bethlehem.* Cophenhagen: Liber Annus.

Stookey, Robert W.
1976　The Holy Land: The American experience, vol. 1: The Christian American concern. *Middle Eastern Journal* 30 (3): 351–68.

Sutton, Constance, and Elsa Chaney, eds.
1987　*The Caribbeanization of New York City.* New York: Center for Migration Studies.

Sweet, Louise E., ed.
1970　*Peoples and cultures of the Middle East,* 2 vols. Garden City, N.Y.: Natural History Press.

Tabash, Robert
1985　Etude de la population Chretienne de la region de Bethleem. Bethlehem. Unpub. MS.

Tafari, Seko
1989　*From the maroons to Marcus.* Chicago: Research Association School Times.

Tannous, Afif I.
1942　Emigration: A force of social change in an Arab village. *Rural Sociology* 7 (1): 62–74.

Tawney, R. H.
1926　*Religion and the rise of capitalism.* New York: Harcourt, Brace.

Todaro, Michael P.
1969    A model of labor migration and urban unemployment in less-developed countries. *American Economic Review* 59:138–48.

Trimingham, J. Spencer
1979    *Christianity among the Arabs in pre-Islamic times.* London and New York: Longman.

Tristram, H. B.
1866    *The land of Israel: A journal of travels in Palestine.* London: Society for Promoting Christian Knowledge.

Tshelebi, Evilya
1980    *Travels in Palestine (1648–1650).* Jerusalem: Ariel.

Tsimhoni, Daphne
1976    *The British Mandate and the Arab Christians in Palestine, 1920–1925.* London: School of Oriental and African Studies, University of London.

1978a   The Arab Christians and the Palestinian Arab national movement during the formative stage. In *The Palestinians and the Middle East conflict,* ed. Gabriel Ben-Dor, 73–98. Ramat-Gan (Israel): Turtledove.

1978b   The Greek Orthodox Patriarchate of Jerusalem during the formative years of the British Mandate in Palestine. *Asian and African Studies* 12:77–121.

1983    Demographic trends of the Christian population in Jerusalem and the West Bank, 1948–1978. *Middle East Journal* 37 (1): 54–64.

Turner, Victor, and Edith Turner
1978    *Image and pilgrimage in Christian culture: Anthropological perspectives.* New York: Columbia University Press.

Udovitch, Abraham L.
1977    Bankers without banks: Commerce, banking, and society in the Islamic world of the Middle Ages. In *The dawn of modern banking,* ed. Center for Medieval and Renaissance Studies, 255–74. New Haven, Conn.: Yale University Press.

Van Arkadie, Brian
1977    *Benefits and burdens: A report on the West Bank and Gaza Strip economics since 1967.* New York: Carnegie Endowment for International Peace.

Vilnay, Zev
1975    *Legends of Judea and Samaria (The West Bank of the Jordan River),* vol. 2. Philadelphia: Jewish Publication Society of America.

Volney, Constantin Francois Chasseboef de
1787    *Travels through Syria and Egypt in the years 1783, 1784, and 1785.* London: C. G. J. and J. Robinson.

Ward, Robin, and Richard Jenkins
1984    *Ethnic communities in business.* Cambridge: Cambridge University Press.

Watson, James
1975    *Emigration and the Chinese lineage: The Mans in Hong Kong and London.* Berkeley: University of California Press.

Webb, Beatrice
1956    *Diaries, 1924–1932.* London.

Weber, Max
1958    *The Protestant ethic and the spirit of capitalism.* New York: Charles Scribner's.
Weingrod, Alex
1965    *Israel: Group relations in a new society.* New York: Praeger.
Weingrod, Alex, and P. Mendes-Flohr
1976    *Jewish-Arab relations in Jerusalem.* Jerusalem: Hebrew University.
Werbner, R. P.
1977    *Regional cults.* New York: Academic.
Wickberg, E.
1965    *The Chinese in Philippine life, 1850–1898.* New Haven, Conn.: Yale University Press.
Wiest, R. E.
1979    Anthropological perspective on return migration: A critical commentary. *Papers in Anthropology* 20:167–87.
Williams, Judith R.
1968    *The youth of Haouch el-Harimi.* Cambridge: Harvard University Center for Middle Eastern Studies, Monograph 20.
Willmott, W. E.
1966    The Chinese in Southeast Asia. *Australian Outlook* 20:252–62.
Wilson, Mary C.
1987    *King Abdullah, Britain and the Making of Jordan.* Cambridge: Cambridge University Press.
Wood, Merry Wiesner
1981    Paltry peddlars or essential merchants? Women in the distributive trades in early modern Nuremberg. *The Sixteenth Century Journal* 12 (2): 3–13.
Wright, Thomas
1969 [1848] *Early travels in Palestine, comprising the narratives of Arculf, Willibad, Bernard, Saewulf, Sigurd, Benjamin of Tudela, Sir John Maundeville, de la Brocquière, and Maundrell.* New York: Ams.
Zamir, Meir
1981    Population statistics of the Ottoman Empire in 1914 and 1919. *Middle Eastern Studies* 17 (1): 85–106.
Zenner, Walter P.
1971    International networks in a migrant ethnic group. In Spencer, *Migration and anthropology,* 36–48.
1972    Some aspects of ethnic stereotype content in the Galilee: A trial formulation. *Middle Eastern Studies* 8 (3): 405–16.

# Index